THE SCHOOL SAFETY HANDBOOK

HOW TO ORDER THIS BOOK

BY PHONE: 800-233-9936 or 717-291-5609, 8AM–5PM Eastern Time

BY FAX: 717-295-4538

BY MAIL: Order Department
Technomic Publishing Company, Inc.
851 New Holland Avenue, Box 3535
Lancaster, PA 17604, U.S.A.

BY CREDIT CARD: American Express, VISA, MasterCard

BY WWW SITE: http://www.techpub.com

PERMISSION TO PHOTOCOPY–POLICY STATEMENT

Authorization to photocopy items for internal or personal use, or the internal or personal use of specific clients, is granted by Technomic Publishing Co., Inc. provided that the base fee of US $3.00 per copy, plus US $ .25 per page is paid directly to Copyright Clearance Center, 222 Rosewood Drive, Danvers, MA 01923, USA. For those organizations that have been granted a photocopy license by CCC, a separate system of payment has been arranged. The fee code for users of the Transactional Reporting Service is 1-56676/96 $5.00 + $ .25.

THE SCHOOL SAFETY HANDBOOK

Taking Action for Student and Staff Protection

EDITED BY

Kenneth E. Lane, Ed.D.
California State University, San Bernardino

Michael D. Richardson, Ed.D.
Georgia Southern University

Dennis W. Van Berkum, Ed.D.
Moorhead State University

TECHNOMIC PUBLISHING CO., INC
LANCASTER · BASEL

The School Safety Handbook
a **TECHNOMIC**®publication

Published in the Western Hemisphere by
Technomic Publishing Company, Inc.
851 New Holland Avenue, Box 3535
Lancaster, Pennsylvania 17604 U.S.A.

Distributed in the Rest of the World by
Technomic Publishing AG
Missionsstrasse 44
CH-4055 Basel, Switzerland

Copyright © 1996 by Technomic Publishing Company, Inc.
All rights reserved

No part of this publication may be reproduced, stored in a retrieval system, or transmitted, in any form or by any means, electronic, mechanical, photocopying, recording, or otherwise, without the prior written permission of the publisher.

Printed in the United States of America
10 9 8 7 6 5 4 3 2 1

Main entry under title:
    The School Safety Handbook: Taking Action for Student and Staff Protection

A Technomic Publishing Company book
Bibliography: p.

Library of Congress Catalog Card No. 96-60023
ISBN No. 1-56676-397-5

*To Megan and Austin Lane
Chad and Brandi Richardson
Jessica, Emily and Andy Van Berkum*

Contents

Foreword by James M. Smith   xiii
Preface   xvii
Acknowledgements   xix
Prologue   xxi
Contributors   xxix

PART I: ROOTS OF VIOLENCE

1. The Impact of Violence in Schools   3
DONALD F. DeMOULIN

- Introduction 3
- School Crime and Violence 4
- School Violence Statistics 4
- Weapons in the Schools 7
- Conflict Resolution 11
- Conflict Resolution Strategies 12
- Teaching the Teachers 14
- Conclusion 17
- Author's Perspective 20
- References 20

2. Psychological Aspects of Safe Schools   23
ROBERT NIELSEN

- Introduction 23
- Involving Students to Create a Safe Environment 35
- References 39

3. Bullying: Concerns for School Administrators   41
JOHN H. HOOVER and RONALD OLIVER

- Bullying Defined 42
- Findings from the Midwest Bullying Studies 43
- Prevention and Treatment 50

Summary 52
References 53

4. School Violence: Everybody's Problem — 55
PAUL M. KINGERY

Perpetration and Victimization 55
Interpersonal Violence 57
Witnesses of Violence 59
Coping Mechanisms 60
Rural School Violence 61
References 65

5. Outside Agitators — 67
WILLIAM McFARLIN and MURDELL WALKER McFARLIN

Introduction 67
Perceptions and Attitudes 71
Summary 78
References 79

PART II: LEGAL ISSUES

6. A Dilemma: Dress Codes, Safety and Discrimination — 83
KENNETH E. LANE, MICHAEL D. RICHARDSON,
DENNIS W. VAN BERKUM and STANLEY L. SWARTZ

Introduction 83
Review of Court Cases 84
Conclusions 90
References 91

7. Sexual Harassment in the Schools: A Safety and Liability Issue for All Administrators — 93
SANDRA SIMPSON

Introduction 93
Legal Basis: Establishing and Defining the Issue 94
Civil Rights Act of 1991: Punitive Damages
   for Sexual Harassment 97
Title IX: Sexual Harassment within the Schools 98
Landmark Cases under Title IX 99
Eleventh Amendment Immunity 102
Liability under § 1983 103
Tolling the Statute of Limitations 107
Legal Problems for Education 108

The Responsibilities of School Officials 110
Conclusion 112
References 113

8. **The Politics of "Zero Tolerance" Legislation in Michigan Public Schools: Origins, Implementation and Consequences**   **117**
   BEVERLEY B. GELTNER and JOHN S. GOODEN

   National Context for the Reform 117
   Background to Public Act 328 118
   Senate Bill 966/Public Act 328 121
   Reactions to "Zero Tolerance" Law prior
      to Its Implementation 123
   Lessons to Be Learned: Questions to Be Asked 133
   References 134

9. **Creating Safe Schools: Policies and Practices**   **137**
   MARILYN L. GRADY

   Introduction 137
   Demographics 138
   Causes 140
   Definitions 141
   Problems and Responses 142
   Alternative Schools 144
   Legislation 145
   Programs 146
   Caveats 149
   Prevention 150
   Recommendations 157
   References 158

PART III: STRATEGIES FOR MAKING SCHOOLS SAFE

10. **Creating and Keeping Safe Schools: The Roles of Parents and Community**   **163**
    CAROLYN L. WANAT

    Introduction 163
    Research about Parental/Community Involvement 164
    Program Initiatives Respond to School Violence 165
    Differences in Parental Involvement in Academics
       and Safe Schools Programs 168
    A Process for Parental and Community Involvement 173

x   Contents

  Other Basic Requirements in a Safe Schools Process 176
  Conclusion 179
  References 179

11. **The Involvement of Community Agencies
    in the Development of Safe Schools**   **181**
    HARBISON POOL and DOUGLAS W. POOL

      Safe Schools—Perception, Reality, Response 181
      Addressing the Problem: Before, During, and After 182
      Involvement 184
      Volunteers 186
      The Real World as It Is Now 191
      An Alternative Paradigm 196
      A Somewhat Immodest Proposal 199
      Conclusion 205
      References 207

12. **School-Based Intervention:
    The Tucson, Arizona, Model**   **211**
    GAIL BORNFIELD and ROGER PFEUFFER

      Introduction 211
      School-Based Intervention Programs 213
      Conclusions 227
      References 227

13. **Technology to Create Safer Schools**   **229**
    ART TOWNLEY and KENNETH MARTINEZ

      Introduction 229
      The Technologies 232
      Conclusion 236
      References 236

14. **Extracurricular Activities: Asset or Hindrance**   **239**
    JERI L. ENGELKING and MICHAEL R. HOADLEY

      Introduction 239
      Program Needs 240
      Objectives of the Program 242
      Safety in Activities 243
      School Facilities and Equipment 245
      Participant Conditioning 246
      Care and Protection of Participants 247
      Principles Governing Accident/Injury Prevention 248
      References 250

PART IV: CONCLUSIONS AND RECOMMENDATIONS

15. **Educational Reform in Changing Contexts of Families and Communities: Leading School–Interagency Collaboration**   **253**
    LARS G. BJÖRK

    Introduction 253
    The Educational Reform Reports 254
    Changes in Public Expectations for Schooling 256
    Implications for Changing Administrator Roles...........272
    Conclusion 274
    References 275

16. **Violence in Our Schools**   **281**
    M. SUE TOLLEY

    Introduction 281
    Review of the Literature 281
    Analysis, Conclusion, and Implications 318

Epilogue   321

Foreword

JAMES M. SMITH

SELDOM in our careers as professors are we openly invited to critically analyze important work and then compose an unrestricted written review of that material. Certainly, as members of editorial boards for leading journals, we are asked to review a proposed article and then construct a series of suggestions for modification and/or improvement. These suggestions are then sent to the author of the proposed work for analysis and recomposition; however, these comments never appear in print within the body of the journal, nor are they available to the original author with a signature or other means of authentication. When Drs. Lane, Richardson, and Van Berkum requested that I compose a foreword to this text, I was immediately struck with a sense of honor and appreciation. Then, after several hours of contemplation, a feeling of intense responsibility and genuine modesty began to overcome me. After all, what did a faculty member with research interests in school restructuring, site-based decision making, and proactive supervision, have to contribute to a text dedicated to safe schools?

After reviewing the final drafts of the chapters contained within this book, I began to understand the rather circuitous relationship that a person with my experiences might have to the myriad concepts, considerations, and prognostications contained within the body of this work. After all, like many of my colleagues, I was raised in a small community in the midwestern United States. The school district that provided me twelve years of education was certainly one that offered safety and security to all its students. Upon the conclusion of any school day, the families that sent their children to my elementary, junior high and high school seldom worried about the safe return of their young sons and daughters. Embedded within the literally hundreds of conversations I can recall from my childhood, I can recollect none that focused on the fear of violence, weapons, gang membership or student harassment. Although I vividly remember discussions regarding paddlings, suspensions, extra basketball or football drills (i.e., running the stairs or completing a series of extra forty-yard dashes) and the fear of hair length and skirt length violations, none of these discussions create a picture of threatened or disturbed youth. The young men and women with whom I completed high school were concerned largely about finding the right college to attend, the right job to select or the right person to marry.

As I reflected upon my childhood as a public school student, two pertinent questions came to mind with respect to schools of today: What critical changes have occurred in our schools during the past twenty-five to thirty years? Why are these institutions no longer the bastions of safety that society once believed them to be? Possibly, Dr. Lars Björk best describes this transition in his chapter dedicated to families and communities. Clearly, when 73% of Americans polled believe that problems originating in society have produced a profound negative effect on the performance of school children and schools in general (Elam, 1990), educational professionals alone cannot shoulder the blame for this changing pattern of school life. Likewise, we as educators cannot ignore this massive change in societal structure. Schools of today are different; kids of today are different; parents of today are different; and, indeed, society of today is very different. To repeat an often quoted and somewhat sarcastic phrase, "Beaver Cleaver does not live here anymore!"

In light of these changing societal patterns, a book dedicated to safe schools and school safety in general is tremendously timely. Chapters from this work are dedicated to the basic identification of school violence, the differences between urban and rural school safety, the legal mandates for school safety, dress code concerns for reasons of gang identification, safety issues for extracurricular activities and extracurricular sponsors, and examples of schools and school districts that have implemented comprehensive safety planning into their daily operational actions. As scholars and practitioners alike, the authors and editors of this text labor to make no apologies for the many issues that surround school violence; rather, they dedicate their time, energy and effort to creating illuminating strategies and solutions to the tumultuous nature of life in modern schools.

Many who read this foreword will find the thought of an entire text dedicated to school safety a highly depressing notion. As one who examines school reform and school restructuring on a daily basis, I too find the need for such a text far less than uplifting. Graduate students enrolled in my classes often chide me for the belief that schools can and will become less bureaucratic, more student-centered and increasingly cooperatively led (Smith, 1993; Smith & Cairns, 1995). These same students have gone so far as to say that I frequently view the world through "rose-colored glasses." After carefully reviewing this text, possibly the rose-colored glasses analogy is most appropriate. To make schools increasingly more safe, we all must hope for change. As educators, we all must believe that different strategies and different actions can and will make a positive difference in how schools are operated. If teachers, principals and superintendents hope to create new learning communities; first and foremost, those communities must be ones that exude safety. We must optimistically view the material contained within this text as a means to create new and different schools. These new schools must be schools of safety and inclusion — not schools of violence and discrimination. The ideas, concepts and methodologies included in this text offer precisely such a smorgasbord of options to create schools that function within this realm of difference.

In keeping with the majority of texts in the field of education or any discipline within the social sciences, *The School Safety Handbook* offers thousands of options to consider for inclusion within a school or school district. It has been my experience that successful schools will specifically focus on one or two of these considerations and will, in turn, implement them both carefully and methodically. All schools and school districts in America are not alike; therefore, appropriate strategies for one district would be totally inappropriate for another. The beauty of this text is that ideas and strategies are free-flowing. Each chapter forces the reader to consider his or her school and then, concomitantly, to consider how that school might be made into an institution of greater safety. Teachers, principals, superintendents, school board members and parents alike will find many pertinent considerations within the sixteen chapters of this work. The key for successful utilization of this material is to read, reflect and then implement the strategies that specifically address local concerns. Although I feel certain that this text will be used as required reading in numerous graduate classrooms across the country, its greatest contribution to the profession will remain within the parameters of local school examination and local school implementation.

As noted at the beginning of this foreword, seldom are professors given an open invitation to critique written material and then publish their responses. I hope that this response reflects my sincere belief that

The School Safety Handbook will serve as a valuable contribution to the professional literature in the field of teacher education and educational leadership. Without books of this nature how would school leaders ever hope to overcome the skyrocketing statistics of gang activity, adolescent homicides, and physical and mental abuse perpetrated upon young children (Hechinger, 1992)? Indeed, there is hope—that hope lies firmly within the confines of this text!

REFERENCES

Elam, S. M. (Ed.). (1990). *The Phi Delta Kappa Gallup polls of attitudes toward education.* Bloomington, IN: Phi Delta Kappa.

Hechinger, F. M. (1992). *Fateful choices: Healthy youth for the 21st century.* New York: Carnegie Corporation.

Smith, J. M. (1993). Teacher empowerment in rural schools: Where do we begin? In J. R. Hoyle & D. M. Estes (Eds.), *NCPEA: In a new voice* (pp. 312–323). Lancaster, PA: Technomic Publishing Co., Inc.

Smith, J. M. & Cairns, D. V. (1995). Site-based management and rural public schools: A principal's dilemma. In M. Richardson, J. Flanigan & K. Lane (Eds.), *School empowerment* (pp. 227–246). Lancaster, PA: Technomic Publishing Co., Inc.

Preface

THIS book grew out of the authors' investigations of issues impacting school administrators in the 1990s, particularly the effect school violence has had on schools, students, community, parents, faculty, staff and administrators. We believe that the authors of the various chapters have provided a conceptual framework for the examination of the issues impacting on *safe schools,* including the social environment, the legal issues and the strategies for creating safer schools.

We are grateful to the authors for sharing their insight, knowledge and wisdom regarding this very controversial, sensitive and potentially destructive subject. The information contained in this volume is not a recipe for the creation of safe schools dictating the "one best way" to control and eliminate violence in schools. Rather, the editors have attempted to present a variety of viewpoints that ask more questions than provide definitive answers. We hope that the volume will serve as a catalyst for continued discussion and deliberation among and between the numerous stakeholders in this vital area.

Acknowledgements

THE editors acknowledge the support of the Mental Health Association of the San Bernardino (CA) County. We also wish to thank Terri King and Donna Colson for their assistance in the preparation of this manuscript. Their diligence and talents permitted this book to be completed on schedule.

Prologue

KENNETH E. LANE
MICHAEL D. RICHARDSON
DENNIS W. VAN BERKUM

INTRODUCTION

WHAT exactly is a safe school? We can define a safe school as an educational environment in which teachers can concentrate on teaching and students can concentrate on learning without concern for their physical or mental safety. For the purposes of this discourse, school safety includes the physical facility, the people in the environment and the systems for maintaining that safety.

School authorities are expected to maintain a safe school environment. Established by a combination of federal and state laws, case law at all levels and regulatory language developed by various federal and state agencies, this expectation is understood but difficult to meet. The courts have not always clearly given administrators the authority to control the school environment, protect all students and protect themselves from lawsuits.

School safety issues are varied, depending upon the locale and population of the school affected; however, there are generic school safety issues that demand the attention of school personnel as they endeavor to provide a safe, educational environment. A key issue is violent use of weapons, regardless of the age or social class of the students involved; however, as this volume demonstrates, other issues such as dress codes aimed at banning gang attire, drug abuse, vandalism, racial and ethnic animosity, bullying and sexual harassment are also threats to a safe school environment as well.

Weapons in Our Schools

The issue of weapons includes both the bringing of weapons onto school campuses and the use of weapons to injure students or adults. Kilpatrick (1992) estimated that there are 525,000 attacks, shakedowns and robberies in public high schools each month in this nation and that there are approximately 135,000 students who carry guns to school daily. In California alone, the number of reported crimes committed on school campuses is increasing. Between the 1986–1987 and the 1988–1989 school years, reported crimes increased from 157,597 (Smith, 1989, p. 23) to 174,478 (Kneedler, 1990, p. 48). According to Kneedler (1990), of the 174,478 crimes reported in 1989–1990, 62,000 were property crimes like vandalism and arson, which resulted in $24 million in damage to our schools. Additionally, 11,000 cases of weapon possession were reported and over 1000 guns were confiscated from K–12 students.

In a Louis Harris poll (Harris, 1993) sponsored by the Joyce Foundation in Chicago and prepared for the Harvard School of Public Health, 59% of the students surveyed said that guns were easily available, and 35% said it would take them less than an hour to obtain a weapon. Among the other findings in the survey (conducted between April 19 and May 21, 1993) were

- Twenty-two percent of the students claimed that they carried a weapon to school during the past year, with 4% saying that the weapon was a gun.
- Thirty-nine percent said that they knew someone personally who had been killed or injured from gunfire.
- Nine percent said they had fired a gun at somebody.

John Burton (1993), Child Attendance and Welfare Officer for the San Bernardino (CA) County Superintendent's Office, stated in May of 1993 that there had been over 800 students expelled from classrooms in San Bernardino County during the 1992–1993 school year for weapons offenses. Over sixty of those students were from grades K–6. It is worth noting that in 80–90% of the cases involving students bringing guns to school, the guns were brought from home (Burton, 1993).

What should not be overlooked is that weapons are used on school campuses in some cases by outside gunmen. Students and teachers have been shot and killed on school campuses by adult gunmen in urban and rural areas across this country. Included in this tragedy are Stockton, California; Winnetka, Illinois; Greenwood, South Carolina; Little Rock, Arkansas; and Washington, D.C.

Impact on School Campuses

The impact of violence on school campuses in seen in various ways.

Disaster drills similar to tornado drills have been developed and are practiced routinely in some schools. In these drills students are taught to hit the floor in the event of gunfire. Also, some schools have eliminated faculty restrooms to force teachers and staff to circulate through the student restrooms. Uniformed officers have become as much a part of the school environment as the administrator. In addition, many schools have removed student lockers to eliminate potential hiding places for weapons.

Metal Detectors

The most controversial remedy for creating safe schools is the introduction of the metal detector into the school setting. After two students were shot and killed by a fifteen-year-old gunman in a school that Mayor David Dinkins of New York City was to visit in less than one hour, Mayor Dinkins was faced with the personal reality of his recent $50 million cut in the security budget for New York schools. Within two days, Dinkins restored $28 million to place metal detectors in New York's forty most dangerous schools (*Los Angeles Times,* March 13, 1992). In the midst of cries concerning invasion of privacy rights, the Attorney General for the state of California issued an opinion in 1992 stating that metal detectors in schools were constitutional.

Creating the Safe School

Numerous suggestions have been made for ending violence on school campuses. The suggestions have come primarily from the federally funded National School Safety Center (NSSC) and the United Federation of Teachers in New York. Additionally, school boards have begun to implement dress code policies directed toward eliminating the ability of gang members to identify one another on school campuses.

Violence Recommendations

NSSC has recommended a six-step strategy program for creating safe schools as a result of the Urban School Safety Practicum (*USA Today,* December, 1988, pp. 6–7):

(1) Involve the public in the schools.
(2) Improve school leadership skills.
(3) Keep youths from bringing guns and other weapons to school.

(4) Make schools and the surrounding community drug-free.
(5) Halt negative gang activity.
(6) Improve discipline of youth in schools and at home.

Stuart Greenbaum (1989), communications director for NSSC, also recommended additional preventative security measures:

(1) School districts should coordinate a local school security committee to plan and regularly update school safety and security measures.
(2) School site administrators must acquire "crime-resistance savvy" and take greater responsibility in working with the school board and school district to implement site security programs.
(3) Schools must develop a comprehensive crisis management plan that incorporates resources available through other community agencies.
(4) A school communications network should be established that links classrooms and school yards with the front office as well as local law enforcement and fire departments.
(5) School staff should be informed and regularly updated on safety plans through inservice training.
(6) Parents and community volunteers should be used to help patrol surrounding neighborhoods and supervise the campus before, during and after school.
(7) Access points to school grounds should be limited and monitored during the school day.
(8) Students should be taught to take responsibility for their own safety by reporting suspicious individuals or unusual activity on school grounds and by learning personal safety and conflict resolution techniques.

Cryer (1989) outlined the recommendations agreed to by New York's United Federation of Teachers and New York Mayor Koch to create safe schools:

(1) Increase the number of security officers to staff the elementary schools and special education sites.
(2) Assign security officers to after-school activities, including those held outdoors.
(3) Install two-way, talk-back systems in every classroom to allow conversations to be heard in the office.

(4) Initiate a program to install electromagnetic door locks in every school to hamper intruders.
(5) Provide every secondary school student with a photo identification card.
(6) Request that the police department assign officers to schools in high-crime areas during the time students arrive at school and when they are dismissed at the end of the day.
(7) Urge the state legislature to increase the penalties for those who assault school employees.

Administrator's Response

Does this nation believe that no cost is too great to protect children and ensure their safety? Do we, as a nation, honor and cherish our constitutional right to freedom of expression, even expression exercised by what we wear or how we wear it? These are the fundamental questions facing the school administrator.

How can school leaders realistically regulate weapons and student dress to ensure that the regulations will have the desired effect? While the courts have historically given the schools considerable latitude in their efforts to regulate student behavior, the relationship between the probibition and the targeted problem must be carefully addressed.

Since the majority of gang members are also members of racial and/or ethnic minority groups, the issue of racial/ethnic discrimination must be addressed. Clothing styles associated with gangs or gang activity might more accurately represent a form of expression or identity that is only secondarily associated with a gang. A case for discrimination might be effectively made when a dress code policy impacts some groups more adversely than other groups. Remember the three keys to effective relationships with students: firmness, fairness and consistency.

If dress can be directly attributed to an inappropriate behavior that disrupts the school environment, then and only then, is its regulation justifiable; however, courts will likely require schools and school administrators to demonstrate "imminent danger" before a school or district ban on attire is acceptable. Attire bans that are indiscriminate or are not directly related to creating and maintaining safe schools will not be supported. Mere speculation or anticipation of danger would probably not be acceptable to the courts. Likewise, the courts will not hesitate to declare school policies unconstitutional if they are racially or ethnically discriminatory. The challenge for school administrators is to develop policies that are congruent with these specifications and that help promote school safety! Two principles should govern the policy development process: 1) Is there a direct link between the attire being regulated and disruption of the school environment, and 2) is the prohibition specific enough to cover the attire that poses the threat to safety without infringing student rights?

The following guidelines are suggested for use by school principals when developing dress codes:

(1) Expert opinion or actual experience should be used to demonstrate the relationship between a specific form of attire and the potential threat to the school environment (Gee & Sperry, 1978).
(2) Dress that is prohibited should usually not be that worn by the student population in general (Lane & Stine, 1992).
(3) Reference to specific sports teams or trademarks should not be included in the language of dress code policy (Lane & Stine, 1992).
(4) Student attire should be recognized as a legitimate form of personal expression. Regulations that exceed what is clearly necessary to control disruption or violence should be considered an abridgement of the freedom of expression and open to legal challenge.

Preparation Programs in Educational Administration

Programs of educational administration prepare people to become the school administrators of tomorrow. As a result of changing school climates and community ethos, some difficult questions must be addressed by these preparation programs:

(1) Are preparation programs addressing the needs of the site administrator?
(2) Are programs willing to change course work or even the transition process through programs in order to meet the needs of the school administrators of the future?
(3) What are the responsibilities of a preparation program for helping potential and practicing school administrators deal with school safety issues?

For the most part, the traditional preparation programs for school administrators address theoretical skills rather than practical needs. A major criticism that school administrators constantly reiterate is that professors are out of touch with the reality of the present-day school setting and the demands it places on the administrator. Whether or not the perception is factual, professors must understand that the perceptions are real and that the needs of the potential and practicing administrator must be addressed. To say that school administrators have too narrow a viewpoint does not alleviate the problem. Preparation programs are viewed as, in a large measure, irrelevant to the current role of the school administrator. Students will transit through preparation programs because that is the only way to obtain an administrative endorsement, and consequently an administrative position; however, that does not mean that they are in agreement with the preparation provided them.

CONCLUSION

The school administrator is faced with leadership problems on a daily basis. In today's environment, these problems force one's attention to guaranteeing school safety. In fact, the state of California now has a constitutional amendment that holds the principal responsible for creating a safe school environment. Thus, issues of safety are as large a challenge as issues of school curriculum.

The pressures on school officials to maintain a safe school environment cannot be overstated. Pressure to ensure students' rights and freedoms are in no measure comparable. Most experts agree that gangs and the violence that they engender are only symptoms of larger societal problems. The belief that schools control the effects of these problems by metal detectors and by regulating what students wear or how they wear it is hopeful at best and hopelessly simplistic at worst. Schools that engage with their communities in efforts to resolve the problems that create violence in the schools and that create gangs will be more effective than schools that attempt to regulate the artifacts of their existence through metal detectors and dress codes.

Schools cannot hope to encourage students to become responsible and fully participating citizens when they appear to be disposed and even anxious to restrict their rights in the school setting. The extent to which the school is an artificial or contrived environment helps determine the extent to which it is important or meaningful in the lives of children.

Finally, the violence and gang problems that take place on school campuses do not have their genesis in the school environment; rather, the roots are established in the community and the home. Society has yet to deal with this issue but has, instead, left it to the schools for remediation. The harsh reality is that schools will be unable to end violence and gang activity on campuses until parents and communities become active participants in the education of children.

REFERENCES

Bannister v. Paradis, 136 F. Supp. 185 (1970).
Boggers v. Sacramento City Unified School District, 25 Cal. App.3d 269 (1972).
Breen v. Kahl, 419 F.2d 1034 (7th Cir. 1969).
Burton, J. (1993, May 12). Personal interview. San Bernardino, CA.
California State Department of Education. (1986). *Students' rights and responsibilities handbook.* Sacramento, CA: California State Department of Education.
Cryer, R. (1989). Understanding: The key to curbing violence. *Thrust for Educational Leadership,* 18:14–16.
Gee, E. G. & Sperry, D. J. (1978). *Education law and the public schools: A compendium.* Boston: Allyn & Bacon, p. 59.
Greenbaum, S. (1989). Safe schools and quality schooling: The public responds. *Thrust for Educational Leadership,* 18:17.
Harris, L. (1993). *A survey of experiences, perceptions, and apprehensions about guns among young people in America.* Boston, MA: Harvard University School of Public Health.
Karr v. Schmidt, 460 F.2d. 609, 613 (5th Cir. 1972).
Kilpatrick, W. K. (1992). *Why Johnny can't tell right from wrong.* New York: Simon & Schuster.
King v. Saddleback, 445 F.2d 932 (1971).
Kneedler, P. (1990). Securing your campus. *Thrust for Educational Leadership,* 20:48–50.
Lane, K. E. & Stine, D. O. (1992). Dress codes and association. In W. Camp, J. Underwood, M. J. Connelly & K. E. Lane (Eds.), *Principal's handbook for school law.* Topeka, KS: National Organization on Legal Problems of Education.
Ledger v. Stockton Unified School District, 202, Cal. App.3d 1448 (1988).
Massie v. Henry, 455 F.2d 779 (4th Cir. 1972).
Olff v. Eastside Union, U.S. App. 305 F. Supp. 557 (1969).
Scott v. Board of Education, Union Free School District #17, 61 Misc.2d 333, 305 S.C. 601 (1969).
Smith, D. (1989). The Little Hoover Commission report. *Thrust for Educational Leadership,* 18:23
Tinker v. Des Moines Independent Community School District, 393 U.S. 503, 89 S.Ct. 733 (1969).
Totsiello v. Oakland Unified School District, 197, Cal. App. 3d, 41, 45 (1972).
Wallace v. Ford, 346 F. Supp. Ark. (1972).

Contributors

Dr. Lars G. Björk is an Associate Professor of Educational Administration at the University of Kentucky in Lexington, Kentucky.

Dr. Gail Bornfield is an Assistant Professor of Educational Administration at Minot State University in Minot, North Dakota.

Dr. Donald DeMoulin is at the University of Memphis in Memphis, Tennessee.

Dr. Jeri Engelking is the Associate Dean of the School of Education and an Associate Professor of Educational Administration at the University of South Dakota in Vermillion, South Dakota.

Dr. Bev Geltner is an Associate Professor of Educational Administration at Eastern Michigan University in Ypsilanti, Michigan.

Dr. John Gooden is an Associate Professor of Educational Administration at Georgia Southern University in Statesboro, Georgia.

Dr. Marilyn Grady is an Associate Professor of Educational Administration at the University of Nebraska in Lincoln, Nebraska.

Dr. Michael Hoadley is the Director of InTEC and an Associate Professor of Health and Safety Education at the University of South Dakota in Vermillion, South Dakota.

Dr. John Hoover is an Associate Professor of Special Education at the University of North Dakota in Grand Forks, North Dakota.

Dr. Paul Kingery is the chair of the Department of Kinesiology & Health Promotion in the College of Education at the University of Kentucky in Lexington, Kentucky.

Dr. Kenneth E. Lane is a Professor of Educational Administration at California State University, San Bernardino (CSUSB), and the Coordinator of Planning and Distance Learning for the Coachella Valley Campus of CSUSB in Palm Desert, California.

Mr. Ken Martinez is an Assistant Principal at Cajon High School in San Bernardino, California.

Ms. Murdell Walker McFarlin is an educational consultant from East Point, Georgia.

Mr. William McFarlin is the Principal of Usher Middle School in Atlanta, Georgia.

Dr. Robert Nielsen is an Assistant Professor of Counseling at North Dakota State University in Fargo, North Dakota.

Dr. Ronald Oliver is with the National Resources Center for Youth Services at the University of Oklahoma in Norman, Oklahoma.

Mr. Roger Pfeuffer is an Assistant Superintendent for the Tucson Unified School District in Tucson, Arizona.

Mr. Doug Pool is a Deputy Sherrif in Humboldt County, California, who works actively with the DARE (Drug Abuse Resistance Education) program.

Dr. Harbison Pool is a Professor of Educational Administration at Georgia Southern University in Statesboro, Georgia.

Dr. Michael D. Richardson is a Professor of Educational Administration at Georgia Southern University in Statesboro, Georgia.

Ms. Sandy Simpson is an Administrator at the San Bernardino City Unified School District in San Bernardino, California.

Dr. Stanley Swartz is a Professor of Education at California State University, San Bernardino, California.

Ms. Mary Sue Tolley is the Principal of Joseph Martin Elementary School in Hinesville, Georgia.

Dr. Art Townley is an Associate Professor of Educational Administration at California State University, San Bernardino in San Bernardino, California.

Dr. Dennis W. Van Berkum is an Associate Professor of Educational Administration at Moorhead State University in Moorhead, Minnesota.

Dr. Carolyn Wanat is an Assistant Professor of Educational Administration at the University of Iowa in Iowa City, Iowa.

PART I

ROOTS OF VIOLENCE

CHAPTER 1

The Impact of Violence in Schools

DONALD F. DeMOULIN

INTRODUCTION

AGES ago, Plato believed that as long as the young generation was and continued to be well brought up, our ship of state would have a fair launch. Otherwise, the consequences were better left on the boat. Today, his belief still holds merit. Violence is in the mainstream of the American culture. In the early history of the expansion westward of this country, there was more violence per capita than in the American society today; however, the nature of violence and its impact on groups of people has emphatically changed (Andrews, 1993).

Over the last decade, we have learned what is required to produce a positive environment and to provide the building blocks so children can learn in an instructionally effective school. We know that where we have increased the intensity of the right kind of instruction, student achievement increases. However, in order to increase this intensity, we also have to improve the conditions under which children come to school to actively engage in that instruction. It is the intersection of these two conditions that strengthens the nature of successful student achievement. Without the proper intersection of these two, we will have failed in teaching these students to become effective citizens in the twenty-first century (Andrews, 1993).

A key element of both of these dimensions, proposed in a study started by Ron Edmonds (1979) called the Effective Schools Research, is a safe and orderly environment. As the problems of our towns, cities and country grow, they spill naturally into our schools. The presence of weapons, drugs, gangs and violence in schools has caused school officials to be ever more conscious of student safety; it becomes more burdensome with each act perpetrated against our children.

> Violence is a public health and safety condition which results from individual, socio-economic, political and institutional disregard for basic

human needs. Violence includes physical and non-physical harm which causes damage, plain, injury, and fear. Violence disrupts the school environment and results in the debilitation of personal development which may lead to hopelessness and helplessness. (Dear, Scott & Marshall, 1994, p. 4)

This chapter addresses the impact that violence has on school operation. It also provides successful conflict resolution strategies that have been incorporated around the nation. It also provides approaches by administrators, teachers, students and parents to minimize the occurrence of violence.

SCHOOL CRIME AND VIOLENCE

Childhood has usually been viewed as a time of innocence, but for many children, this is no longer the case. Violence has become a part of their everyday lives, especially for children living below the poverty level who see violence in their neighborhoods, as well as in their homes.

Many children are exposed to violence on television, which has become more common since deregulation of children's television. It is estimated that youngsters between the ages of five and fifteen will view over 13,000 killings on television. In addition, the media (radio, television, newspapers and magazines) constantly give graphic accounts of murders, rapes, abuse and other violent acts now happening in our world. Because war, weapons and power are glorified and international conflicts are solved through fighting, children are exposed to situations that dramatize violence as an acceptable and sometimes thrilling way to handle conflicts (Carlson-Paige & Levin, 1992). Equally damaging to children is the exposure to racial and cultural tensions, which can put an entire school into a state of crisis. Meek (1992) reported that a far greater amount of school crime and violence is racially related than anyone cares to admit. Hate crimes increased fourfold during the first four months of 1992 compared to the same time period in 1991, and many hate crimes go unreported.

SCHOOL VIOLENCE STATISTICS

The thought that violence in schools is merely a reflection of violence in society is not a very comforting thought to educators at any level. Statistics and examples show that children are using violence to solve their conflicts. What used to be solved by shouting is now solved by shooting, as evidenced by the following:

(1) In Washington, D.C., a fifteen-year-old was killed by his best friend in an argument over a girl.
(2) In Kresserville, Pennsylvania, a nine-year-old boy shot and killed a seven-year-old playmate after she told him she was a better Nintendo player than he was.
(3) The number of gunshot wounds to children under age sixteen doubled in large cities between 1987 and 1990.
(4) There was a 125% increase in the number of murders of young people under age nineteen between 1984 and 1990.
(5) There were over 800 gang-related shootings in 1992 (Carlson-Paige & Levin, 1992).

The 1978 National Institute of Education study, *Violent Schools–Safe Schools*, has been credited as the first large-scale investigation of school crime and violence. Statistics from both this study and the 1989 *School Crime Supplement* to the national crime survey showed that school crime consisted mostly of nonviolent larcenies, rather than violent attacks or robberies. Until 1993, the bulk of school crime was basically "furtive misbehavior"—theft of unattended property, fights between students that broke up when teachers appeared, graffiti on bathroom walls and so forth (Toby, 1983). A 1983 Department of Justice report also found that theft was more common than assault or robbery of both teachers and students; however, this report (Toby, 1983) further stipulated that:

(1) Rates of assaults or robberies for students were twice as high for junior high schools as senior high schools.
(2) Schools in larger cities had a higher incidence of school violence.
(3) Four percent of all secondary school students surveyed reported that they had stayed home from school out of fear at least once in the past month.
(4) Twelve percent of secondary school teachers reported that they had hesitated to confront misbehaving students in the past month.

In 1991 in the state of Florida, 546 students were asked about violence they had seen at school. Results indicated that 83% had witnessed fighting, 16% had seen students assault teachers, 20% had seen a student pull a knife on someone and 7% had witnessed someone being threatened with a gun (Kadel & Follman, 1993).

Currently, the frequency of violence on school campuses appears to be a critical problem of increasing proportions, perhaps fueled by a 300% increase in news media coverage of school violence in the past few years. A majority of educators believe that violent crime in the United States has increased dramatically during the past twenty years and that students increasingly feel unsafe at school; however, educators and students are surprised when information presented on school violence is contradictory, especially when reports indicate that incidents of violent crime are not on the increase. Even more interesting are the data recently released from the National Educational Longitudinal Study, which showed that, between 1980 and 1990, there was a 12.2% decrease in the number of students who reported feeling unsafe at shool and an 8.1% decrease in the proportion of tenth graders nationwide who reported that they felt unsafe at school (Furlong, 1994).

National statistics from government and private sources, however, indicate that youth violence in general is on the increase. The Centers for Disease Control and Prevention reported that in the fall of 1991, one in twenty students carried a gun at least once a month. The 1991 National Goals Report stated that one out of every four high school seniors reported that they had been threatened with violence; 14% said that they were injured in school. A 1993 *USA Weekend* survey of 65,000 students across the nation revealed that 55% of the students in grades 10-12 know that weapons are regularly brought to school; 79% of the respondents reported violence often occurs from insignificant things such as bumping into someone (Weaver, 1994).

Public sentiment about school violence is influenced by the increased media coverage. Five major newspapers (*Los Angeles Times, The New York Times, Washington Post, Wall Street Journal* and *Christian Science Monitor*) were surveyed for articles that focused on school violence published between 1982 and the present. Of the 349 articles printed during this time period, many of the articles listed statistics without a primary source and many included sensational incidents designed to substantiate the pervasiveness of the problem. Thus, media coverage may accurately report increased public awareness and concern about school violence, but it may not accurately reflect what is actually happening on school campuses (Furlong, 1994).

School crime and violence statistics should not be equated with violent juvenile crime in general. Because there are no current national data on the actual level of violent crime committed by juveniles, researchers rely on the number of arrests reported by the FBI's *Uniform Crime Reports* of youth under age eighteen as an indicator. Juvenile arrests for violent crimes have increased dramatically since 1987. Although youths under the age of twenty comprised only 14% of the FBI's survey population, this age group accounted for 30% of violent crime victimizations. Further, such teen victimizations were more likely to occur in or around school, with schools having gangs reporting higher victimization rates (Allen-Hagen & Sickmund, 1993).

While generalized national data are available (though frequently misleading), states and local communities usually do not have localized information about school crime in their area on which to base decisions about policies and resource allocation. The Clinton administration's Safe Schools Act of 1993 requires schools and districts wishing to qualify for funding to assess and report the incidence of school crime and violence; therefore, statewide standardized reporting systems must be developed and consistently administered to provide accurate data on school crime from all districts. An effective system such as this requires standardization, training for all personnel involved, monitoring and assistance in reporting procedures. Without clear standards, schools may use different definitions of what constitutes a crime or violent act and may unintentionally underreport or overreport the incidence of crime on their respective campuses.

WEAPONS IN THE SCHOOLS

Gun violence in schools is a major problem. New York City schools operate a security force costing $60 million per year. Some California schools holds "bullet drills" to teach the students to hit the floor in case of gunfire (Weaver, 1994). Each day, public school systems are confronted with the problem of weapons in the school. A "weapon" usually refers to a gun or knife but can be identified as any instrument used to attack another person. This includes firearms, switchblades, knives, swords, metal knuckles, billy clubs, sandbags, slingshots, daggers, acid, loaded or blank cartridges and/or ammunition, broken glass, pencils and so on. A weapon, therefore, can take on unlimited forms.

However, it is the dramatic increase in the use of firearms at schools that has brought the issue of school safety to the forefront of the public's attention (Kadel & Follman, 1993).

Nationwide, between 1986 and 1990, at least seventy-five people were killed with guns at school, over 200 were severely wounded by guns, and at least 242 people were held hostage at school by gun-wielding assailants. Based on a national study of students, the National School Safety Center estimated that 135,000 adolescents carried guns to school daily in 1987. An estimated 270,000 others carried guns to school at least once during the school year (Kadel & Follman, 1993).

Presently, California is the only state that publishes annual data on school gun confiscations. There the number of gun incidents reportedly increased 40% from the 1987-1988 school year to the 1988-1989 school year. During a four-year period from 1989 to 1993, a 100% overall increase in gun-related incidents was reported, including a 50% rise in gun-related incidents in elementary schools and an 80% increase in middle schools. The most staggering statistic was a 142% increase in gun-related incidents at the high school level during the same period.

With an estimated 400,000 adolescents carrying handguns to school yearly, there is a tremendous potential for even greater rates of deaths, injury and violence. As it stands now, at least thirty-five states have schools that have already been the scene of shootings or hostage situations.

In an effort to stop the infiltration of weapons at school, many school district personnel have stepped up their efforts to insure the safety of their schools. Stronger penalties have been written into board policies, and metal detectors have been installed at the school entrances of many city schools. Security officials and police have been hired by many school districts in an effort to educate students about the dangers and rules concerning weapons and at the same time enforce these rules. Motivational speakers have been used to speak to the students about the dangers of weapons, much in the manner of a "Say No to Drugs" platform. Possibly, the strongest deterrent thus far has been to increase searches of lockers, school property and, sometimes, even students.

Although it would seem logical to practice all of the aforementioned techniques, several cases of litigation have come forth from students and parents claiming an infringement of their civil and constitutional rights. School personnel, already fearful of the threat of weapons at school, also fear litigation for their actions.

In 1969, the United States Supreme Court, in *Tinker v. Des Moines,* concretely outlined the rights of students in public schools. Writing for a seven-justice majority, Justice Fortas stipulated that although the rights of students could be modified or curtailed by school policies, students did not shed their rights at the schoolhouse gate. These rights were secure, however, only so long as their exercise did not materially or substantially interfere with the educational mission or disciplinary processes of the school (Yudof, Kirp & Levin, 1992). This ruling established the boundaries for future litigation.

In 1985, a fourteen-year-old student was accused of violating a school rule against smoking cigarettes in a school lavatory. When the student denied the accusation, the assistant vice-principal searched her purse. The student filed suit against the school district and, thus, began what is now considered the landmark case for search and seizure, known as *New Jersey v. T.L.O.*

The Supreme Court held that public school officials need only a *reasonable cause,* rather than a probable cause to justify a search of a student. The Court also noted that this standard would spare teachers and school administrators the necessity of schooling themselves in the details of probable cause and permit them to regulate their conduct according to the dictates of reason and common sense. The Supreme Court ruled that reasonableness of the search is to be determined by a two-pronged test:

(1) Whether the action was justified at its inception
(2) Whether the search as actually conducted was reasonably related in scope to the circumstances that justified the interference in the first place

The Court also found that the warrant requirements of the Fourth Amendment do not apply to school authorities. Thus, searches without warrants have been found to be permissible if the official had reasonable grounds to believe that a student possessed evidence of illegal activity or activity that would interfere with school discipline and/or order (Frisby & Becklam, 1993).

One way school officials have tried to deter students from bringing weapons to school and to minimize student searches is through the use of metal detectors. While the Supreme Court has upheld the use of metal detectors to screen passengers at airports and state courthouses, the issue of metal detectors in schools has yet to reach the highest court. If and when the Supreme Court does hear a case on metal detectors in schools, it will most assuredly use the two-prong criteria between students' privacy rights and the schools' rights to maintain a safe environment to resolve the issue.

Ironic, but true, is the fact that schools that use metal detectors and other forms of security measures open the door for the possibility of litigation if the measures fail, but at the same time, school officials could be held liable if nothing were done to prevent weapons on school grounds—a catch-22.

The sad truth is that the incidence of students having weapons on school campuses is on the rise. Students bring weapons to school for many reasons such as 1) to show off, 2) out of fear, 3) for protection, and 4) simply as a way of life (gang-related). The school system does, indeed, reflect societal attitudes and values that can change drastically in a short period of time. A perfect example illustrating the thinking of many students in urban schools is captured by a teenage boy in a southern school who, when asked his concern about carrying a weapon, responded that he would "rather be judged by twelve which be carried by six." It is this attitude among the youth that is in drastic need of renewal. However, not all weapons are brought to school by students. On May 20, 1988, a woman walked into an elementary school in a quiet suburb of Chicago carrying three handguns. Before she left, five children had been wounded and an eight-year-old boy was dead. The only possible way to have prevented this would have been to have secured the entire school's perimeters—something that was not feasible. Since that time, there have been numerous instances of this nature occurring around the country. So, in essence, educators and students are internally and externally at risk.

We, as educators, know logically that we cannot build a fortress surrounding the school, nor can we search each and every person who goes into or out of the school at all times. We can, however, take some important steps to improve school safety. Messing (1993) suggests that school officials can do the following:

(1) Develop a sound school policy regarding weapons.
(2) Provide all staff members suitable and appropriate training on policy implementation.
(3) Plan for crisis intervention.
(4) Continue security measures already in place (improving where needed or incorporating where deficient).
(5) Establish and/or enhance conflict resolution programs.

The problem of weapons at schools is not going to go away soon. Increased searches, metal detectors, extra security devices and personnel will help; however, the real change will come from the school personnel drastically improving the teaching of conflict resolution strategies so students can have alternative means of solving problems peacefully.

CONFLICT RESOLUTION

Historically, school personnel have assumed the responsibility of teaching students peaceful means of resolving conflicts only in a superficial manner. Today, because conflicts among students are escalating due to family, economic and/or social stress, school personnel need to drastically increase their efforts. Children bring unresolved tensions into the school environment, and the resulting conflicts, if not ended peacefully, may end in violence (Messing, 1993).

More and more students are resorting to violent means to solve their disputes. Education can be essential in counteracting this rising problem of violence as a choice. Educators can reverse this trend by providing students, staff and the community with the skills and strategies necessary to promote nonviolent means of conflict resolution.

Conflict resolution is a method of resolving disputes; it uses a set of formal procedures to improve communication, promote empathy, increase sensitivity, encourage acceptance of ethnical/racial diversity and develop negotiating skills. Knowledge of this process enables a person to anticipate and prevent certain types of conflict. It stresses a "stop and think" attitude. The conflict resolution process results in the ability to solve conflict in a positive way and creates opportunities for creative problem solving (Messing, 1993).

Conflict resolution has roots in the peace movement and collective bargaining of the 1960s. Programs began to appear as part of the curriculum in isolated schools in the 1970s; however, it was not until the 1980s that conflict resolution strategies began to gain popularity. In 1982, the Martin Luther King, Jr. Law and Public Service Magnet High School in Cleveland initiated one of the first student mediation programs in Ohio: Winning Against Violent Environments (WAVE). Even though this program was successful and won national acclaim, duplication of this success spread slowly in Ohio and throughout the nation (Stephens, 1993).

It is estimated that only 2000 schools nationwide have incorporated the use of conflict resolution into their curriculum. The programs tend to fall into three general categories:

(1) Those that train teachers to learn how to encourage students to state their complaints in such a way that it leaves open the possibility of resolving the problem through peaceful means: this is done mostly through the use of "I" messages such as, "I feel really angry when you call me names," which prevents the constant hurling back and forth of insults.
(2) Those that train students how to do the mediating by learning techniques from their teacher or trained instructors: when conflicts arise, student mediators step in and deal with the problem first. Student mediators handle everything from playground squabbles to gang fights.
(3) Those that use a special conflict resolution curriculum in classrooms (mostly in the upper grades): classes are structured to either offer conflict resolution as a subject itself or to integrate it into the existing curriculum (Williams, 1991).

Endorsements for these types of programs have come from the American Psychological Association in their report on youth violence. In addition, this report urged Congress to finance school programs for violence prevention from early childhood through adolescence.

CONFLICT RESOLUTION STRATEGIES

Conflict resolution is a general descriptor for a group of strategies that include mediation, negotiation, conciliation, alternate dispute resolution (ADR), and arbitration. These strategies have been evolving since the mid-1960s and have played an increasingly significant role in our society (Messing, 1993).

Mediation

Mediation is one of the oldest forms of conflict resolution and refers to a structured process in which a neutral third party gets involved to assist two or more disputing parties reach an agreeable, peaceful agreement. At the very heart of mediation is the idea that the mediator, acting as a facilitator, helps the disagreeing parties work together to identify common interests and goals. It is the responsibility of the disputing parties to make recommendations, determine the final outcome and find mutually agreeable solutions to the dispute (Messing, 1993). Student mediation can range from on-the-spot, informal interventions to sit-down, scheduled mediation sessions (Stephens, 1993) Mediators are sometimes chosen by their peers and must spend hours training and practicing problem-solving and communication skills. Mediators are forbidden from assigning blame, passing judgment or showing favoritism and must agree to confidentiality (Meek, 1992). They also agree not to impose their views of settlement, but to help the disputing parties communicate more effectively and in a peaceful way. Some of the communication rules mediators follow include the following (Meek, 1992):

(1) State your own feelings clearly, without being accusatory—begin with "I feel . . ." instead of "You always . . ." to ensure honest communication.
(2) Never interrupt or finish another person's sentences.
(3) Concentrate on what is being said to you, rather than on your response.
(4) Maintain eye contact with the other person.
(5) Ask questions for clarification.
(6) Repeat the other person's ideas for understanding.
(7) Never put anyone down.

Negotiation

Negotiation refers to voluntary problem solving or bargaining carried out directly between the disputing parties without the use of a third party. They try to reach a compromise that is agreeable to all parties without the benefit of a mediator. Some steps in the negotiation process can include the following:
(1) Say what you think the problem is.
(2) Say what you want to happen.
(3) State what the limits are.
(4) Work out an agreement.
(5) Ask if everyone is happy with the solution.
(6) Repeat steps 1–5 if necessary.

Arbitration

Arbitration refers to voluntary or required submission of a dispute to a third party who is neutral. The arbitrator renders a decision after hearing arguments from both sides and assessing the evidence. In binding arbitration, the parties agree to an assigned arbitrator and are legally bound by the decision (Messing, 1993).

Conciliation

Conciliation refers to informal voluntary negotiations in which a third party tries to bring the disputing parties together. Communication is encouraged to reduce tension, relay information between parties and provide assistance, when needed, for a safe environment in which to reach some sort of compromise. Conciliation can be a step that occurs before formal mediation or arbitration so that potentially volatile situations can be negotiated before they get out of hand (Messing, 1993).

Alternate Dispute Resolution

Alternate dispute resolution (ADR) refers to alternatives to the traditional court process. ADR attempts to use mediation, negotiation or arbitration to settle civil cases in informal sessions with magistrates or judges before going to trial. It encourages agreements on the part of the disputing parties (Messing, 1993).

TEACHING THE TEACHERS

Teachers and administrators are constantly involved in conflicts of varying degrees throughout the school day. At times, the conflicts are so minor and routine that the educator is not aware of what he or she is doing. Mediation of conflicts frequently fall on the educator to resolve, when in fact another party can assist or deal with the conflict just as effectively. In most cases, however, teachers are expected to teach and/or model conflict strategies before they have been properly trained and may, in fact, complicate the conflict situation.

Educators should share conflict resolution responsibilities with students, teachers, staff, or administrators. Educators must also understand that they are role models for their students. If they cannot resolve their own conflicts or ask for help from others, students will be reluctant to go to them for assistance.

Mediators must be seen as valuable tools in conflict resolution before presenting the mediation process to the students. This strengthens a mediator's position and maximizes the chance for a successful solution.

Conflict resolution does not happen by accident nor can it be ignored or deemed as "not my job, I am here to teach." In the past, teachers have often handled disputes or violent confrontations by imposing a solution or some form of discipline on the participants. This may have temporarily solved a problem; however, it probably accomplished nothing toward the long-term goal of developing positive conflict resolution skills in those involved. Allowing the students to solve their conflicts involves defining the problem, brainstorming possible solutions, using negotiation skills and choosing solutions that satisfy both sides (win/win solutions).

One of the most dramatic success stories comes from a middle school in Albuquerque, New Mexico. Gang-related violence had been plaguing their school. The administration persuaded gang leaders to meet twice a week for a month. They agreed to a set of rules for the mediation sessions and negotiated everything from fear for the safety of their families to unfair treatment by the school administration. After a month, the gang leaders and the principal signed an agreement stating that they would try to solve future disputes by peaceful means. The fighting soon ended and the gangs continued to hold mediation sessions. This is just one example of how conflict resolution strategy, when taught successfully, can reduce violence and can be the long-term solution to ending school violence.

Carlson-Paige and Levin (1992) conducted a study of conflict resolution skills in urban districts. They developed the following conflict resolution guidelines for teachers:

- Guideline 1: Teachers can help children understand the problems that cause their conflicts in terms that make sense. For young children, this will mean helping them define their problems in terms of physical objects and concrete actions. With age and experience, children slowly learn to see problems in a larger context—in more abstract terms that involve underlying motives, feelings and intentions—and from more than their own point of view.
- Guideline 2: Teachers can help children see that their problems

have two sides. While it is difficult for young children to do this on their own, a teacher may show them the two viewpoints in the immediate context of the problem they are having.
- Guideline 3: Teachers can help children see the whole problem and how their behavior contributed to it. After a conflict occurs, they can help children look at the specific actions that led to the problem and what effects the children's actions had on others. Teachers can also try to enter into the heat of the conflict to help children think of what will happen if they do what they are headed toward. As children develop, they become better able to link cause and effect and to predict the results of their actions.
- Guideline 4: Teachers can help children think of winning solutions when they have a hard time coming up with solutions of their own. They can offer several winning solutions by suggesting a variety of ways in which children can share positive solutions that worked for them in the past. In addition, once children have tried out a winning solution, teachers can assist in its overall evaluation.
- Guideline 5: Teachers can suggest winning solutions that recast the situation in some creative way to include children's joint participation. Helping children find inclusive solutions can lead to more joint participation and cooperation as opposed to traditional win/win solutions.
- Guideline 6: Children should have many opportunities to explore what happens in conflicts in which one or both parties lose. While most conflict resolution programs focus on win/win solutions, younger children are still working on what happens as conflicts worsen and on what hitting, fighting and name calling can lead to in the process. It is often outside actual conflicts that teachers can help children see how bad leads to worse in a conflict and then help children use what they have learned when they have conflicts. It is easier for children to work on conflict-solving skills when they are not caught up in the heat of their own conflicts. They need many opportunities to experiment with their developing skills. Classroom activities may include class meetings, mock trials, literature involving conflict, puppets and role-playing.
- Guideline 7: Teachers can help young children see what they need to do to put their positive solutions into practive. To do

this may require direct intervention in children's conflicts, helping them move from the conflict to the solution. Negotiation, while critical to the resolution of conflict, is a difficult concept for children. Teachers may need to monitor the negotiation process to see if the children agree with each other's ideas, showing them that negotiation is a mutual process.
- Guideline 8: From an early age, no matter what developmental skills children have, one of the most important things that we can do is instill in them a sense of empowerment—that they can do things to create more positive social relationships. The more children try out their skills and experience success in resolving their own conflicts, the more they will see themselves as empowered and successful and the more skills will evolve.

CONCLUSION

The principal is the key player in establishing communication practices internally with the students and teachers and externally with the community (DeMoulin, 1991). The literature suggests that the principal can minimize the potential for violence by

(1) Sending a clear message to the student body and the community that acts of violence, gangs, weapons and drugs will not be tolerated within the schools
(2) Keeping the lines of communication open and networking with other administrators of schools in his or her area and state to keep abreast of problems that they may be facing
(3) Keeping communication open with students, encouraging them to feel free to come forward and letting other administrators know of any drugs or weapons being brought to school
(4) Preplanning actions in case a particular situation occurs in his or her building, thinking of situations he or she could encounter and planning possible strategies
(5) Keeping in constant contact with local law enforcement officials to keep informed of trends or suspicions they might have
(6) Taking a proactive approach to discipline, establishing positive relationships with possible troublemakers, and keeping his or her finger on the "pulse" of the student body
(7) Providing inservice training for teachers and staff about gangs,

drugs and weapons and about effective strategies for dealing with potentially violent students
(8) Keeping abreast of the latest legal implications by reading current administrative periodicals—however, when in doubt, consulting the school district's attorney
(9) Teaching students the skills necessary to make decisions resulting in appropriate outcomes
(10) Teaching students how to seek nonviolent solutions to their problems by working collaboratively with others
(11) Providing educators with the means to model problem-solving behavior

Students have a stake in minimizing violent situations. Van Steenbergen (1994) provides the following roles students can play in violence prevention as suggested by the CTC School Violence Advisory Panel:

(1) Students should learn to listen to other students.
(2) Self-esteem and personal social responsibility can be improved when students are provided opportunities to help others.
(3) Students need to see more people from their own generation doing things that matter.
(4) Students should be able to ask questions "straight up" and get a "straight" answer.
(5) Peer pressure works.
(6) Students can be recruited and trained to identify strengths and weaknesses in their school, teach each others to solve conflicts and mediate differences, encourage personal and social responsibility among students, enhance self-esteem in themselves and others and identify potential student leaders.

Van Steenbergen (1994) also offers suggestions for what families can do to curb violence. These include
(1) Building emotional resilience in families and emphasizing strengths
(2) Creating a family environment rich in protective factors, including caring, setting clear expectations, providing consistency and nurturing
(3) Providing supportive relationships
(4) Creating an emotional, protective shied through caring, responsible adults who have well-defined roles

(5) Developing a neighborhood watch
(6) Talking and listening to children and reassuring them that they are okay
(7) Keeping informed and informing children
(8) Taking time to review their family's ways of resolving conflict responsibly
(9) Discussing with their family ways to resolve conflict responsibly
(10) Learning how to seek help, support and assistance

The role of the family in violence prevention is much more important than the role of the school; however, without the school, the family's success may be limited. The school and community need to work together to support the family and its effort to prevent violence. Currently, there are numerous programs being used in schools to try to provide this support in violence prevention. Below are three examples that might provide models for beginning this supportive coalition.

Community-Based Youth Violence Prevention Program

This program was developed at Temple University. It uses an educational curriculum and a mass media campaign. The developers tracked the extent of penetration of the program and found that the media campaign produced the most beneficial results (Hausman, 1992).

Positive Adolescents' Choices Training

This program specifically targeted the black adolescent to improve communication, problem-solving and negotiation skills. This program demonstrated success in improving meaningful dialogue among inner-city youths (Hammond, 1991).

Natural Helpers Program

This program encourages prosocial peer support for a broad spectrum of adolescent problems, including drug use. The developers utilize extensive peer support groups to assist troubled youths in facing their problems while attempting to elevate their self-respect. The program tries to encourage earned self-esteem (Hicks, 1992).

AUTHOR'S PERSPECTIVE

Not long ago, parents worried about their children's education with regard to how well they could read, write and do math. Today, they fear that their children will be severely injured or not come home at all due to increased school violence, especially the increase of weapons at school.

School districts are responsible for maintaining a safe atmosphere conducive to learning, not only for students, but for teachers as well. The potential for violence is making school personnel more aware of the school's responsibility to protect its students *and* teachers. Parents and memebers of the community must also take a proactive role in addressing the causes of, and solutions to violence, if the violence in our schools is ever going to end. As stated by McPartland and McDill (1987),

> Too often the problem of violence in schools becomes entangled in a vicious cycle of scapegoating, finger pointing, and avoidance of responsibility by individuals and those segments of society that must work together to solve the problem. (p. 86)

Supported by a strong coalition between schools, parents and the community, families may be able to incorporate the conflict resolution strategies necessary to reduce the potential for violent activity of our nation's youth.

REFERENCES

Allen-Hagen, B. & Sickmund, M. (1993). Juveniles and violence: Juvenile offending and victimization. *U.S. Department of Justice Fact Sheet*, 3:1–4.

Andrews, R. (1993). Superintendents' role in leadership. Modified from introductory remarks at Superintendents' conference, Columbia, Missouri.

Carlson-Paige, N. & Levin, D. E. (1992). Making peace in violent times. *Young Children*, 48(1):4–13.

Dear, J. D., Scott, K. & Marshall, D. (1994). An attack on school violence. *School Safety*, 4–7.

DeMoulin, D. F. (1991). School administrators in the twenty-first century. *Journal of School Leadership*, 1(1):54–58.

Edmonds, R. (1979). Effective schools for the urban poor. *Educational Leadership*, 37:15–27.

Frisby, D. & Becklam, J. (1993). Dealing with violence and threats of violence in school. *NASSP Bulletin*, 10–15.

Furlong, M. (1994). Evaluating school violence. *School Safety*, 23–27.

Hammond, R. W. (1991). Preventing violence in at-risk African-American youth. *Journal of Health Care for the Poor and Underserved*, 2(3):359–373.

Hausman, A. J. (1992). Patterns of teen exposure to a community-based violence prevention project. *Journal of Adolescent Health*, 13(8):668-675.

Hicks, G. F. (1992). Natural helpers needs assessment and self-esteem. Pro-social foundation for adolescent substance abuse prevention and early intervention. *Journal of Alcohol and Drug Education*, 37(2):71-82.

Kadel, S. & Follman, J. (1993). Reducing school violence in Florida. *Southeastern Regional Vision for Education* (ERIC Document Reproduction Service No. ED 355, 614).

McPartland, J. M. & McDill, E. L. (1987). *Schools and violence.* Garden City, New York: Doubleday.

Meek, M. (Fall, 1992). The peacekeepers—Students use mediation to resolve conflicts. *Teaching Tolerance*, 46-52.

Messing, J. K. (1993). Mediation: An intervention for counselors. *Journal of Counseling & Development*, 72:67-72.

Stephens, J. B. (Winter, 1993). A better way to resolve disputes. *School Safety*, 12-13.

Toby, J. (1983). *Violence in schools.* Washington, D.C.: United States Department of Justice: Research in Brief.

Van Steenbergen, N. (Winter, 1994). Letter to the editor. *School Safety*, 6-22.

Weaver, M. T. (Winter, 1994). Gazing into a crystal ball. *School Safety*, 8-11.

Williams, S. K. (October, 1991). We can work it out. *Teacher Magazine*, 22-23.

Yudof, M., Kirp, D. & Levin, B. (1992). *Education policy and the law.* St. Paul, MN: West Publishing Company.

CHAPTER 2

Psychological Aspects of Safe Schools

ROBERT NIELSEN

INTRODUCTION

"IF you build it, they will come." The underlying concept in the popular movie *Field of Dreams* (if a physical area is created for a specific purpose, that purpose will be realized) can be applied to an educational environment, as well as an athletic field. If we create a physical space that is appropriate for healthy learning to take place, it will. More than just the physical surroundings, however, that space symbolizes the dedication, desire and energy of the people involved within it. The management and the team must work closely together to create the necessary atmosphere if those within that space are to feel a willingness to be there. When people enjoy what they are doing and feel free to accomplish the tasks at hand, they will more naturally involve themselves with the challenges of those tasks. They will appreciate the significance of their involvement. William Glasser (1969) stated, "Unless we can provide schools where children, through a reasonable use of their capabilities, can succeed, we will do little to solve the major problems of our country" (p. 6). He went on to say that students need to "learn to be responsible for each other, to care for each other, and to help each other, not only for the sake of others, but for their own sake" (p. 14).

All living creatures are confronted by both the environment that surrounds them and the environment within them. Although the external environment usually receives the major focus, it is the internal environment that plays the predominant role in our lives. Changes to both the external and the internal environments are important when attempting to improve the quality of life, yet often the internal is overlooked in an attempt to manipulate the external.

A common desire is to have an external environment available to meet our every need; therefore, great efforts to change "things" outside ourselves may become the focus for solving all of our distress. Although positive change in our external environment can be healthy, internal change must also take place in order for our lives to be fulfilling. Our emotional well-being may not be as dependent on the external environment as we sometimes are prone to believe.

Just as "beauty is in the eye of the beholder," the way in which we perceive our external environment also becomes an individual issue. Our perceptions of that which is outside of ourselves lead to how we feel about those surroundings and, probably to some degree, how we feel in general. These feelings constitute our psychological state and are more dependent on our subjective perceptions of the "things" outside of ourselves than the objective reality of what those "things" actually are.

Feelings don't just happen. Feelings are triggered not only by the stimuli around us, but by how we interpret the stimuli. All the senses play a part in how the human organism experiences life. Sight, hearing, touch, smell and taste all serve to receive stimuli and transmit them to the brain. The brain serves to translate those stimuli into what the individual will experience as various levels of either pain or pleasure. Since pleasure normally includes the absence of pain, psychological safety (or a feeling of security) assumes the absence of any perceived significant threat.

In order for students to feel safe in any surrounding, there must be a reality component to that safety.

> Not only does a school's environment affect learning, but more than any other setting it influences how students—especially high school students—conform to society. School's internal life influences how all students behave, often more powerfully than the home or community. It is unlikely that a student immersed in a school environment of delinquency will form a more responsible view of society at large. (Rapp, Carrington & Nicholson, 1992, p. 61)

For students to consistently feel safe, they need to perceive that their environment is safe—physically and psychologically. Although the student's physical safety is addressed in the other chapters of this book, the psychological or emotional safety of the child is just as important. In psychoanalytic terms, psychological threats are threats to a person's "ego" or the concept of his or her worth as an individual. A manifestation of this concept is when a child is afraid that he or she will be ridiculed, criticized, teased or otherwise treated in a way that is demeaning. Children develop defenses or "coping mechanisms" that allow them to deal with the anxiety brought about by these threats. Often, the defense will be successful in dealing with the anxiety, but it can simultaneously cause dysfunctional or socially maladaptive learning and behavior to take place if the defense mechanism is the child's *only* means for dealing with the stress.

In the real world, there is no absence of anxiety evoking stimuli, just levels of the threat they pose. Certainly, there are times when we are confronted by a high degree of these undesirable circumstances and there are other times when the degree of threat in our lives seems to be very small. When the degree appears small, we are said to feel more secure or "safe" within our environment. What we want is for students within the schools to experience, most often, these feelings of safety and security, which result from minimal to no levels of threat existing in the environment.

Even though the school has a tremendous influence on a child's self-concept or emotional well-being, safety for a student extends beyond the realm of the school yard. For example, if the child believes that he or she must behave in a certain way in order to be given food, then there is a threat to the physical well-being if those expectations are not met. Physical safety is threatened; further, the concept of self-worth may also be involved. The child may take on the self-concept belief that goes something like this: "If I don't behave in the way my parent expects me to, that parent may not give me dinner because he or she doesn't love me. If she or he doesn't love me it is because I am not worthy of his or her love." The threat that comes from the child's parents offering "conditional love" is a definite threat to the child's self-concept.

As explained, the realm of psychological safety within the school is much more than an issue of appropriate physical facilities. Not only do the physical surroundings need to offer everyone a healthy environment, but the emotional atmosphere conveyed by the people within the system also plays an enormous role in the perceptions of all who are involved. People who feel accepted by those around them also feel stronger and more capable of accomplishment than if they are confronted by an environment that is perceived as threatening. Psychological safety, therefore, is extremely important for youth.

Even though many children learn maladaptive ways of social interaction that result in behavior problems within the school setting, sometimes these problem behaviors are a sign that the student is experiencing conflict, frustration or a threat of some kind. School personnel are often sensitive to this and are willing and able to intervene in order to understand better the reasons behind the child's behavior. There are hundreds of examples of school personnel (teachers, administrators, counselors, nurses, secretaries, cooks and janitors, etc.) who have established relationships with students who have struggled with behavior problems. In some cases, the behavior problems diminished or even completely disappeared because an adult established a link with the student that offered the student acceptance and understanding, which in turn helped him or her feel emotionally "safe."

Abraham Maslow (1962) has written volumes on human needs. He states that people strive to meet the most basic needs first. Examples of basic needs are the need for food, liquid, oxygen and sleep. Maslow proposed a hierarchy of needs that exist within the individual. When an individual's basic needs are not met, the person concentrates on fulfilling those needs first. If a person is very hungry, for instance, she or he will strive to satisfy the need to eat before seeking self-esteem fulfillment. Next on Maslow's hierarchy are the safety needs. According to Frank G. Goble (1970)

> . . . Children need a predictable world; a child prefers consistency, fairness and a certain amount of routine. When these elements are absent he [she] becomes anxious and insecure. Freedom within limits rather than total permissiveness is preferred; in fact, it is necessary for the development of well-adjusted children. . . . (p. 40)

It becomes clear that in order for children to meet safety needs, they need to experience appropriate, yet well-defined boundaries. Children need to know what is expected of them and simultaneously have the freedom to express who they are in a socially acceptable way. They need to be able to experiment, explore and make mistakes without feeling as though they have failed. When students experience relationships that convey these attitudes, they will have established an element of psychological safety within an otherwise threatening world. According to Glasser (1969), "We must get [students] responsibly involved from early childhood in an educational system in which they can succeed enough to function successfully in our society" (p. 10). The key to this kind of involvement becomes the psychological safety that offers them freedom to learn and grow.

Appropriate boundaries that are well defined give the student space to grow, yet offer a degree of order necessary for security and a feeling of safety. An analogy might be the boundaries of a race track. If the race track is lined on each side by concrete walls, a mistake by the driver may well be a catastrophe. If the race track has no boundaries, just an open area in which cars drive around, it becomes a demolition derby. In order that there is an appropriate direction and an order to the race, the track must be well defined and have boundaries such as straw bales that will give a bit when the driver makes a mistake, yet will clearly indicate that he or she has taken a turn that it would be good not to take in the future. A positive piece of learning has taken place, yet the individual is not destroyed in the process.

As children grow and develop physically, they also go through developmental or psychological stages that are unique unto themselves, yet have characteristics that are common to the development of all human beings.

> Although research has demonstrated the important effects of school counseling, many counseling interventions have not adequately taken into account the developmental differences that influence children's performance in school. Counselors and other educators, for example, have often failed to consider that children characterized as discipline problems may be at different developmental stages from their classmates. (Brake & Gerler, 1994, p. 170)

Eric Erikson (1963) described eight life stages and presented them as focus points in an individual's emotional development. He also stated that these stages were not absolutely distinct and that there were times when emotional needs from earlier stages would resurface later in the person's life. These stages are summarized in Table 1.

As stated in Table 1, the first stage is trust versus mistrust, and although it is centered on the first year of life, mistrust and a feeling of threat may emerge in later life stages if the environment being experienced is one which triggers that feeling.

Students within the school system may not trust those around them and this will have a negative impact on their current emotional growth. The same concept holds true in the second of Erikson's stages. If students do not feel free to express themselves, they are probably feeling the threat of rejection. They will not feel safe enough to develop their own identities, which is all important according to Erikson's fifth stage. Again, their perception of their environment becomes critical in their healthy emotional development.

The influence of American society on our youth today is not generally observed as "safe" and free of physical threat. Movies and television entail major time involvements for our young people, creating a focus on danger and violence that is experienced by most children on

Table 1. Psychosocial development stages.

Trust vs. mistrust (0–1)
   Consistency and order in care leads to trust. Unpredictable care leads to mistrust.
Autonomy vs. doubt (1–3)
   Support for exploration of skills leads to autonomy. Lack of support and rejection leads to doubt.
Initiative vs. guilt (3–5)
   Expression of self freely through language and activities leads to initiative. Restrictions may lead to a sense of guilt.
Industry vs. inferiority (5–11)
   Constructing and organizing freely leads to being industrious. Failure to meet other's expectations to produce or perform on a regular basis may lead to a sense of inferiority.
Identity vs. role confusion (11–18)
   Understanding and accepting the sameness of self leads to identity. Confusion and lack of self-understanding may cause internal role conflict.
Intimacy vs. isolation (young adulthood)
   Linking with others emotionally leads to intimacy. Isolation may be a result of competitive and hostile behavior.
Generativity vs. stagnation (middle age)
   Preparing, or giving back to, the next generation leads to emotional wellness. Focus mostly on self creates stagnation.
Integrity vs. despair (old age)
   Satisfaction with one's life leads to integrity. Despair comes from perceiving life as unsatisfying or worthless.

Source: Adapted from Erikson, 1963.

a daily basis. Although movies and television dramas are not reality, they are reinforced, unfortunately, by reality as it is reported by the media. Not only are youth exposed to violence, but much of it is glorified and presented as desirable. It becomes understandable (though not acceptable) that, when conflicts between individuals occur and problem-solving skills are not well developed, violent action becomes the first alternative explored in dealing with conflict. "In desperation, [students] may repeat what was done to them or retaliate in some other way. They may create new alliances to deal with adversaries and thus perpetuate or escalate conflict" (Dysinger, 1993, p. 301). In this way, threat creates more threat, and any previously perceived "safe" environment becomes the exact opposite. "At times, teachers have reported an entire classroom so disrupted by peer struggles that learning is impossible" (Dysinger, 1993, pp. 301–302).

"It is important to stress that violence is a psychologically complex phenomenon whose origins are difficult for the average lay person to explain, understand, or predict" (Houston & Grubaugh, 1989, p. 27). Although most teachers and other school personnel may not be well equipped to control violent behavior, they are educationally prepared to implement developmental and proactive programming that will reduce the atmosphere that encourages violence. Many, if not most, colleges and universities, currently have implemented appropriate curriculum that includes guidance units that are preventative in nature. These programs enhance the atmosphere of safety and security, help the student build healthy self-concepts, and help the student to be a part of the healthy school atmosphere.

Goble (1970) noted clearly the influence of society on our youth. He stated,

> In our pathology and problem-centered culture, the emphasis is continually on the deficiencies, the shortcomings, the mistakes, and the inadequacies of people. Yet psychological tests with children have clearly revealed that when tired children were given a word of praise or commendation, an upward surge of new energy was evident. (An endless number of cases can be cited where the praise and encouragement of the child by his [her] teacher has significantly influenced his [her] course and development in life.) Conversely, when children were criticized or discouraged, their available physical energy declined dramatically. (p. 157)

The key to healthy emotional development becomes a healthy educational environment that offers consistency, acceptance of differences, an opportunity for adequate autonomy and optimal chances for individual successes to take place regularly. "Safe schools are orderly and purposeful places where students and staff are free to learn and teach without the threat of physical and psychological harm" (California State Department of Education, 1989).

The school must do its part to create a healthy educational environment. Not only is it important for teachers, administrators, counselors and other support staff to be actively aware of this, it is also important that students themselves offer this environment to each other. Guidance programs and peer programs can play an important role in the creation and implementation of a healthy school environment, and some of these programs will be offered as examples later in this chapter.

Schools can't do everything necessary to create a healthy, safe environment in which to grow. The community, and especially the home, impact strongly on students' feelings of safety. Students bring their values, needs and attitudes to school with them every day, and much of what they bring has been learned outside the school environment. Parent and community programs are valuable, but often they are not available, or those who can benefit from them most are not involved. The responsibility again falls back on where the students spend most of their active time—in the school.

Robert J. Havighurst (1972) proposed six developmental life stages and described common tasks within each stage. He stated that it is important that people who are of school age (six to eighteen) learn wholesome attitudes toward themselves and others. Getting along with peers, defining their gender roles, and establishing values consistent with socially responsible behavior are all of primary importance in this stage of the person's life.

It is the nature of social learning that it takes place in the presence of groups of people. The school brings people of similar ages together. Therefore, the school becomes the social agency most responsible for the developmental growth of the individual. It is within the school that social learning is given the conditions necessary to take place. Students will develop good or poor peer relations, establish positive or negative gender roles and develop constructive or destructive value systems. The social atmosphere of the school, as perceived by the student, goes a long way in determining the feeling of security and safety necessary for healthy development to take place. The school can actually be an oasis of safety for students experiencing the realities and the harshness of the outside world.

Proactive strategies that enhance the possibilities for a healthy psychological environment today are becoming much more the focus than the reactive strategies that have been so prevalent in the past.

> A proactive strategy is an attempt on the part of the administrators, teachers and other members of the instructional team to conceptualize, design, and implement measures to foster the development of positive behavioral and social skills, and to eliminate inappropriate behavior patterns within the school. The aims of proactive strategy are to decrease the opportunity for, and the likelihood of, violent outburst(s). (Houston & Grubaugh, 1989, p. 31)

In essence, if we can increase the opportunity for students to feel psychologically safe within the school, we will have also increased the likelihood that retroactive measures to deal with disruptive or violent behavior will not be necessary.

In a paper presented at the annual meeting of the American Alliance for Health, Physical Education, Recreation and Dance, components of a safety program for the elementary schools were presented by Daniel E. Della-Gustina (1990). Della-Gustina suggested a number of elements that are necessary for the effective implementation of an organized program to foster student's feeling more secure within the school environment. He outlined inservice programs for all school personnel, defined responsibilities of each, provided structure for administration and organization, established procedures for reporting and data gathering regarding safety issues and conducted evaluating procedures for the program. He specifically stated that

> This is the responsibility of all employees of the school district, and must be a collaborative effort. Collaboration is not merely cooperation. Collaboration means to solicit respect and act upon the input from all levels within the school district. Active participation in the decision making process is the fundamental concept of collaboration. (p. 4)

Through a collaborative effort, the school can be experienced as a caring place.

> In caring environments conflicts would occur, but they would not escalate into violence because one of the main concerns of the individuals would be not to hurt other members of the caring network. To accomplish this, youngsters need to learn how to solve interpersonal problems (conflict resolution curricula could help accomplish this), mediate problems among their peers (mediation program could help accomplish this), and also to be involved in the school's overall climate and well-being. To create caring environments schools need to be responsive to the students' needs and interests, so that they become student-centered. Caring communities also need to be aware of their structural problems (e.g., racism, poverty) and be willing to discuss them to find solutions. (Cueto, Bosworth & Sailes, 1993, p. 16)

It is clear that in order for people to feel safe and secure in the school setting, all people involved in that setting must take an active role in creating an atmosphere that *is* safe and secure. Many educators, philosophers and theorists have presented opinions regarding the composition of such an environment. Carl Rogers (1983) studied the conditions necessary for personal change and growth in the process of counseling and summarized these conditions by identifying three major components. "Rogers was the first to identify counselor genuineness, unconditional positive regard, and empathic understanding as necessary and sufficient conditions of therapeutic change" (Beale, 1993, p. 284).

Rogers was speaking of a therapeutic counseling relationship when he identified the three prime elements. These same conditions, however, if present in the school environment, will offer those involved optimal chance for positive development. Rogers (1983) clearly applied these concepts to the educational system when he stated,

> We have described the methods, techniques, and the program for a person-centered teaching approach. However, we cannot describe the more fundamental and critical interpersonal climate that must exist day by day if such a program is to succeed. Here, within the climate of unconditional positive regard and respect, empathy and personal genuineness, a community of people emerges, sharing the hopes, the fears, the excitement and courage to have an impact on a deadening, human wasteland.[1] (p. 174)

Genuineness means that the people are direct, honest and appropriate in their dealings with others. The agendas (boundaries) involved in the social structure are clear and understandable; there are no hidden agendas. True feelings, as well as straight cognitive thoughts, are shared among each other, and there is a respect for each other in that sharing. "Power plays" and "psychological games" are not a part of the environment; thus, people can learn truly to trust each other. Conflict is not eliminated, but there is an understanding that it is dealt with through resolution and problem-solving processes rather than aggressiveness or violent behaviors.

Unconditional positive regard means that people honor each other simply because they believe in the qualities of humankind. It does not mean that people accept all behaviors and attitudes that are displayed or expressed by others. There is an understood dignity and respect for the person, although there may not be an acceptance of that person's actions. The essence of the individual is recognized even when the individual has acted in an unacceptable way. For instance, when a student throws a brick through the classroom window, obviously, the behavior is not accepted; yet the student can be accepted as a valid and worthy human being. The behavior will have its consequences for the student, but the student will not be shamed or belittled. In this way, the student is held accountable for her or his behavior, yet will continue to be cared for and nurtured by those around her or him.

Withdrawing nurturing (or withdrawing caring) from someone because she or he has behaved in an unacceptable way does nothing to

---

[1] Reprinted with the permission of Simon & Schuster, Inc. from the Macmillan College text *Freedom to Learn for the 80's* by Carl Rogers. Copyright ©1983.

change that person's behavior. What it does is shame and belittle the individual, which is a threat to his or her ego, and therefore will contribute to the student's perception of insecurity and lack of emotional safety.

Unconditional positive regard is a difficult concept to grasp and an even more difficult concept to put into practice, yet it is the cornerstone of a strong bridge between people. It is what holds relationships together, and it is what makes for strong emotional environments. Families that practice this concept, for instance, are strong and supportive. Those that do not, develop family disputes and conflicts that last throughout their lifetimes. These family members simply do not believe in each other's worth and do not treat each other as worthy human beings. The same, unfortunately, can be true in the school. If people within any system, do not honor the worth of the others (all others) within that system, the atmosphere will convey distrust and threat. It will not offer the feelings of safety that foster growth and development. Through unconditional positive regard (as it has just been defined), a healthy, supportive atmosphere can evolve and flourish.

Accurate empathy means that one person has a good understanding about how another person is feeling. Accurate empathy involves trying to put oneself in another's place by asking the question, "If I were _____, how would I feel?" The concept does not mean that they feel sorry for or have sympathy for each other. Having accurate empathy is having the ability to get in touch with other people on an emotional level without actually experiencing their feelings. For example, if someone is in deep sorrow, we can understand how she or he is feeling and respect the person and the feeling he or she is experiencing. We do not have to be experiencing sorrow ourselves, and we do not have to feel "sorry for" the person who is in emotional pain.

Accurate empathy means that, even though there is no way we can know exactly how others are experiencing their lives, we can understand something about the feelings they are having in the process. It is not possible to know "just how they feel," yet trying to understand their feelings can go a long way in developing the unconditional positive regard discussed earlier. For instance, the student who threw the brick and broke the classroom window may have been "acting out" from his or her emotions in a very unacceptable way. Although his or her behavior was unacceptable, we may be able to help him or her better if we try to understand the emotional frustrations that led to the behavior to begin with. Although the person is responsible for his or her behavior and there is an appropriate consequence for it, understanding may help the individual recognize where positive change can take place so that we will not have simply acted on the behavior and punished the person; punishment would likely cause more resentment and hostility. If he or she is held responsible for the behavior, and at the same time we try to show accurate empathy for the frustrations that he or she is experiencing, we are in a much stronger position to offer him or her support and guidance in dealing with the *cause* of the behavior rather than dealing only with the behavioral result or "symptom" of the frustrations.

Through genuineness, unconditional positive regard and accurate empathy, we set up an atmosphere of working together rather than against one another. Psychological safety is enhanced and developmental proactive involvements take place. Everyone has a part to play in creating the atmosphere in which they find themselves. Through taking responsibility for our own feelings and behaviors, we demonstrate and model these attitudes and behaviors for those around us.

At the present time, there is a strong movement throughout the United States to develop comprehensive developmental counseling programs within the school systems. No longer is the counselor only responsible for reactive (or retroactive) programs and service-oriented tasks. Individual counseling still has its place for personal, social, emotional, educational and vocational concerns, but a much larger component of the counselor's responsibilities involve coordinating and facilitating a guidance team approach whose major focus is on the developmental, proactive guidance process within the school. The results of this approach are intended to offer a "student-focused" environment that is organized to demonstrate an inviting, caring, growth-enhancing and unified effort on the part of all people within the system. In essence, it is an environment that is emotionally safe for learning and developing.

Instrumental in creating a psychologically safe environment within the school is an effective program for counseling and guiding the student. A comprehensive developmental guidance and counseling program is usually included as part of the school's curriculum. It is constructed by a guidance team and made up of selected school personnel that often includes students, teachers, counselors, administrators and support personnel. The "team" develops the program and all people within the system help to implement it.

In organized efforts to develop effective comprehensive school counseling program models, many states have drawn on the work of other states and adopted or modified already proven components for inclusion in their model; therefore, common threads run through most of the current developmental school counseling programs presently being implemented in the United States. For example, Minnesota and North Dakota, both, include personal/social development, educational development and career development as domains with delivery through the Guidance Curriculum, Individual Planning, Responsive Services and System Support.

Components within the Guidance Curriculum are such activities as classroom presentations and group guidance, where personal/social development, educational development and career development are the focus. Individual Planning involves appraisal, advisement and placement. Responsive Services include consultation, personal counseling, crisis counseling and referral. System Support includes such things as program evaluation, public relations, professional development and community outreach.

When the entire school population supports and has a part in implementing a comprehensive developmental guidance and counseling program, the school atmosphere has a better chance of becoming one which is positive and proactive in its approach to the learning environment. Students and school personnel are working together to help create a healthy and safe psychological environment.

INVOLVING STUDENTS TO CREATE A SAFE ENVIRONMENT

Perhaps the best way to involve students in helping to create their own psychologically safe environment is to invite them to be a part of that process. A comprehensive educational program that protects and enhances the learning environment must have active input from all people involved within the system, especially the students. When students take an active role in the "system," they have a vested interest in seeing that it "works." Students should be included on curriculum committees, crisis teams, management teams, advisory committees, guidance teams, mediation teams and any other school-based body that involves making decisions or recommendations to the system, which affect the process of education. There are some major reasons why this is so very important.

First, we learn from students' perceptions of their environment. Students experience their surroundings much differently than do the adults who are involved within the system. It is impossible for school personnel to predict how students will perceive the school atmosphere. The best way to understand how decisions and programs will affect students is to ask them. The best way to plan for positive change is to involve in the planning those people for whom the change is being made. Much can be learned from students. Listening in an accepting and serious way can help in constructing positive change within the system. If students do not feel safe, free to learn and secure in their surroundings, we should not simply guess at the reasons why. We must ask the right questions of the right people: students are the right people.

Second, involving students in the process empowers them in a very positive way. When people think that they have no voice in decisions that affect them and no way to constructively present their views, they seek more aggressive ways of making themselves heard or they give up. There is no vested interest in what the system requires, so reactions to the system rather than actions within the system occur. Typical reactive behaviors include: 1) avoidance—cutting classes or skipping school; 2) acting out—behaving in socially unacceptable ways, rebelling against the system; 3) unhealthy indulgences—drugs, alcohol, indiscriminate and careless sexual behavior, dyssocial involvement such as cult or gang membership; and 4) conforming—doing just what the closed system expects, with no creativity, no individual identity and no personal growth. These are just some of the common behaviors exhibited by people who feel disempowered within a system.

When students feel they have a voice in what is expected of them, when they feel others listen and act on some of what they have to say and when they invest themselves in the process of change, they also feel empowered. With the feeling of empowerment, creativity is enhanced, individuality is honored and growth can occur. Positive action within the system is achieved, and negative reaction to the system declines. Students do not generally want to react in a destructive way to what they have had a part in creating.

The third reason for active student involvement in the structure of the system is to enhance the feeling of unity and cooperation. When we feel as though we are working with others, an atmosphere of trust can be built. With trust comes the feeling of psychological safety.

Peer Programs

Some of the best examples of student involvement within the system are exhibited in peer programs. Within these programs, school personnel work with students who in turn work with other students. Peer programs have taken on a multitude of forms and have focused on a variety of system concerns; however, they all have four basic components: selection, training, implementing and evaluating.

Selection of peer program members is somewhat determined by the nature of the process in which they will be involved. For instance, if the process is peer mediation or conflict resolution, the members might be selected differently than if the focus is for senior high students to talk with elementary students about friendships. Regardless of the nature of the peer "helper" group, some general suggestions are presented:

(1) Allow all students within the selected population to apply. For example, if the peer "helper" group is determined to be senior high school athletes who will work with junior high students on the importance of study skills, then all athletes, not just the excellent students or the "star athletes," should be accepted applicants.
(2) Select by a committee that is representative of the school population. Teachers, administrators, counselors and certainly, other students should be on the committee making the selections.
(3) Select a good "mix" of students to be in the group. Diversity is the key here. The student's popularity is no more important than any other characteristic. Sometimes it is the student we might least expect to make a good "peer" helper who emerges as exceptional.

The second component of peer programs is the training of the peer group. The school personnel responsible for the training should be very familiar with the process involved. There are numerous examples of training modules available, but the focus is clearly on interpersonal skill development and sensitivity to those with whom the peer helpers will work. It is during the training that a feeling of belonging, unity and trust can develop among the members of the group. Peer helpers do not help only those with whom they work, they often grow significantly via the process. Peer helpers feel important and valuable; they feel empowered. Through these experiences, they can help other students within the system feel worthy also.

The third component of peer programs is the actual process of helping. The process is dependent on the role for which the peer group has been trained. For example, if the peer group is trained in conflict mediation, the peer helpers will be involved in helping resolve conflict

Table 2. Resource catalogs for guidance and counseling materials.

- Allyn & Bacon Education Catalog; Dept. 894, 160 Gould St.; Needham Heights, MA 02194-2310
- Auson Schloat; 175 Tompkins Ave.; Pleasantville, NY 10570-9973
- Book & Counseling Resource Catalogue: American Counseling Association; 5999 Stevenson Ave.; Alexandria, VA 22304-3300
- Career Planning & Guidance; Meridian Education Corporation, Dept. CG-95; 236 E. Front St.; Bloomington, IL 61701
- Childswork Childsplay; The Center for Applied Psychology, Inc.; P.O. Box 61586; King of Prussia, PA 19406
- Educational Media Corporation (for counselor educators, teacher educators & special services); Box 21311; Minneapolis, MN 55421-0311
- Education Media Corporation: Resources for Helping Professionals; Box 21311; Minneapolis, MN 55421-0311.
- Educational Video Network; 1294 19th St.; Huntsville, TX 77340
- Elementary Drug Catalog; NIMCO; 117 Hwy 815; P.O. Box 9; Calhoun, KY 42327
- Guidance Club for Kids; Ready Reference Press; P.O. Box 5249; Santa Monica, CA 90409
- The Gilford Press: Special Instructor's Edition; 72 Spring St.; New York, NY 10012
- Love Publishing Company Catalog of Books; 1777 South Bellaire St.; Denver, CO 80222
- Marco: Materials for teachers, counselors, and parents; 1443 Old York Road; Warminster, PA 18974-1096
- Outstanding Resources in School Psychology & Special Education; Gilford Publications, Inc.; 72 Spring St.; New York, NY 10012
- Pro-Ed 1994 Catalog: Tests, Materials, Books & Journals; 72 Spring St.; New York, NY 10012
- Psychology on Video; Insight Media; 2162 Broadway; New York, NY 11024
- Research Press; Dept. 95; P.O. Box 9177; Champaign, IL 61826
- School Counselor Catalog 6-12; Paperbacks for Educators; 426 West Front St.; Washington, MO 63090
- School-to-Work Resource Catalog; Center on Education & Work Center; Pub. Unit, Dept. A; Univ. of Wisconsin-Madison, 964 Educational Science Building; 1025 W. Johnson; Madison, WI 53706
- Sunburst: Health, Home, & Family Life; a) Videos for grades K-8; b) Videos for grades K-12; Sunburst Communications; 39 Washington Ave.; P.O. Box 40; Pleasantville, NY 10570-0040
- Teacher Education: Diversity/Educational Psychology; 2162 Broadway; New York, NY 10024.

when it occurs among other students within the system. If they are trained to conduct preventative units on chemical involvement, they will be organized to implement that process. Through this program, students see that other students are involved in creating a healthy learning environment. Many students will listen to their peers when they will otherwise simply dismiss the same words from a teacher or another adult.

Finally, an evaluation of the peer program will need to be done. Is it meeting the needs of the students? Are the peer helpers being trained well? Is the program doing what it is intended to do? What improvements might be made?

Peer programs can go a long way in creating an empowering and, therefore, a more psychologically safe, environment. When people feel that they count, that they have the opportunity to be heard and understood and that they have worth within a system, they also feel more safe and secure within that system.

Peer programs are just examples of guidance-related activities that can help create a more psychologically safe school environment. There are a multitude of materials available to draw upon for implementing developmental guidance units and programs within the school system. Table 2 presents an extensive yet partial list of catalogs that offer examples of these units. Offerings are available in printed form, videotapes, audiotapes and computer software.

REFERENCES

Beale, A. V. (1993). Contemporary counseling approaches: A review for the practitioner. *The School Counselor,* 40(4):282–286.

Brake, K. J. & Gerler, E. R., Jr. (1994). Discovery: A program for fourth and fifth graders identified as discipline problems. *Elementary School Guidance & Counseling,* 28(3):170–181.

California State Department of Education. (1989). *Safe schools: A planning guide for action.* Sacramento, CA: The Department.

Cueto, S., Bosworth, K. & Sailes, J. (1993, April). Promoting peace: Integrating curricula to deal with violence. A paper presented at the annual meeting of the American Educational Research Association in Atlanta, GA (ERIC Document Reproduction Service No. ED 362 463).

Della-Guistina, D. E. (1990, March). Organizing safety in elementary schools: Components of the process. A paper presented at the annual meeting of the American Alliance for Health, Physical Education, Recreation and Dance, New Orleans, LA, March 28–31, 1990 (ERIC Document Reproduction Service No. ED 322 085).

Dysinger, B. J. (1993). Conflict resolution for intermediate children. *The School Counselor,* 40(4):301–308.

Erikson, E. H. (1963). *Childhood and society* (2nd ed.). New York: Norton.

Glasser, W. (1969). *Schools without failure.* New York: Harper & Row.

Goble, F. G. (1970). *The third force: The psychology of Abraham Maslow.* New York: Pocket Book.

Havighurst, R. J. (1972). *Developmental tasks and education* (3rd ed.). New York: David McKay.

Houston, R. & Grubaugh, S. (1989). Language for preventing and defusing violence in the classroom. *Urban Education,* 24(1):25-37.

Maslow, A. H. (1962). *Toward a psychology of being.* New York: Van Nostrand.

Rapp, J. A., Carrington, F. & Nicholson, G. (1992). *School crime and violence: Victims' rights* (ERIC Document Reproduction Service No. ED 362 950).

Rogers, C. (1983). *Freedom to learn for the 80's.* Columbus: Charles E. Merrill.

Chapter 3

Bullying: Concerns for School Administrators

JOHN H. HOOVER
RONALD OLIVER

YOUNG people arrive at our schoolhouse doors shouldering onerous burdens. As principals and superintendents can readily attest, social problems increasingly have become a daily responsibility of educators. Order must often be brought from the chaos of children's lives before the cognitive work can begin; *in loco parentis* is a responsibility with profound implications in today's world.

One of the most demanding tasks facing educators is the design of physically and psychologically safe environments, an endeavor addressed at length in this volume. The current chapter is dedicated to a related problem — schoolyard bullying. Though bullying captures fewer newspaper headlines or minutes on the nightly news than do either drug problems or gang violence, many American students are harassed frequently enough by their peers to be troubled by it in school (Hoover, Oliver & Hazler, 1992). It is only in the past ten years, however, that bullying has been regularly addressed by researchers, practitioners and the media.

Despite the fact that it is often seen as trivial, expected or even marginally acceptable behavior by some adults (Arora & Thompson, 1987), bullying is viewed as a serious problem by many students (Hoover, Oliver & Hazler, 1992). We estimate that up to 15% of American schoolchildren are chronic bullying victims. Harassment by bullies may result in such extremely low quality of school life that mental health and academic performance are affected (Hoover, Oliver & Hazler, 1992; Hoover, Oliver & Thomson, 1993). About a fifth of students report that their ability to perform academically is reduced by bullying (Hoover, Oliver & Thomson, 1993).

It is perhaps dismaying that, with the full plates already before them, school officials must now worry about whether Abel calls Baker a "ninny." Yet it is important to examine bullying objectively in order to determine the degree to which it affects schooling. In the remainder of this chapter, several aspects of bullying are examined. First, the term is defined. Second, results of a series of midwestern investigations of bullying are examined. Each category of outcome data is organized with a review of results followed by specific implications for the administration of schools. Finally, prevention and treatment suggestions are outlined.

BULLYING DEFINED

Most simply, bullying is the physical or psychological harassment of one individual by another. If the harassment of one student is perpetrated by a group of students, experts often use the term "mobbing" (Pikas, 1989). An uneven distribution of power is implied by both bullying and mobbing. That is, victims are either physically or emotionally unable to defend themselves.

Though related to other forms of aggression, bullying can be distinguished from more overt forms of violence on several dimensions. The behaviors involved with bullying tend to be verbal in nature, at least as described by observers and victims (Hazler, Hoover & Oliver, 1992; Hoover, Oliver & Hazler, 1992). Bullies tend to pick targets with care—it may be that it is socially acceptable to harass certain unfortunate students. Male Norwegian and Swedish bullies received peer ratings that were as positive as those obtained by a sample of well-adjusted children in the same student population (Olweus, 1978). Aggressive youngsters, on the other hand, tend to be feared by classmates and are thus rated as unpopular (Foster, DeLawyer & Guevremont, 1986). Bullying has characteristics reminiscent of both more overt forms of aggression and also the types of intergroup pressures more often associated with racism and sexism.

Bullying is initiated by a process of "defining" a person out of the group. The person to be picked on is symbolically designated as less than human, the hated and feared "other" (Mihashi, 1987). This may occur in one of several ways. A potential bullying victim may be forced to perform a humiliating act, the execution of which sets them apart and serves as grounds for future ridicule. For example, Mihashi (1987) described a Japanese student whose peers marked his face with a felt tipped pen and subsequently forced him to dance in the school halls. Or a victim might be "defined" by a rumor that he/she has performed an embarrassing act. Several middle and high school female students, for example, related to us how rumors were spread that they were sexually promiscuous. ("They say I'm easy.") No way existed to counteract the gossip without publicly raising the very painful subject, thus drawing unwanted attention during an extremely vulnerable period.

Physical or psychological characteristics of a student might be stressed frequently in interactions with peers. In such a situation, the victim's entire identity may become associated with real or putative stigmata. For example, a student with wide-set ears may be nicknamed "Dumbo" and forever after "be" Dumbo to classmates. A sixth-grade classmate of the lead author was called only "Boxer" (after a cartoon character) nearly continuously by most of her classmates.

In the paragraphs below, data from a series of studies conducted in the rural Midwest are reviewed with an eye toward highlighting bullying problems which may be of interest to school administrators. Other research, most of it conducted in Europe, will be reviewed when necessary to make a point.

FINDINGS FROM THE MIDWEST BULLYING STUDIES

Along with colleagues Rich Hazler and Keith Thomson, we initiated an investigation of bullying in rural and small-town midwestern schools. The primary focus of the project initiated in 1989 was to replicate Scandinavian research on bullying in the rural midwestern United States (see, Olweus, 1978). In addition, we conducted a detailed examination of students' perceptions of bullying problems in their schools. Rural and small-town schools were targeted because they were relatively free of the inter-group pressures more commonly associated with large urban schools; inter-group conflicts would easily confound generalizations regarding mobbing. Findings from the Midwestern studies are laid out in the sections on prevalence, severity of the problem, the nature of bullying behaviors, risk factors and student attitudes about the performance of school personnel in ameliorating bullying.

Prevalence and Severity

Results of Studies

Approximately 80% of high school students reported experiencing bullying during their schooling. The late elementary and middle school years were implicated by a majority of respondents (Hoover, Oliver & Thomson, 1993). When fourth- through eighth-grade students were asked the same question, 90% across gender reported peer harassment. High school students may have reported lower rates of bullying overall because some portion of the sample may have forgotten or discounted earlier episodes.

Prevalence estimates decrease if the severity of bullying is controlled. We asked students to rate the degree to which bullying pejoratively affected them in the physical, social, somatic, academic and emotional domains. When the midpoint of a scale averaged across the five domains was used to define serious trauma, 14% of the high school sample could be so categorized.

As might be expected, victims reported that most trauma from bullying occurred in the emotional domain, followed in order by the social, physical, academic and familial. A gender difference was observed with females more emotionally traumatized than males (Hoover, Oliver & Thomson, 1993). Strong reaction to peer rejection by females has been observed in other contexts and may result from a greater affiliative need on their part. It is also possible that males underreport trauma out of a culture-based fear of appearing weak.

The majority of students in rural and small-town midwestern schools reported personal victimization by bullies. The problem appeared to increase rapidly in the late elementary years and declined during high school; in other words, it was at its worst during the middle school or junior high years. The best estimate is that a sixth of American students are traumatized by bullying to the point that it pejoratively affects their school performance. Though the data are not directly comparable due to differences in data collection procedures, midwestern results exceeded the range reported in European studies for students who were "seriously" bullied (once per week or more). The figures ranged from a low of 3% in Norway to a high of about 8% in Great Britain and Ireland. Figures as high as 20% for students bullied "sometimes" have been reported in English investigations (Smith, 1991).

Implications for School Officials

Bullying is a severe problem for 10-15% of the most vulnerable students. Victims are reportedly affected in many aspects of their lives, including academic learning. A situation in which the quality of life is low for a tenth of students is unacceptable, and it is clear that increasing pressure will be placed on schools to reduce the problem of bullying (National School Safety Center, 1988a). The problem of mobbing is likely to directly affect, at a minimum, the areas of curriculum development, school discipline policies and the current wave of school reform.

Bullying Behaviors

Results of Studies

Students identified many behaviors with bullying, but overall the nature of bullying had a distinctively verbal flavor, at least as portrayed by student victims:

> The case of one 15-year old girl is classic. "I was made fun of because of the way I looked . . . now I'm being talked about. It really hurts." Other common forms of bullying included . . . "name calling," "putting me down," "teasing," and "saying I'm stupid." "Just ignoring me" and "talking about me a lot" also surfaced as painful experiences for teenagers. . . . (Hazler, Hoover & Oliver, 1992, p. 20)

Statistical analyses matched the written comments of students listed above. Ridicule and verbal teasing were the behaviors receiving the highest ranking among five behaviors listed on a survey form. Across gender, the teasing and ridiculing forms of bullying were rated as the most commonly experienced. Female respondents picked it significantly more often than did male respondents (Hoover, Oliver & Hazler, 1992).

Several female students from the high school sample penciled in comments on their questionnaires such as "they just ignored me," so this behavior was addressed in a survey of fourth through eighth graders. Female victims frequently (62.5%) picked this statement ("leaving you out of activities or not playing with you") as a bullying description. Members of the elementary and middle school sample also identified teasing as the behavior most commonly employed by bullies. Younger males, though still reporting teasing as the most common form of bullying (87.3%), also identified the experience of physical attacks with some frequency (62.0% of those reporting personal victimization) (Hoover, Oliver, & Thomson, 1993).

The bullying which goes on in school is largely made up of teasing and other verbal harassment, though significant physical violence appears in the mixture among younger males. In addition, female students appear to utilize social ostracism frequently as a means to harass others.

The verbal nature of bullying deserves attention for several reasons. First, students expressed a great deal of ambivalence about it. We correlated bullying behaviors with the "severity" items mentioned above, expecting to find that students receiving physical harassment would be more traumatized by mobbing. No relationship between bullying behaviors and perceptions of harm by victims were observed. We interpret this to mean that, at least to our most vulnerable students, verbal harassment can be extremely traumatic—words as well as sticks and stones can harm children.

Many respondents endorsed the statement that most bullying was not done to hurt—it was done in fun (Oliver, Oaks & Hoover, 1994). Yet a subset of the same sample, which portrayed teasing as harmless, also rated it as a bullying behavior and reported traumatization! Like much in life, it probably matters most whether the person is on the receiving or delivering end as to whether one perceive teasing as nasty behavior or harmless verbal playfulness. In talking to students, we were struck by the confusion about this. Students asked, "How do we know when Sara is bothered by our teasing?" At one school, a student stood up and said, "You've been teasing me about my weight for years and I've always hated it." Her classmates who saw her as a good sport seemed nonplused by the vehemence of her reaction.

Implications for School Officials

The primary role of teasing in the behavioral "mix" of bullying has a great deal of significance for the operation of school programs. Verbal bullying among preteens may serve as precursors to other, more insidious forms of harassment. Students and teachers frequently commented on the early age at which teasing contained sexual content. We can't help but wonder whether widely accepted teasing is a laboratory for later development of sexual harassment. Most bullying was done by boys, according to respondents, whether victims were male or female (Hazler, Hoover & Oliver, 1991). Hate crimes are rising faster among school-aged persons than among any other group (Bodinger-deUriarte,

1991). Could mobbing of an individual within a racial, cultural or ethnic group be a precursor to outwardly directed bias?

Students found it difficult to understand the dynamics of teasing and other forms of interpersonal conflicts. It is probable that a developmental sequence exists in the ability to comprehend interpersonal nuances of humor and teasing. Thus, it may be difficult to broach these issues with young children. Cognitively immature thinkers find it hard to "take the other's point of view" in interpersonal disputes (Carlson-Paige & Levin, 1992), a necessary prerequisite for reasoned dialogue about teasing. Yet, based on student responses, we believe that discussion of such interpersonal issues is essential. It is incumbent upon researchers and practitioners to develop language about harassment and teasing that is accessible to children and that this dialogue, once initiated, be maintained throughout the school years. These issues seem to mesh nicely with social studies or mental health curriculums. The topics of teasing and verbal harassment deserve a great deal more discussion and research than they have so far elicited.

School officials are already dealing with an emerging conflict between protecting the rights of groups with less power and free speech (Splitt, 1992). It is possible that this issue could surface in the context of bullying given its verbal nature.

Considerable physical violence was noted by males representing a late elementary and middle school population. The degree of physical risk is an aspect of life in school which cannot be ignored by those resposnsible for the well-being of young people.

What Increases Students' Risk for Victimization?

Results of Studies

Males and females across ages selected similar factors which they felt exacerbated their risk of harassment and these corresponded to a list generated by students rating the risk factors for others (Hazler, Hoover & Oliver, 1991). Members of all groups endorsed the statement that victims "just didn't fit in." Characteristics which motivated students to rate themselves as outcasts fell generally into either physical or social categories.

Social factors selected frequently by students were lack of social skills, emotionality and choice of friends. Physical or appearance factors selected frequently across gender included facial appearance (most common among females), the clothes they wore, overweight, too short (older males only) and physical weakness. Perhaps unexpectedly, physical weakness was picked frequently by males (picked among the five most common reasons for being harassed) and females (in the top ten). Perhaps, the importance of physical prowess among females in athletics and in the ability to ward off unwanted attacks has increased in recent years. Weakness was one of the few characteristics systematically observed among male victims in Scandinavia (Olweus, 1978).

Among the younger sample (Hoover, Oliver & Thomson, 1993), "too weak" (identified as a factor by 32% of male victims) and "short tempered" (29%) appeared among the top five selections by males only. Two factors appeared among those most commonly identified by elementary and middle school girls: "the way my face looked" (30%) and "I was too heavy" (13%).

Olweus argued forcefully that the problem of bullying falls mainly within the characteristics of bullies. He identified physical weakness as the only distinguishing characteristic of male victims in the Scandinavian studies, maintaining that perceptions of students notwithstanding, it is bully characteristics that motivate bullying not attributes intrinsic to scapegoats.

Implications for School Officials

Midwestern students felt that certain characteristics increased their risks and the risks of others for attaining the status of bully victim. The main implication of these data is that administrators and their support staff might be able to target some students for mental health screening, though certainly this must be done sensitively.

Female students who fall outside accepted parameters for appearance (physical or clothing), or believe that they do, or who believe they are overweight, or are too emotional, appear to be at increased risk for peer abuse. Females may also be bullied if they maintain friendships with other outcast students.

Patterns among males were similar to those reported by females, except that facial appearance was seldom picked, while physical weakness and short-temperedness were frequently nominated. It is possible that "short-tempered" among boys plays a role similar to "cried – was emotional" among girls; these may be characteristics that reinforce bullying via eliciting a reaction that may be sought by some bullies.

Attitudes Supporting Bullying

Results of Studies

Students were asked to endorse statements that could be construed as supportive of bullying or that would explain the failure to intervene in the bullying of others. We were interested in the role of bullying for perpetrators. In two studies a variety of factors were cited by students. By far, the most commonly defended position was one of blaming the victim. A majority of respondents endorsed the statement that "victims brought on the bullying themselves" (62%; unless otherwise stated, data are reported across sexes).

Substantial numbers of students agreed that bullying made victims tougher (61%) and that bullying helped students by teaching them what was acceptable to the group. Nearly half of the male respondents agreed with the latter statement (44.7%), while less than a third of females endorsed it (30%). A subset of students may bully others or fail to intervene because bullies occupy higher social strata (44.6% of males; 69% of females), or because intervention on behalf of a low-status individual would result in one's own loss of status (48% agreement).

Implications for School Officials

Educators must be aware that many students harbor attitudes that could be seen as supportive of bullying or that militate against defense of weaker members of the group. It is unlikely that anti-bullying campaigns will be effective until a fundamental change in student ideology occurs. This will require consistent, rigorous and long-term efforts.

Students' Views of the Response of School Personnel

Results of Studies

High school students were asked to rate the performance of school personnel in responding to bullying episodes. Most students (69%) rated school officials' responses as "poor." The item evoked many written additions, including such comments as, "They could care less" (Hazler, Hoover & Oliver, 1991, p. 148). While only 2% felt that school officials handled bullying problems well, several noted on surveys that school officials may not have known about bullying:

"Teachers don't know about the teasing that goes on . . . even though they should have been aware and done something about it" (Hazler, Hoover & Oliver, 1992, p. 22). Several students' responses were bitter—fairly or unfairly, believing school personnel shared the blame for their plight.

Implications for School Officials

The views of victims of bullying toward school officials can only be described as latently (and sometimes overtly) hostile. This may be taken as evidence that, at least in the schools we studied, no noticeable intervention was taking place. As bullying is increasingly seen by members of the public as problematic, failure to take a proactive stance may prove to be a community relations disaster.

PREVENTION AND TREATMENT

It is beyond the scope of this chapter to present prevention and amelioration programs in depth. However, emerging principles of anti-bullying campaigns are addressed below, particularly those with salience for school officials. The categories of prevention and treatment programs are somewhat arbitrary—merely ways to divide information into friendlier "bits." In reality, an effective schoolwide or districtwide anti-bullying effort will be multifaceted, involving proactive disciplinary policy, information, changes in curriculum, teaching methods and the management of school programs.

At a minimum, school officials must educate themselves about the problem and, as Batsche and Knoff (1994) argued, quit believing the mythology that "kids will be kids." Other actions fall into the categories of evaluation, informational campaigns, mediation, counseling and changes in attitude about the worth of individuals.

Evaluation

Effective anti-bullying efforts include technically sound, ongoing program evaluation. Students can be surveyed and interviewed to assess baseline levels of bullying and other problems related to quality of life. This could be part of a larger, continuing effort to manage programs in a manner responsive to users.

Survey data could be employed to determine baseline levels of bullying to compare with post-intervention measures. There may be a tendency among some officials to shy away from such efforts because they have the potential for generating interest in a problem that might otherwise remain "underground." However, this concern must be balanced against the harm that may accrue to vulnerable students. In addition, the public will likely raise the issue in years to come; it will likely not go away.

The type of data gathered should allow officials to target adult supervision to times and places where students are most vulnerable. For example, mobbing tends to occur in areas of low supervision, such as hallways, playgrounds, bathrooms and lunchrooms. Effective program evaluation will reveal "hot" spots in the building to which increased adult attention can then be allocated.

Informational Campaigns

The Norwegian Ministry of Education sponsored a nationwide anti-bullying campaign which was initiated in 1983. The program, which has been described elsewhere (Olweus, 1991, 1993; Olweus & Alsaker, 1991), included an information mailing to every Norwegian householder. Mailings were followed up by ongoing informational meetings for teachers, parents and students. Olweus concluded that schoolwide efforts should include clear rules against bullying, parent and teacher participation as well as support for chronic victims. He also stressed the importance of creating a safe environment in schools.

Informational publications, legal advice and resources such as films are available from the National School Safety Center (NSSC) located at Pepperdine University.[2] We have shared shared one of their videotapes, *Set Straight on Bullies* (1988b), with groups of parents, teachers and students and have found it to be an effective conversation-starter.

Peer Mediation and the Peaceful School Movement

Alternatives to traditional discipline practices that stress the skills of negotiation hold a great deal of promise as part of an anti-bullying package. No data have been collected specifically addressing the relationship between mobbing and peer mediation, but it seems reasonable

---

[2]National School Safety Center, 16830 Ventura Blvd., Suite 200, Encino, CA 91436.

to assume that mediation may prove effective as part of an anti-bullying campaign. In situations where there is a clear victim and perpetrator, it is probably not appropriate to force a scapegoat to negotiate with bullies. In such situations, victim-offender mediation may be the more effective model (Umbreit, 1991).

Group and Individual Therapy and Training

Several models for the support of victims and the reduction of aggression among bullies have become available in the past few years. Pikas (1989) outlined a specific procedure, called the Common Concerns Method, for counseling bullies and their victims. Oliver, Oaks and Hoover (1994) explored the relationship between family counseling and patterns of parenting among the parents of both victims and bullies.

Another method which may hold promise is to use cognitive retraining procedures to teach more adaptive responses to bullies and chronic scapegoats. For example, victims could be taught to think through a teasing episode in a more adaptive manner; bullies could be taught to better manage thoughts that have lead to aggression (Eggert, 1994; Feindler & Ecton, 1986; McGinnis & Goldstein, 1984).

Communitarian Ideals

A successful anti-bullying campaign may require building a greater sense of community within a school's walls. Procedures designed to bring handicapped students into the mainstream of school life may also prove useful in reducing and preventing bullying. Peer tutoring (Ehly & Larson, 1980) and cooperative education (Johnson & Johnson, 1994) are examples of approaches in which development of connectedness among students is stressed.

SUMMARY

We have proposed that bullying is a severe problem in schools, including many schools which seem otherwise untouched by the pandemic violence in the United States. This type of child-on-child aggression affects the quality of school life for many and severely affects about a sixth of rural midwestern students. The difficulty of solving bullying problems lies in its subtlety; for example, the fact that much of it is verbal behavior, and the degree to which it has become ingrained in American culture.

Little doubt remains that bullying negatively affects both victims and bullies. As school officials attempt to mold institutions which are responsive to the needs of their consumers, they must look for solutions to mobbing and bullying. "Boys will be boys" is no longer acceptable given evidence that up to 15% of middle school students report themselves traumatized by abuse from peers.

REFERENCES

Arora, C. M. & Thompson, D. A. (1987). Defining bullying for a secondary school. *Educational and Child Psychology*, 4:110-120.

Batsche, G. M. & Knoff, H. M. (1994). Bullies and their victims: Understanding a pervasive problem in the schools. *School Psychology Review*, 23:165-174.

Bodinger-deUriarte, C. (1991). Hate crime: The rise of hate crime on school campuses. *Research Bulletin*, 10:1-6.

Carlson-Paige, N. & Levin, D. (1992). When push comes to shove: Reconsidering children's conflict. *Child Care Information Exchange*, 5:34-37.

Eggert, L. L. (1994). *Anger management and youth: Stemming aggression and violence.* Bloomington, IN: National Educational Service.

Ehly, S. W. & Larson, S. C. (1980). *Peer tutoring for individualized instruction.* Boston: Allyn & Bacon.

Feindler, E. L. & Ecton, R. B. (1986). *Adolescent anger control. Cognitive behavioral techniques.* New York: Pergamon.

Foster, S. L., DeLawyer, D. D. & Guevremont, D. C. (1986). A critical incident analysis of liked and disliked peer behavior and their situation parameters in childhood and adolescence. *Behavioral Assessment*, 8:115-133.

Hazler, R. J., Hoover, J. H. & Oliver, R. (1991). Student perceptions of victimization by bullies in schools. *Journal of Humanistic Education and Development*, 29:143-150.

Hazler, R. J., Hoover, J. H. & Oliver, R. (1992). What kids say about bullying. *The Executive Educator*, 14(11):20-22.

Hoover, J. H. & Hazler, R. J. (1991). Bullies and victims. *Elementary School Guidance and Counseling*, 25(2):12-219.

Hoover, J. H., Oliver, R. & Hazler, R. J. (1992). Bullying: perceptions of adolescent victims in the Midwestern U.S.A. *School Psychology International*, 13:5-16.

Hoover, J. H., Oliver, R. & Thomson, K. (1993). Perceived victimization by school bullies: New research and future directions. *Journal of Humanistic Education and Development*, 32:76-84.

Johnson, D. W. & Johnson, R. T. (1994). *Learning together and alone. Cooperative, competitive, and individualistic learning* (4th ed.). Boston: Allyn & Bacon.

McGinnis, E. & Goldstein, A. P. (1984). *Skillstreaming the elementary school child. A guide for teaching prosocial skills.* Champaign, IL: Research Press.

Mihashi, O. (1987). The symbolism of social discrimination. A decoding of discriminatory language. *Current Anthropology,* 28:519-529.

National School Safety Center. (1988a). *Safe schools and quality schooling. The public responds.* Encino, CA: Author.

National School Safety Center. (1988b). *Set straight on bullies.* Encino, CA: Author.

Oliver, R., Hoover, J. H. & Hazler, R. J. (1994). The perceived roles of bullying in small-town midwestern schools. *Journal of Counseling and Development,* 72:416-420.

Oliver, R., Oaks, I. N. & Hoover, J. H. (1994). Family issues and interventions in bully and victim relationships. *The School Counselor,* 41:199-202.

Olweus, D. (1978). *Aggression in the schools. Bullies and whipping boys.* New York: Wiley.

Olweus, D. (1991). Bully/victim problems among school children: Basic facts and effects of a school based intervention program. In D. J. Peppler & K. H. Rubin (Eds.), *The development and treatment of childhood aggression* (pp. 411-448). Hillsdale, NJ: Erlbaum.

Olweus, D. (1993). Victimization by peers: Antecedents and long term outcomes. In K. H. Rubin & J. B. Asendorf (Eds.), *Social withdrawal, inhibition, and shyness in childhood* (pp. 315-326). London, England: Erlbaum.

Olweus, D. & Alsaker, F. D. (1991). Assessing change in a cohort-longitudinal study with hierarchical data. In D. Magnuson, L. R. Bergman, G. Rudinger & B. Torestad (Eds.), *Problems and methods in longitudinal research: Stability and change* (pp. 107-132). Cambridge, England: Cambridge University Press.

Perry, D. G., Kusel, S. J. & Perry, L. C. (1988). Victims of peer aggression. *Developmental Psychology,* 24:807-814.

Pikas, A. (1989). A pure concept of mobbing gives the best results for treatment. *School Psychology International,* 10:95-104.

Smith, P. K. (1991). The silent nightmare: Bullying and victimisation in school peer groups. *The Psychologist. Bulletin of the British Psychological Society,* 4:243-248.

Splitt, D. A. (1992). Rethinking "hate speech" codes. *The Executive Educator,* 14(11):11.

Umbreit, M. (1991, July). Restorative justice: Having offenders meet with their victims offers benefits for both parties. *Corrections Today,* 164-166.

CHAPTER 4

School Violence: Everybody's Problem

PAUL M. KINGERY

VIOLENT crime victimization rates are higher for metropolitan areas than for rural areas. The Bureau of Justice Statistics reports that violent crime victimization rates for white males age twelve and over in the United States during 1992 were 50% in central cities and 29% in rural areas (U.S. Department of Justice, 1994). Rates for black males were 76% in central cities and 51% in rural areas. Rates for white females were 32% in central cities and 19% in rural areas, while rates for black females were 42% in central cities and 18% in rural areas. The U.S. Department of Justice reports that the violent crime rate per 100,000 households for cases involving injury to twelve- to nineteen-year-olds during the years 1987–1989 was 86.2 in urban areas and 47.9 in rural areas (Bachman, 1992). Blacks, males and inner-city youth are clearly at higher risk of victimization from violent crime, and inner-city black males are clearly at the highest risk of victimization (Baker, Mednick & Carothers, 1989).

PERPETRATION AND VICTIMIZATION

The victims of violent crime are often also the perpetrators of violent crime (Kingery, Pruitt & Hurley, 1992). Perpetration and victimization are part and parcel of a deadly cycle. To understand why males are at higher risk for both the perpetration of, and victimization by, interpersonal violence, we will examine the effects of testosterone and socialization toward aggressive self-protection. To understand why inner-city youth are at higher risk, we will examine overcrowding, inadequate parenting, poverty, school failure and a host of other intractable urban blights. To understand why blacks are at higher risk, we must examine the degree to which they are differentially hindered by a constellation of these risk factors. The complexity of considering all such variables simultaneously is daunting.

An analysis was performed specifically for addressing this problem of multiple risk factors as a part of the groundwork laid for writing this chapter. Census data were merged with several other indices compiled from various sources (*Kids Count Data Book,* 1994) using individual states in the United States as the unit of analysis (including the District of Columbia and excluding Hawaii and Alaska). State violent crime arrest rates for juveniles aged ten to seventeen for the period 1985–1991 were correlated with the following variables: the percentage of the population living in metropolitan areas in 1992 ($r = .69$); the percentage of the population under age eighteen from minority racial groups in 1990 ($r = .69$); the percentage of children living in single-parent families from 1985–1991 ($r = .68$); the percentage of students graduating from high school on time from 1985–1991 ($r = -.58$); the percentage of children living in overcrowded housing in 1990 ($r = .56$); the percentage of births attributable to single teens for the period 1985–1991 ($r = .31$); and the percentage of children living in poverty for the period 1985–1991 ($r = .24$). Single parenting, teen childbirth, school failure, overcrowding and poverty are more common in urban than rural areas, placing students in urban areas at higher risk of violence.

These univariate relationships clearly indicate an association between these variables, but they tell us little about how these variables relate to violence in a multifactorial model. Multiple regression of all these variables revealed that 73% of the variance in the juvenile arrests for violent crime can be explained by three of the factors: the percentage of the population living in metropolitan areas, the percentage of all births that were to single teens and the percentage of children living in overcrowded housing. Allowing all variables to enter freely, no variables other than these three explained a significant portion of the variance in arrests. Race was not a significant independent predictor of juvenile crime in the analysis; it was overshadowed by the greater importance of living in a metropolitan area, regardless of race. Thus, we may conclude that the higher rate of violent crime among blacks in the inner city is attributable to the fact that black juveniles have a higher risk of living in a single-parent household under crowded living conditions than do white inner-city youths and that race is not an independent factor.

INTERPERSONAL VIOLENCE

The gap between rates of interpersonal violence in urban and rural areas is likely to be smaller than indicated by crime reports since violence is probably underreported in rural areas. The difficulty in obtaining accurate statistical reporting of violence in rural areas appears on several fronts. Anyone who has lived in a rural area for an extended period realizes that police presence there is minimal. Police do not routinely pass by, they are slow to arrive in a crisis, and there is an implicit assumption that the rural dweller is expected to provide for self-protection through firearm possession and active defense of one's territory. Crimes are dealt with immediately and directly in most cases, often without reporting to a distant authority. Many of the charges in urban areas are for assaulting a police officer or resisting arrest, two events that are as rare in rural areas as are police officers. Thus, reports of crime occurring in rural areas are underestimates.

Further, crimes reported in urban areas reflect overestimates of crimes perpetrated by urban youth. Crime is generally reported by the location of its commission, rather than by the residence of the person committing the crime. This feature of statistical reporting becomes important when we examine the prevalence of violence among youth who are within driving distance of an urban area. Rural youth often go to the city for fun and excitement: drinking, procuring and using drugs and other activities. It is in the city (often under the influence of drugs or alcohol) that their crimes are committed. Those crimes are reported as urban crimes, not as rural crimes. Thus, while more violent crimes are committed in urban areas, the average reader of statistical tables will attribute urban crimes to urban youth, even if they were committed by rural youth. Rural youth may not be much less violent than urban youth. In the final analysis, we must conclude that violent juvenile interpersonal crime is both overreported in urban areas and underreported in rural areas, creating the perception of a gap between urban and rural crime rates that is largely "artificial."

Machismo runs high in rural areas just as it does in the inner cities. Guns and knives are readily available in rural areas, and rural youth may be very comfortable and practiced in using them. A rural youth may be more likely to have actually fired a gun than an urban youth and may be a better marksman. Rural youths may feel more confident about using a weapon because they have the skills, have been taught to look after their own safety needs and have been taught to protect others. We have little information, however, about how rural youth are involved in urban crimes and how their involvement differs from that of urban-dwelling youth.

Although interpersonal violence is much more frequent (higher incidence) in urban areas than in rural areas, it is not necessarily much less prevalent in rural areas. A Department of Justice survey of 21.6 million students (ages twelve to nineteen) conducted in 1989 found that the percentage of students reporting at least one victimization at school was 10% in the central city and 8% in rural areas (Bachman, 1992). A single youth in an urban area may commit more violent acts and may be more often victimized than a rural youth, but the rural youth may be as likely as an urban youth to commit a violent act, carry a weapon or be victimized. Rural and urban youth have the experience of interpersonal violence in common, although the urban youth experiences more of it.

Evidence for a higher incidence or prevalence of interpersonal violence, weapon carrying, victimization and fear among urban students than among rural students has not been uniform. A survey of victimization among eighth and tenth graders in Alabama was conducted in 1987. Urban boys were only marginally more likely to have been attacked at least once in the past year than rural boys (15% versus 14%, respectively) (Nagy & Adcock, 1990). Urban girls were even less likely to have been attacked than rural girls (10% and 12%, respectively). In the same year, the percentage of eighth- and tenth-grade boys who had carried a knife at school was higher in rural Central Texas (40%) than the national average for boys of that age (23%), and in rural Texas boys were twice as likely to carry a handgun to school (6%) as compared to the national average (3%) (Kingery, Mirzaee, Pruitt, Hurley & Heuberger, 1991). The national averages were based on a combination of both rural and urban schools randomly selected to represent all U.S. eighth and tenth graders. This comparison between rural Texas students and U.S. students in general is interesting in light of the fact that the majority of youth in the nation live in urban areas.

Prevalence and incidence data, alike, are generally presented in such a way that they may mask the effects of school size, grade level and proximity to an urban area on interpersonal violence. The primary reason that rural schools have lower violent crime rates may have more to do with their smaller size on the average than with their rural location. Researchers have not directly compared small urban schools with small rural schools.

Within large urban areas, violence is more common where population density is higher. In Los Angeles County schools, for example, the assault rate was 19.7% in districts having more than twenty-five schools, as compared to 4.3% in districts with ten to twenty-five schools (Stefanko, 1988). This holds true similarly, for rural schools; violence is more common in rural schools which are closer to a large city than in more remote rural schools. Rural central Texas students (eigth and tenth graders) living closer to Houston were more frequently assaulted at school than students living further away (Kingery, Mirzaee, Pruitt, Hurley & Heuberger, 1991).

Violence in rural schools may be more prevalent when eighth graders are in attendance centers with high school students rather than when they are in an elementary school or middle school. Rural Texas eighth graders in small schools who attended high school with ninth graders, for example, were involved in significantly more fights than eighth-grade boys who were in middle schools (Kingery, Mirzaee, Pruitt, Hurley & Heuberger, 1991).

WITNESSES OF VIOLENCE

We are also concerned with students who may be neither perpetrators nor physical victims of interpersonal violence but who witness such events or hear of them. The Safe School Study examined student fears in relation to interpersonal violence at school in 1975-1976. Students were asked to indicate, based on a list of places at school, whether they stayed away from various locations because someone might hurt or bother them there. The percentage of students avoiding three or more places at school was 24% in large cities as compared to 14% in rural areas among junior and senior high school students (U.S. Department of Justice, 1994). A similar picture emerges from the data on the percentage of students afraid of being hurt or bothered at school most of the time (4% in large cities as compared to 3% in rural areas). Likewise, the percentage of students staying home out of fear in a typical month was 7% for large cities, as compared to 4% for rural areas.

Similar findings emerged from a comparison of youth attending an inner-city medical clinic and youth attending a resort area clinic

(Gladstein, Rusonis & Heald, 1992). Inner-city youth were more often victims, knew of victims and witnessed more assaults, rapes, knifings, life-threatening events and murders than their resort group counterparts. Over 45% of adolescents in the inner-city group knew someone who had been assaulted with a weapon, robbed, knifed or murdered while 67% knew someone who had been shot. In the resort group, in contrast, only 25% knew someone who had been assaulted, shot or murdered. The students were unlikely to receive counseling after witnessing such events, regardless of whether they were in the inner-city or resort group. Similar findings emerged from a Department of Justice survey of 21.6 million students (ages twelve to nineteen) conducted in 1989. The percentage of students who avoided places at school out of fear or who feared attack was 8% in the central city and 6% in rural areas (Bastian & Taylor, 1991). Witnessing violence has been linked to post-traumatic stress disorder (PTSD) in the same way that victimization is linked to PTSD (Fitzpatrick & Boldizar, 1993).

When a violent event occurs in a smaller school, particularly one attended by local children of a particular age group as is the case in rural areas, the event may receive more notice than if it had occurred in a larger school attended by students drawn from a wider region with fewer inter-family relationships. The attention given to the event may have a direct bearing on the fears produced in children who hear of it. If parents seem frightened by the event, the children are likely to mirror or even magnify the fears of their parents. For these reasons, a violent event in a rural school may have greater impact on students than would the same event in an urban school. Urban students who see violence routinely may develop coping mechanisms. Rural students who see violence less frequently may be more shocked by it, and the events may occur with such low frequency that they never really adapt. These possibilities remain to be examined fully in research studies.

COPING MECHANISMS

When students live in fear of interpersonal violence, one of the coping mechanisms they may adopt is to take action to arm themselves. The 1992 Department of Justice survey determined that the percentage of students who had taken something to school to protect themselves was 3% in the central cities and 1% in rural areas (Bastian & Taylor,

1991). These percentages are low enough that we can safely say the average fearful student does not quickly seek to arm himself for protection. Students are much more likely to arm themselves if they are involved in using or selling cocaine or other drugs, presumably because they deal with violent people and are more fearful (Kingery, Pruitt & Hurley, 1992). The violence problem is closely associated with the drug problem. Although drug use has declined in recent years among adolescents, those who sell drugs are increasingly violent and are more likely to be armed than ever before.

Evidence points to an increase in weapon carrying and interpersonal violence among both urbn and rural youth in recent years. A survey of 1216 school executives drawn from throughout the United States in 1992 compared the percentages of urban and rural principals reporting increases in violence in their districts (Boothe, Bradley & Flick, 1993). More urban than rural principals reported increases in every measure of violence: girls fighting (59% vs. 37% for urban and rural, respectively), boys fighting (43% vs. 25%), school bus violence (24% vs. 21%), incidents involving guns at school (38% vs. 12%), fights between students of different races (20% vs. 6%), student fights at extracurricular activities (14% vs. 12%) and sexual assault (26% vs. 12%).

RURAL SCHOOL VIOLENCE

The only ongoing longitudinal study of rural school violence is being conducted in Central Texas (Kingery, Pruitt & Heuberger, 1996). Surveys conducted in 1987 were compared to identical surveys conducted in the most recent survey year (1994). Weapon carrying at school increased significantly over that period. Knife carrying increased 12% among boys and 79% among girls in eighth and tenth grade. Handgun carrying among boys increased 138% over that seven-year period. The carrying of other types of weapons by boys at school increased 38%.

The increase in weapon carrying is mirrored in the increases in interpersonal violence for the same period among central Texas youth. The prevalence of physical fighting at school (one or more fights involving fists or weapons during the past year) had increased 25%. The prevalence of repeated fighting at school (three or more fights in the past year) had increased 62%. Threats against students at school increased 11%, attacks increased 26% and attempted rape increased

60%. Victimization had increased more rapidly in the school setting than outside the school setting over the seven-year period.

Responding to the Texas survey, 78% of the rural eighth and tenth graders believed they could avoid fighting by joining a gang for protection. Their secondary solution was to carry a weapon. The vast majority of students felt they should fight if someone hit them (80%) or hits someone they care about (74%). Nearly half (46%) had been in at least one fight involving fists or weapons in the past year at school, while 21% had been in at least three fights over that period. Nearly 29% of students in the region had carried a knife at school in the past year, 8% had carried a handgun at school and 15% had carried some other weapon.

Guns were most often obtained from friends, usually from someone eighteen or older. In most cases, it was given to the student for free, while smaller proportions borrowed it, traded something for it, bought it or rented it. Two major rationales were given for carrying a handgun at school: "It made me feel safer," or "I was angry with someone and thinking about shooting him/her." Much smaller percentages of students said, "Carrying a gun showed I could get away with breaking school rules," "helped me get others to do what I wanted," "made me more accepted by my friends," or "I was forced to carry the gun for someone else." Knives were not simply pocket knives, but the more dangerous switchblades, butterfly knives and others. The pocket knives were not innocuous either, for they have often been used in school stabbings.

What Are the Effects?

The effects of violence and drug use on literacy among these rural central Texas students were examined in 1992 (Kingery, Pruitt, Heuberger & Brizzolara, 1996). Literacy was examined using standardized tests in a sample of fifty-nine grade and gender specific cohorts composed of 2980 eighth and tenth graders. Economically disadvantaged cohorts had lower literacy ($r = -.38$). Additional variations also appeared with respect to gender and maturation. After accounting for the variance induced by economic hardship, violence outside school supervision explained 38% of the variance in literacy of tenth-grade male cohorts. Adding drug/alcohol misuse increased the explained variance to 61%. Similar results were found for other groups. Students who were exposed to violence also had lower literacy rates.

Cohorts scoring in the upper tenth percentile of victimization in school had an average literacy score in the lowest tenth percentile. Violence appeared to be rooted in low-performing schools in rural communities beset with economic hardship and drug/alcohol misuse.

Conclusions for the Texas Study

The 1994 rural central Texas survey illustrates the point that conditions which produce violence may be present in rural areas just as they are in urban areas. The conditions which produce violence in rural areas may be different from those at work in urban areas, however. Many are in the rural areas because they cannot afford to live in the city; and precisely because they are so far from the city, they often lack economic and educational opportunities. Government housing is located in urban areas, trapping many who have no access to land or credit. In an equally pernicious way, rural areas often trap those who have access to land, but who have little else. Because their houses and lands hold little financial value, they cannot afford to move to the more prosperous suburbs. The squalor of rural Appalachia or rural Texas may be as damaging as the squalor in inner cities, although it may be of a different nature. Violence is rooted in people who live in poverty and hopelessness, whether they live in inner cities or rural areas.

Recommendations

Solutions are required that address failing schools and communities as they aid rural students in overcoming environmental deprivations associated with living in a rural community. Reductions in levels of interpersonal violence in rural schools may be possible without simultaneously changing the rural communities themselves, however. Various strategies for violence prevention are being tested, although they are less likely to be tested in rural schools than in urban schools. The 1992 survey of school principals mentioned earlier (Boothe, Bradley & Flick, 1993) found that urban principals were more likely to have increased their efforts at violence prevention than rural principals. A higher percentage of urban principals compared to rural principals had increased their enforcement of discipline policies, banned gang clothing and insignias, restricted use of school facilities after hours, issued ID cards to students, instituted mandatory multicultural education, banned racial/ethnic insignias, instituted the use of metal detectors, installed video surveillance cameras, formed volunteer parent patrol groups and instituted the use of school uniforms. Because violence is less frequent in rural schools, administrators may be less prepared to deal with it when it occurs. This may leave students in rural schools vulnerable to more serious harm when they are victimized.

Further, when tested for effectiveness, violence prevention strategies may be less rigorously evaluated in rural than in urban schools. For these reasons, our knowledge of effective strategies for rural school interventions is likely to be limited for some time. We have some evidence that students in rural schools are likely to respond differently than urban students to the same strategies. Therefore, violence prevention strategies also may need to be different. A Harvard study of 2508 ten- to nineteen-year-olds conducted in 1993 asked students whether they would like to see guns taken away from anyone not authorized by the courts to carry them (Harris, 1993). Responses indicated that more urban youth (60%) than rural youth (52%) wanted unauthorized guns prohibited. Those already carrying guns, a larger percentage of rural youth, were less likely to want to have them prohibited. We might expect rural students to feel less favorable to restrictive measures that they consider unnecessary.

To the degree that attitudes are different among rural youth than among urban youth, violence prevention strategies may need to be different also. In an urban school, an adolescent who is wrongfully charged with a crime may assert his innocence to avoid punishment. In a rural Appalachian school, however, a student may shoulder the blame and take the punishment without comment and then turn violently on the student who actually committed the trespass.

Intersectoral solutions to community problems that hinder the development of youth are being sought in urban areas. The schools, courts, social and health service agencies, churches and other groups are working together to meet the needs of youth. This approach takes as its rationale the view that addressing the root of the violence problem will be more effective than a quick fix. The same level of collaboration has seldom been achieved in rural communities with fewer intellectual and financial resources. Change may be more attainable in rural communities, but it may be slower in coming.

Urban dwellers cast longing glances to the rural countryside and imagine a life free of overcrowding, street noise, pollution, violence and other banes of city life. They see wide open spaces, relatively lower land prices, natural scenery, wildlife, a more relaxed lifestyle and other features that are lacking in the city. They imagine tranquility, safety, traditional values and a return to an idyllic past: a safe place to raise their children. Many urban dwellers who relocate to the rural areas surrounding a big city find no safe haven, however (Kingery, Mirzaee, Pruitt, Hurley & Heuberger, 1991). More remote rural areas may be somewhat safer, but the rural areas near large cities do not appear to offer much advantage over the urban areas.

Rural school personnel, as compared to their urban counterparts, must address interpersonal violence prevention with fewer resources, less community support, less information concerning effective approaches and with greater need to ensure local relevance. In order to exert this level of effort, rural school administrators must first acknowledge that interpersonal violence is a real problem in their schools. This first step is particularly difficult in view of the fact that rural parents believe violence is an urban problem and that a rural administrator is a poor manager if he cannot keep modest violence problems in check. The prevalence of these myths on the national level assures that violence prevention program grant funds will seldom reach rural schools. Strong leadership is required against these odds. Our rural school administrators are some of the best and are certainly up to the task. Hopefully, some will soon publish their experiences in school violence prevention so that other rural administrators can learn from them also.

REFERENCES

Bachman, R. (1992). *Crime victimization in city, suburban, and rural areas: A national crime victimization survey report.* U.S. Department of Justice, Office of Justice Programs, Bureau of Justice Statistics (NCJ-135943).

Baker, R. L., Mednick, B. R. & Carothers, L. (1989). Association of age, gender, and ethnicity with juvenile victimization in and out of school. *Youth and Society,* 20(3):320–341.

Bastian, L. D. & Taylor, B. M. (1991). *School Crime: A National Crime Victimization Survey Report.* U.S. Department of Justice, Office of Justice Programs, Bureau of Justice Statistics.

Boothe, J. W., Bradley, L. H. & Flick, T. M. (1993). The violence at your door: Violence has increased markedly in U.S. public schools over the last five years, says our exclusive nationwide survey of school administrators. *The Executive Educator,* 15(2):16.

Fitzpatrick, K. M. & Boldizar, J. P. (1993). The prevalence and consequences of exposure to violence among African-American youth. *Journal of the American Academy of Child & Adolescent Psychiatry,* 32(2):424–430.

Gladstein, J., Rusonis, E. S. & Heald, F. P. (1992). A comparison of inner-city and upper-middle class youth's exposure to violence. *Journal of Adolescent Health,* 13(4):275–280.

Harris, L. (1993). *A survey of experiences, perceptions, and apprehensions about guns among young people in America.* Boston, MA: Harvard University School of Public Health.

Kids count data book: State profiles of child well-being (1994). The Annie E. Casey Foundation (ERIC Document Reproduction Service No. ED 371 063).

Kingery, P. M., Mirzaee, E., Pruitt, B. E., Hurley, R. S. & Heuberger, G. (1991). Rural communities near large metropolitan areas: Safe havens from adolescent violence and drug use? *Health Values,* 15(4):39–48.

Kingery, P. M., Pruitt, B. E. & Hurley, R. S. (1992). Violence and illegal drug use among adolescents: Evidence from the U.S. National Adolescent Student Health Survey. *The International Journal of the Addictions,* 27(12):1445–1464.

Kingery, P. M., Pruitt, B. E., Heuberger, G. (1996). A profile of rural Texas adolescents who carry handguns to school. *Journal of School Health,* 66(1):18–22.

Kingery, P. M., Pruitt, B. E., Heuberger, G. & Brizzolara, J. A. (1996). Violence in rural schools: An emerging problem near the United-States-Mexico border, *School Psychology International* (In Press).

Nagy, S. & Adcock, A. (1990). *The Alabama adolescent health survey: Health knowledge and behaviors of grade 8 and 10 students.* Summary Report. Birmingham, AL: Alabama Department of Health.

Stefanko, M. (1988, August). Trends and comparisons in secondary school vandalism and assault. A paper presented at the annual meeting of the American Psychological Association in Atlanta, GA.

U.S. Department of Justice (1994). *Criminal victimization in the United States, 1992.* U.S. Department of Justice, Office of Justice Programs, Bureau of Justice Statistics (NCJ-145125).

CHAPTER 5

Outside Agitators

WILLIAM McFARLIN
MURDELL WALKER McFARLIN

INTRODUCTION

An understanding of the role the school plays in a community is the first important step in creating a school atmosphere that attracts a limited amount of outside agitation. Each school is different; therefore, each school must identify its role in the total community before a distinct and effective plan for insulating the school environment from outside agitation can occur. Questions that define the school role in the community must be asked: Does the school serve as the central meeting place for community groups, after-school day care or weekend church services? If so, what responsibility must the total community take for its use, for the treatment of school facilities and for school activities?

Some school districts have already addressed this issue by setting forth guidelines for the use of school facilities before and after school (Harrington-Lueker, 1994). Administrators under these circumstances may feel that they have little or no control over the use of school buildings after school hours and on weekends. These administrators usually take the position that the school building is not really for learning and that they have no "ownership" of the environment; therefore, the community values that are conveyed after school usually carry over into the school during the day (Lieber & Rogers, 1994). While the actual use of the school buildings after school hours may not be within the jurisdiction of the building administrator, the school climate evokes an "attitude" that either breeds outside agitation or that generates a respect for school property and the population that uses it. This "attitude" is created by the school administrator who, through his/her personal sensitivity to school "attitude," seeks to develop an unseen but understood control of the school environment at all times. For example, many religious groups seek use of school buildings for Sunday worship services.

Often, these groups tend to leave literature behind that can be found on many a Monday morning. While in isolation, this may be just a careless oversight, such incidents tend to infringe on the students' rights to an education in an environment that is devoid of propaganda and recruitment efforts that threaten the separation of church and state (Bernard, 1994).

This chapter presents both a historical and contemporary review of the changing school environment as it is affected by societal changes in families, communities and social norms. These societal factors can be and often are sources of outside agitation to the school environment. Recognizing the various factors and addressing them is a major step in insulating the school community and making it a safe haven for learning (Ceperley & Simon, 1994).

Background

Crime and violence have found their way into school yards and classrooms. Incidents of violent rampages in schools that have led to deaths and shootings of even kindergartners have become commonplace in America's communities (Prutzman, 1994). From the heartland to the coastlands, violence in schools is as commonplace as expressway accidents. This is a reality that faces all professional educators, parents and students. Everyone now has a right, a role and a responsibility to participate in the planning and implementation of processes that will eliminate outside agitation to the learning process in both the physical and mental senses (Russell, 1994).

Determining how the school will be used cannot be done by the school principal alone, nor can this determination be made by a small group of teachers and/or parents who wish to focus on the issue, independent of the involvement of the entire school community. The role of the school building is different for every school and every community. It is the responsibility of the school administrator to hold small group sessions continuously with various groups within the school and the community to effectively control the negative impact of outside agitators.

How a school administrator goes about garnering support for his/her school is a predictor of the amount of outside agitation that will be focused upon a given school. This chapter will discuss detailed methods of controlling outside agitation. Specific suggestions will be given and probable outcomes and expectations to these suggestions are also detailed in this chapter. However, this chapter will not set forth a prescription to cure outside agitation. There is no one solution. The purpose here is to provide a systematic and holistic approach to curbing a growing problem for all schools—rural, suburban and urban.

Changing Patterns of School Disruption

Disruptive behavior patterns that previously have been confined to the urban, inner-city school districts of northern and eastern cities have spread to all kinds and types of school communities across this country. From Tupelo, Mississippi, to Ames, Iowa and from Spokane, Washington, to Augusta, Maine, crime in schoolhouses has increased tenfold in the past twenty years (Prutzman, 1994). Each day, local, state, regional and national news agencies report increased violence in schools in much the same manner in which daily crime reports are used to report sensational crimes in America's major cities. No one is immune, and no one common institution is spared from vandalism, murder, assault or theft. School administrators of the nineties are charged with more than the challenge of making sure Johnny can read. Keeping Johnny safe in the classroom long enough to learn how to read is a fundamental requirement of the school administrators role in today's school environment (Sautter, 1995).

Accepting the realities of today's school climate is a must for administrators. Many a school climate becomes the target for continual abuse from outside agitators becaue of the failure of school administrators to accept and act upon their new role. Especially in rural areas, school administrators, teachers, parents and community leaders are often slow to accept the changing realities of the once sacred grounds of the school building. Recently, a school superintendent in rural South Carolina visited an urban elementary school in Charleston, South Carolina, to pick up his grandson. The superintendent reported that he walked through the school from front to back and no one questioned his presence or asked for identification. He asked himself if his own schools allowed persons to walk unannounced through his school system in the rural part of the state. He surmised that they probably did (Christensen, 1995). The failure to accept the realities of our society's inability to structure comprehensive and effective security systems often leads to frustrated communities faced with failing, ineffective school environments that eventually impact on the ability of Johnny and Jane to learn (Arndt, 1994).

Financial Incentives

There is also a financial incentive for school administrators to take the leadership in directing community discussion toward the alleviation of "attitudes" that make the school community the target of outside agitation. The more abuse a school facility endures, the greater the cost of repair in both the physical and emotional costs to communities. The rising costs of repairing school buildings eats up a greater and greater percentage of a school's budget, year in and year out. We need only look at the decay of inner-city schools that bear the markings of angry graffiti, broken windows and falling shingles to bear witness to this truth. Our nation's cities have long endured attacks of burglary, hate, anger and rebellion toward established institutions of authority (Smith, 1994). Now, our rural and suburban communities are bearing witness to rising crime, anger and rebellion and youthful slothfulness. School environments of these communities have become the stage upon which society's angry citizens are acting out their hatreds and frustrations. Growing negative behavior patterns are causing an emotional deficit within local communities that have rising dropout and illiteracy rates and an alarming increase in teenage pregnancies (Hill & Hill, 1994).

How school administrators go about addressing these issues is essential to creating a plan for discouraging an "attitude" that provokes outside agitation to the school climate. This chapter will discuss societal problems that feed anger and hate that is focused on the school environment. A concerted effort is made to include all elements of the community in the search for a holistic approach for providing safe and respected school environments. The chapter is divided into three sections: Perceptions and Attitudes, Why Agitators Agitate and Changing Agitation to Admiration.

Perceptions and Attitudes reviews the attitudes and perceptions of schools often held by school administrators, teachers, parents, students and community leaders. This discussion outlines how attitudes and perceptions influence the way school facilities are treated by elements in the community, both hostile and friendly. The premise is that the way in which the school facility is perceived by those it directly and indirectly serves influences the degree of outside agitation against the school and the school population.

Why Agitators Agitate looks at the anger and hatred that permeates our society in general and our schools in particular. The changing value systems of our young is used as the backdrop for this discussion.

Facts and figures on teenage pregnancy, youth crimes, gun sales, media diets and the court system are related to the dropout rate, guns in schools and youth behavior patterns. These relationships serve as a basis for illustrating the changing school environment and the populations schools now serve.

Changing Agitation to Admiration looks at processes that school administrators can use to alter the effects of negative trends of outside agitation on the school environment. Suggestions ranging from greater school involvement in the community to innovative means of reaching agitating elements are explored.

Each section of this chapter is designed to evoke curiosity and encouragement among those seeking solutions that will make America's schools safe havens for learning. While no foolproof or singular solution is offered, hopefully the information presented will bring a fresh perception of the problem, and provide a framework for creating dialogue on the subject among school educators and others. Since the subject is not one that will go away, it is believed that an honest and sensitive approach to identifying the elements that agitate the school climate is necessary so that the problem can be redressed, if not removed.

PERCEPTIONS AND ATTITUDES

With the continual media coverage of violence in schools, it is easy to assume that outside agitation creates the greatest, single threat to creating an environment conducive to learning. While outside agitation is certainly a factor to be taken seriously, the increase in school discipline problems often feed an atmosphere ripe for intrusion. Strategies that seek to improve school discipline experiences for students include in-school suspension programs that provide tutorial services, mentorships, peer group discussions and other small group experiences that promote interaction among young offenders (Stephens, 1994). This kind of suspension program addresses several immediate problems facing the school climate: 1) students are kept in school; 2) students are given reinforcement in their studies: tutoring, group learning, individual attention; and 3) students are relieved of the psychological stigma of being "thrown out of school" (Hill & Hill, 1994).

The perception of in-school suspension is that this method of discipline is not as demeaning as outright suspension. It gives students an opportunity to reenter the mainstream of the school community without facing attitudes of alienation and rebuke from school mates. Parents seem to appreciate in-school suspension because it gives their children a second chance inside the school building. This system has been in place in Atlanta Public Schools for several years and enjoys strong support from school administrators, teachers, students and parents (Linquanti & Berliner, 1994).

The Princeton Peer Leadership group created a design of peer support and intervention in the Atlanta Public School System during the 1990-1993 school terms. Students in four Atlanta inner-city high schools were scheduled to meet in "group classes" throughout the school year. Students at four private schools in the city also participated in parallel programs. Twice a year, students met across school lines and invisible city boundaries and held conferences on their discoveries about each other and their needs. Comments from students indicated strong support for the program. Funding became an issue, and the program eventually was eliminated from the system's strategies for fostering safe school climates.

Inner-city schools suffer from the perception that violence and crime are the rule and not the exception within the schoolhouse. Unfortunately, the stigma has become embedded in the minds of citizens because news reports tend to focus on inner-city violence more than on suburban and rural school disruptions. Changing the perception of inner-city crime and violence in schools will go a long way toward changing the general perceptions of violence in schools everywhere (Arndt, 1994; Linquanti & Berliner, 1994; Toby, 1994).

An effective method of changing this perception is the development of programs in conflict resolution. Conflict resolution programs teach students how to reach agreement at points of disagreement without using violence and/or abusive language and behavior (Hatkoff, 1994). This kind of program resurrects programs used in schools and churches in the 1930s, 1940s and 1950s when children were taught "how to talk with each other with dignity and respect." This is a more sophisticated method of teaching age-old tactics of common courtesy and the respect for the rights of everyone to hold his or her own opinion on a subject without disrespecting the rights of others.

Conflict resolution programs are being used in schools across the country, from small towns to big cities and from kindergartens to high schools. The Martin L. King, Jr. Center for Nonviolent Social Change in Atlanta offers ongoing seminars and workshops for teachers in how to develop and maintain programs in conflict resolution. Programs are available in every state in support of nonviolent conflict resolution strategies for schools. For example:

- Three-fourths of San Francisco's public schools have student conflict managers.
- In New York City, more than 100 schools with about 80,000 students have some kind of program.
- In Chicago, all students take a dispute resolution course in ninth and tenth grades.
- In New Mexico, a statewide mediation program involves 30,000 students.

In addition, in Ann Arbor, Michigan, a conflict management curriculum reaches all of the city's students (Arbus, 1994; Berlowitz, 1994; Hanson, 1994).

The effectiveness of conflict resolution programs seems to be in the ability of these programs to actually cause changes in the behavior of participants. Positive results arising from conflict resolution programs are spiraling (Trevaskis, 1994). Such results can be extended to address outside agitation against the school environment. Once students and teachers are comfortable with the principles used in conflict resolution programs, efforts can be made to address the elements of the community that seek to threaten the safety of the school environment (Townley, 1994).

Why Agitators Agitate

We all can identify those external factors that prey on the school environment: drugs, guns and gangs. Like a sitting duck, the school facility has been used as the backdrop for violence in almost as many movies as John Wayne made in his entire career. In the late 1960s, the use of drugs by high school students began to attract the attention of school and community leaders. Yet the lack of political strength needed to begin immediate intervention fostered the belief that this plague would not spread on its own, and if let alone, like other fads among the young, drugs would pass out of the lives of our youth. One of the greatest mistakes made by school administrators has been a national failure to begin the war on drugs at the schoolhouse doors (Hughes, 1994).

That mistake now realized, we must begin to fight just as hard as we can to curb the "need" for drugs to chase away the realities of life that face so harshly so many of our young. The relationship of drugs to theft, fights and burglaries is well documented (Hughes, 1994; Lieber & Rogers, 1994). Today, school personnel have had to assume the role of social worker, surrogate parent and policeman, as well as teacher and mentor. Each day, more students go to school afraid that they may become the victim of random violence than ever before in our history. Combating these traits of violence and hatred have become as necessary in the schoolhouse as preparing a lesson plan on subject-verb agreement.

Despite the desperate appearance of our school climate, efforts are being made to address these elements of distraction to the learning environment. Many schools are now employing social workers to go out into the community and work with parents and with young people who need help in developing effective life skills. Improving the self-esteem of young people is a key to curbing the violence that so often walks into the schoolhouse with them. Community groups are beginning to work with young people to develop ways of improving self-respect and self-worth (Berlowitz, 1994; Miller, 1993). The Houston Center at Clemson University assists in the sponsorship of youth groups across the state of South Carolina to help middle school students learn more about themselves, including career opportunities and educational experiences that can enhance their lives.

Self-esteem could be described as an appreciation of self-worth, that is, having a positive attitude by evaluating oneself highly and being in control of our own lives. This definition simply describes what teachers and administrators must foster in students who are victims of drug abuse and parental abuse and who are candidates for violent and disruptive behavior (Reasoner, 1994). At the same time, administrators and teachers must set examples for those students who fail to adopt appropriate behavior and continue to allow outside elements to influence their behavior in schools. As our society continues to become more and more violent, so will our schools. The findings of social and school research reveal that high self-esteem promotes improvement in personal behavior (Lieber & Rogers, 1994; Linquanti & Berliner, 1994; Hill & Hill, 1994).

Improving self-esteem alone will not effectively eliminate the outside factors that agitate the school climate. Community intervention for the protection of the school facility must be active and proactive. Committed law enforcement must discourage loitering and abuses such as graffiti and littering on school grounds. Schools must be kept attractive, well lighted and well secured to discourage mental images of degradation and depression that feed violent behavior patterns. Active campaigns against drug use and weapons in schools must be continually visible and involve teachers, students, school staff and citizens. Signs that display school rules and regulations should be placed in large letters in well-lighted areas all around the school. Morning and afternoon school announcements should include rules and warnings against disruptive behavior.

Afternoon and evening school activities should be well supported by teachers and staff to show a continual interest in the school and its students. When faculty and staff are present outside school hours, students and parents feel that school personnel appreciate the community and what happens in it. These kinds of signals warn against and help to ward off unacceptable behavior among students and nonstudents who visit the school environment. The improvement of the school environment against outside agitation is a total community effort. No one element is exempt. Civic leaders must lend their support through ordinances that prohibit use of the school facility for activities that are not representative of the school's goals and missions. City councils must develop appropriate restrictions on the use of school facilities that foster divisiveness in the community. Law enforcement agencies must monitor school behavior patterns and work with school officials in the developing programs of rehabilitation of offenders.

School officials must use leadership in setting the tone of the school climate and present consistent and fair behavior when dealing with all students and other participants in the school community (Sautter, 1995). Teachers must accept their role as mentor, surrogate parent, confidante, disciplinarian and role model, not only on the school campus, but also in the community. Students must also share in the responsibility of reshaping their school environment by conducting themselves in positive and progressive ways. Each participant must assume responsibility for eliminating undesirable elements from the school community and work to maintain a safe and healthy environment for learning (Stephens, 1994).

Changing Agitation to Admiration

Efforts to eradicate undesirable elements from the school environment may take years to evoke results. Perhaps, an entire generation of students from pre-kindergarten through twelfth grade will have to experience a variety of methods before tangible results can be achieved in this area. A return to the era of exaltation and fond memories of the school experience may not yet be in sight; however, individual moments of fond memories of school can still be found among recent high school graduates. Some of the most common methods of combating outside agitation against the school environment have been discussed in previous sections of this chapter. Creating a complete turnaround in the nation's schools will require a new approach to improving academic performance. Schools must begin to provide opportunities for students to take ownership of their schools. Activities that increase student involvement and attachment to schools will support efforts to curb agitation to the school environment.

Several activities have been tested across the country that have produced recognizable results in student behavior and, in turn, improved the overall school climate.

- after-school academic programs: drama club performances, peer counseling camps, dropout reentry projects: these kinds of activities keep students involved and focused on subjects that are important to their personal development. Dropout reentry projects reintroduce former students to the school environment without the peer pressure of matriculating students. Often, law enforcement officers and school social workers identify dropouts whose profiles indicate possible success if intervention can occur. These young people are often eager to identify with a group whose experiences reflect their own. The intimidating factors that face reentry students into the mainstream day school are absent in after-school and weekend academies designed specifically to meet their social, cultural and academic needs of this group (Linquanti & Berliner, 1994).
- community involvement: Civic and social organizations that meet in school facilities can create an atmosphere of unity and association with the school community. A greater knowledge of school facilities and the conditions that foster either positive school environments or negative atmospheres are witnessed first-hand by a community's citizens. Such experiences can create a greater sense of understanding and support for schools in communities where the school facility becomes a center for community activities (Smith, 1994).
- athletic competitions: Traditionally, young people gravitate to

sporting events. Using this communal form of entertainment can be effective in fostering healthy school spirit between rival schools, communities and neighborhoods. Intramural sporting events can be inexpensive to sponsor. Local merchants are often eager to promote their businesses by donating equipment, refreshments and so forth in support of athletic events. Early afternoon track meets, field sport competitions and just about any game that offers young people an opportunity to strive for perfection can be used to discourage and eventually eliminate negative behavior patterns among students, dropouts and other identified groups whose energies need to be channeled into productive experiences (Reasoner, 1994).

When a community begins to take control of its environment, especially with a focus on improving the school climate, a new attitude begins to foster itself in the behavior patterns of both children and adults. This kind of change begins with the leadership role of the principal and the administrative team. School administrators are challenged to reach out to the community, civic leaders, religious leaders, promoters of social and cultural events and parents to create teams of community persons committed to the improvement of the school environment. Outside agitation, political influences and cultural differences begin to take a back seat to efforts that clearly focus on the common improvement of a school and the community in which it must function (Hill & Hill, 1994).

Most research supports the contention that stable and supportive leadership is the determining factor in developing and sustaining an effective discipline program (Batsche & Knoff, 1994). However, school administrators should consult with district and state officials to be certain to adhere to state and national statutes. One key is for development of a schoolwide plan to make punishments for infringements uniform for all students. Such a plan also fosters a consensus in determining the punishing "weight" of offenses, categorizing offenses by strength of seriousness and incorporating corrective measures for each offense. The sixth goal of the National Goals for American Education (King, 1994) provides a sound premise for the development of a discipline plan that every community can tailor to the uniqueness of its environment:

> Goal 6 – Safe, disciplined and drug-free schools: By the year 2000, every school in America will be free of drugs and violence and will offer a disciplined environment conducive to learning. Schools, families, com-

munities must work together to counteract negative social influences and create safe and orderly schools.

To begin to achieve Goal 6, schools can create student appreciation for citizenship by developing discipline plans that promote personal responsibility for behavior and respect for individual differences and that emphasize the individual's responsibility to self and community. Discipline plans should

(1) Set realistic timelines for implementation
(2) Create uniform reporting systems
(3) Include representation from teachers, students and school staff: clerical, custodial and cafeteria personnel
(4) Communicate policies clearly to staff, parents, students and the community
(5) Be written and accessible for public review

SUMMARY

For effective implementation, every plan developed to eliminate outside agitation from the school environment should begin with an internal audit of the total school environment. Usually, an outside auditor can objectively assess the communication processes; facility factors that foster discord and invite abuse and disruption to the school climate; staff and faculty apathy and support; administrative leadership effectiveness; and community support and parental involvement. Information that can aid in providing an analysis of these factors is crucial to the development of a comprehensive school discipline plan. Regardless of the thoroughness of an internal audit by an outside evaluator, all parties in the school community must commit to the improvement of the school climate. Without this commitment, no plan will effectively begin to reverse the negative trends of drugs, alcohol abuse, teen pregnancies or increased dropout rates for any school.

Leadership in the school hierarchy is the key to producing a setting that is ripe for change. Inservice training and staff development should be an ongoing practice for teachers and staff. As school leaders implement discipline plans and adopt school effectiveness practices, inservice training will teach personnel to stay on the cutting edge of changes that influence the support of improved school environments. Outside agitation can be identified quickly and corrective measurements can be implemented immediately when the approach to inservice training focuses on the realities of an individual school environment. Once such activities become commonplace within the school community, change will become more evident, learning will increase and schools can again capture the respect and admiration of total community.

REFERENCES

Arbus, J. (1994). Building a successful school conflict resolution program. *Primary Voices K–6*, 2(4):6–11.

Arndt, R. C. (1994). *School violence in America's cities*. NLC Survey Overview (ERIC Document Reproduction Service No. ED 377 291).

Batsche, G. M. & Knoff, H. M. (1994). Bullies and their victims: Understanding a pervasive problem in the schools. *School Psychology Review*, 23(2):165–174.

Berlowitz, M. J. (1994). Urban educational reform: Focusing on peace education. *Education and Urban Society*, 27(1):82–95.

Bernard, J. (1994). School violence and the law: The search for suitable tools. *School Psychology Review*, 23(2):190–203.

Ceperley, P. & Simon, K. (1994). Are our schools safe? AEL Policy Brief (ERIC Document Reproduction Service No. ED 373 420).

Christensen, J. (1995, January). Personal interview. Anderson, SC.

Hanson, M. K. (1994). A conflict resolution/student mediation program: Effects on student attitudes and behaviors. *ERS Spectrum*, 12(4):9–14.

Harrington-Lueker, D. (1994). Hanging onto hope. *American School Board Journal*, 181(12):16–21.

Hatkoff, A. (1994). Safety and children: How schools can help. *Childhood Education*, 70(5):283–286.

Hill, M. S. & Hill, F. W. (1994). *Creating safe schools: What principals can do*. Thousand Oaks, CA: Corwin Press.

Hughes, H. W. (1994). From fistfights to gunfights: Preparing teaching and administrators to cope with violence in schools (ERIC Document Reproduction Service No. ED 366 584).

King, E. F. (1994). Goals 2000: Educate America Act. *School Law Bulletin*, 25(4):15–27.

Lieber, C. M. & Rogers, J. (1994). Challenging beliefs and bureaucracies in an urban school system. *Education and Urban Society*, 27(1):45–70.

Linquanti, R. & Berliner, B. (1994). Rebuilding schools as safe havens: A topology for selecting and integrating violence prevention strategies (ERIC Document Reproduction Service No. ED 376 600).

Miller, R. W. (1993). In search of peace: Peer conflict resolution. *Schools in the Middle*, 2(3):11–13.

Prutzman, P. (1994). Bias-related incidents, hate crimes, and conflict resolution. *Education and Urban Society*, 27(1):71–81.

Reasoner, R. W. (1994). Self-esteem as an antidote to crime and violence (ERIC Document Reproduction Service No. ED 373 281).

Russell, A., (Ed). (1994). Our babies, our future. *Carnegie Quarterly,* 39(2).

Sautter, R. C. (1995). Standing up to violence. *Phi Delta Kappan,* 76(5):k1-k12.

Smith, F. L. (1994). Fighting back. *Executive Educator,* 16(10):35-37.

Stephens, R. D. (1994). Planning for safer and better schools: School violence prevention and intervention strategies. *School Psychology Review,* 23(2):204-215.

Toby, J. (1994). The politics of school violence. *Public Interest* (116):34-56.

Townley, A. (1994). Conflict resolution, diversity, and social justice. *Education and Urban Society,* 27(1):5-10.

Trevaskis, D. K. (1994). Mediation in the schools. ERIC Digest (ERIC Document Reproduction Service No. ED 378 108).

PART II

LEGAL ISSUES

CHAPTER 6

A Dilemma: Dress Codes, Safety and Discrimination

KENNETH E. LANE
MICHAEL D. RICHARDSON
DENNIS W. VAN BERKUM
STANLEY L. SWARTZ

INTRODUCTION

IF ever a controversy presented school officials with a dilemma, gang attire dress codes is the consummate issue. Ensuring student safety at the expense of First Amendment rights of students to express themselves presents fascinating predicaments for school officials. The presumption that student dress is related to student behavior is not new. Gangs have been present in the United States since the Revolutionary War, and gangs today are patterned after the so-called "gangsters" of the 1920s as well as the ethnic "street corner gangs," which formed in our early urban centers. Early gangs were typically associated with deteriorating neighborhoods, limited access to jobs and recreation, reduced educational opportunity and impoverished living conditions (Thrasher, 1927).

What is new is the growing number of school districts attempting to develop restrictive student dress codes to curb gang activity. These efforts have taken on a sense of considerable urgency in areas where gang activity threatens the safety of the school environment. Though gang members are known to intimidate others in various ways, their clothing has been a primary form of gang member identification. While the courts have consistently reiterated the authority of school personnel to maintain a reasonable, safe atmosphere in which all students can be educated, the courts also have reinforced student civil rights.

Each local school board can establish policies regarding dress codes and school safety issues for its district and its schools. By developing and implementing policies that prohibit gang or gang-related attire, school officials are asked to weigh two considerations that appear to be on a collision course—the school board's responsibility to ensure a proper learning environment weighed against the individual rights of students. The proper balance of the two competing extremes creates a volatile situation which affects students, parents, school administrators, the community and school board members.

The enactment of school board policies concerning gang attire dress codes raises numerous questions for serious consideration and deliberation. The issue of gang attire dress codes and their impact on student's rights and safe schools has received its first federal court decision. The case of *Jeglin v. San Jacinto Unified School District* (1993), heard before the United States District Court, C.D. California, resulted in a split decision on July 28, 1993. The court ruled that gang attire dress codes for grades K–8 were unconstitutional but for grades 9–12 they were constitutional.

This chapter addresses the gang attire dress question from both the school safety and students' rights perspectives, beginning with a review of court cases. Several recommendations based on an examination of the legal implications of gang attire dress code versus students' rights are made.

REVIEW OF COURT CASES

A lawsuit challenging the constitutionality of gang attire dress codes was filed in *Jeglin v. San Jacinto Unified School District*. Until this historic case, school officials had typically relied on cases which addressed freedom of expression and general dress codes. The Jeglin case presented school officials with the equivalent of boxing's "split decision." The court ruled that school policies restricting gang attire dress codes at the K–8 level were unconstitutional because students at that age did not understand or comprehend the substance of their dress. However, for ninth- to twelfth-grade students, the court specified that a school district could constitutionally restrict student dress because students did comprehend the significance of their behavior. Naturally, nobody seems satisfied with this decision. It has served to raise additional questions and generate confusion over the issue of safe schools and students' rights. A review of some of the cases regarding students' rights and gang attire may serve as a foundation from which to discuss further gang attire dress codes.

Tinker v. Des Moines

The U.S. Supreme Court Case of *Tinker v. Des Moines* (1969) ranks as a landmark case in educational law due to the magnitude of the ruling granting freedom of expression for students. The Supreme Court ruling made it quite clear that students did not lose their constitutional rights when they entered the schoolhouse doors. As a result, school officials could no longer discipline students' symbolic expression of opinion unless the school officials could show that there would be material interference with, or substantial disruption of, the school's normal routine. This case was cited prominently in the court's opinion in *Jeglin v. San Jacinto*.

Hair Length Cases

The courts have been divided in their response to lawsuits over the right of students to wear hair at a length of their choosing. For instance, the right to wear one's hair at any length cannot be found in the meaning of the Constitution, according to the decision rendered in *Karr v. Schmidt* (1972); a case also cited in the court's opinion in *Jeglin v. San Jacinto*. The school district has the right to govern students' dress, as well as hair length and conduct, according to the decisions rendered in the *King v. Saddleback* (1971) and the *Olff v. Eastside Union* (1969) cases. An opposing view was expressed in *Massie v. Henry* (1972) when the court ruled that the school carries the burden of deciding whether the necessity to infringe upon a student's freedom in setting hair length policies is warranted. Likewise, in *Breen v. Kahl* (1969), the right of students to wear their hair at any length or in any manner was declared an appendage of personal freedom protected by the Constitution.

Dress Code Cases

The courts' rulings have been inconsistent and ambiguous with regard to the establishment and implementation of dress codes. In *Scott v. Board of Education, Union Free School District #17* (1969), girls were prohibited from wearing slacks to school due to an issue of taste and style, not of safety, order or discipline. In *Bannister v. Paradis* (1970), the court ruled that it was unconstitutional for a school district to prohibit students from wearing "dungarees" (or jeans) since wearing them did not pose a danger to the health and safety of others, did not cause a disturbance or incite disciplinary problems. However, if attire is immodest, such as short skirts more than six inches above the knees, the courts have ruled that a school can prohibit students from wearing such clothing (*Wallace v. Ford*, 1972).

In *Olesen v. Board of Education of School District No. 228* (1987), a dress code prohibiting male students from wearing earrings was ruled constitutional. Part of the reason for this decision rested on the ability of the school district to establish a rationale for the policy. The rationale stipulated that the policy was related to the goal of curbing gang activity in and around the schools.

Safe Schools

The federal courts consistently have upheld the school district's right to establish regulations for the day-to-day operations of schools. The safety issue specifies that school officials have the right to demand conduct that is conducive to the fulfillment of its responsibility to educate.

However, the courts are not clear concerning the administrator's authority to control the school environment to protect all students and to protect themselves from litigation. In 1988, the court found in the *Ledger v. Stockton Unified School District* case that the California constitution is not self-executing because it does not supply a right to sue for damages; rather, the constitution expresses a general right without giving any specific rules for enforcement. On the other hand, the California Supreme Court ruled in *Totsiello v. Oakland Unified School District* (1972) that the law imposes on school authorities a responsibility to supervise the conduct of children, because of students' tendencies to engage in aggressive and impulsive behavior that could lead to harm to the students. The responsibility of the school to create a safe and orderly school environment has been established by a combination of federal and state laws, case laws at all levels, and regulatory language developed by various federal and state agencies. Although the expectation of student safety is understood, in actual practice the standard is difficult to meet.

Primarily because the violence that takes place on school campuses does not have its origin in the school environment, school administrators are often on the outside looking in on the behavior of students. The roots of student violence are found in the community and the home. However, society has yet to address the issue of student crime; and as a consequence, schools are a convenient source of remediation attempts. Schools have responded by dealing with the symptoms instead of the causes of violence. An increasingly frequent response has been to restrict the display of gang colors and to implement dress codes aimed at banning what are believed to be gang attire, in the belief and hope that violence on the school campuses will end. Any effort that curbs gang activity will positively affect safety and the school environment.

While the courts have historically given the schools considerable latitude in their efforts to regulate student behavior, the relationship between the prohibition and the targeted problem must be carefully addressed. If dress can be directly attributed to an inappropriate behavior that disrupts the school environment, then, and only then, is its regulation justifiable. However, courts will likely require schools to demonstrate "imminent danger" before a district ban on attire is acceptable. Attire bans that are indiscriminate or are not directly related to creating and maintaining safe schools will not be supported. Mere speculation or anticipation of danger would probably not be acceptable to the courts. Likewise, the courts will not hesitate to declare school policies unconstitutional if they are racially or ethnically discriminatory.

Gang Association Cases

The issue of association revolves around the issue of gang activity and the dress that gangs wear to identify themselves. The rationale for addressing the issue of association rests with the concern that all activities that endanger students on the way to, while at, and on the way home from school be eliminated. Therefore, if a student's manner of dress has the potential of causing violence on campus, then that clothing can be eliminated. A clear example of this responsibility was demonstrated in *Boggers v. Sacramento City Unified School District* (1972) when a high school student was attacked by a group of gang members and seriously injured. The court found that the school was liable for damages because it was aware of the gang problem and had neglected to take any action to protect the students. The least action would have been to restrict outward displays of gang affiliations.

School District Dress Code Policies

The issue of association and gang attire becomes confusing when reviewing school board policies. In southern California, many school boards have adopted policies that specifically address gang attire to the point of prohibiting certain styles of clothing. However, some school districts have gone beyond this limit by specifically naming certain professional sports team clothing and enjoining student use of such clothing; because gangs identify themselves with the clothing and the sports teams. Some school districts have chosen to bypass the issue by declaring all sports-organization-related clothing unallowable. An irony of such policies is that it even makes the wearing of one's own school athletic team's clothing a violation of board policy.

Framing the Constitutional Concerns

Admittedly, there is genuine, realistic concern for the safety of students on school campuses, particularly since schools have become the focal point for increased violence. This safety concern has been directly and specifically related to gang activity and the influence of gangs on schools and students. There is no denial that gang activity has resulted in disruptions on school campuses, including the deaths of students. Sadly, some of the deceased students were not members of gangs; but died as the result of gangs and their violent impact on society, particularly the school society. It, therefore, became axiomatic that any effort that curbs gang activity would positively impact the safety of the school environment. It has been suggested by many parents and school officials that no cost is too great to protect children and ensure their safety. However, school officials also honor and cling tenaciously to the constitutional protection of freedom of expression, even expression exercised by what we wear or how we wear it.

The primary question is constitutional: Do school districts have the constitutional right to mandate dress codes at the expense of students' rights to free speech? Most school policies on gang attire are so vague that almost any article of clothing could conceivably be ruled gang attire by school officials. Certain districts prohibit wearing "colors," which could lead school officials to ban certain colors at the school such as reds and blues that represent two of the largest gangs in southern California, the Crips and the Bloods. Such colors do not automatically signify that the student is a gang member; however, school administrators have no valid means for determining gang membership. Consequently, any obviously detectable sign of gang membership is subject to suspicion and ultimately to censorship.

Students have a right to dress according to the clothing available to them, but not at the expense of conduct which is prejudicial to the general order of the school. Limitations on gang attire often contribute to other problems. David Piercy (1992), assistant to the superintendent in Eugene, Oregon, suggests that one of the myths concerning gang attire is that all gang members dress in a certain way when in actuality they do not. For low socioeconomic students, banning certain clothes may interfere with their right to an education, because they may not have the financial resources to buy new clothes consistent with a school district's decision to ban "colors" or certain types of apparel.

The vagueness of the policies may eventually lead more school districts into court. Then the school district shoulders the burden of proving that the policy on gang attire does not discriminate against students and does indeed contribute to a safe school environment.

Framing the Response

In approving policies regarding student dress, school officials must show a connection between the appearance and the negative behavior or distraction from the educational function of the school. To dislike how someone looks is not enough. Questions are legitimately raised about what can be realistically regulated and whether the regulation will have the desired effect. The courts have historically given the schools considerable latitude in their efforts to regulate student behavior; however, the courts have consistently required the schools to determine the relationship between the prohibited activity and the problem targeted by the regulation. This seemingly simple test in theory has not been as simple in application.

General guidelines for schools and districts to follow in establishing dress codes, especially gang attire dress codes, should be the ability to withstand judicial scrutiny as outlined by Gee and Sperry (1978). School officials must not judge students on appearance alone. If dress can be directly related to an inappropriate behavior that disrupts the school environment, its regulation is justifiable. However, there is no evidence that the courts would support districts that enforce bans on attire that are indiscriminate or cannot be shown to be directly related to creating and maintaining safe schools.

Policies developed to deal with gang activity must not be vague; rather, they must explicitly state the items to be banned and give a rationale for their actions. There is some evidence that some policies have been developed with the notion that extreme circumstances require extreme measures. An abridgement of the rights of the individual might be justified in the interest of the greater good.

The history of our country is replete with examples of institutions that advocated sacrificing the rights and freedoms of individuals to advance the goals of society. On the other hand, our courts have not hesitated to step in when institutions have appeared reactionary or overly repressive. Although the rights of students overall cannot be restricted due to the behavior of a few, the fine line between protecting students' rights and ensuring a safe school must be carefully weighed before arbitrary action is taken to control the behavior of the few.

CONCLUSIONS

The problems associated with the conflict between students' rights, demonstrated by dress as a form of freedom of expression; and protection for students, manifested by attempts to regulate dress, place schools once again on the horns of a dilemma. The pressures on school officials to maintain a safe school environment cannot be overstated; however, similar burdens to ensure students' rights and freedoms are often not comparable. The weight of public opinion appears to fall on the side of doing whatever is necessary to accomplish the goal of safe schools.

In many ways, the assumption that regulating student dress will control gang violence is a classic example of the "quick fix" or "one best way" mentality that seemingly permeates education. Most experts agree that gangs and the violence that they engender are only symptoms of larger societal problems. Any belief that schools can control society's problems by regulating what students wear or how they wear it, is hopeful at best, and hopelessly simplistic at worst. School officials who engage with the community to resolve the problems that create gangs, gang violence and unsafe schools will be more effective than school officials who attempt to regulate the artifacts through dress codes. Schools cannot hope to encourage students to become responsible and fully participating citizens when they appear to be disposed and even anxious to restrict students' rights in the school.

All of this leads us to a few questions. If the ultimate purpose of education is to enable students to achieve, then does passing gang attire dress codes enable us to accomplish that objective, or does it simply deal with symptoms rather than the causes of school violence? Where are the data that show that adopting gang attire dress codes has reduced the incidence of violence in our schools?

Though we are committed to providing a safe learning environment, abridging a constitutional freedom to do so is too great a cost. Balancing these issues is a difficult task, but one that comes with living together in a free society.

Later, you might want to look at ways to soften students' attitudes toward dress codes. There is some general law . . . I forget the name of it. It states that if a person feels a freedom has been unduly taken away from him or her, he or she will strongly rebel against the rule. A lot of research had addressed this. It explains the urge to touch something that has a "do not touch" sign. Anyway, the research explains that when a person is given a reason for the rule, for example, "Do not touch, object is very fragile," he or she is many times more likely to abide by the rule.

If students receive a *sincere* explanation as to why there is a ban on gang attire, and perhaps if they *vote* on it, they will be more supportive and abiding of the school and its rule.

REFERENCES

Bannister v. Paradis, 316 F. Supp. 185 (1970).
Boggers v. Sacramento City Unified School District, 25 Cal. App.3d 269 (1972).
Breen v. Kahl, 419 F.2d 1034 7th Cir. (1969).
California Department of Justice. (1990). *Law in the school.* Sacramento: State of California.
California State Department of Education. (1986). *Students' rights and responsibilities handbook.* Sacramento, CA: The Department of Education.
Gee, E. G. & Sperry, D. J. (1978). *Education law and the public schools: A compendium.* Boston: Allyn & Bacon.
Jeglin v. San Jacinto Unified School District, 827 F. Supp. 1459 (1993).
Karr v. Schmidt, 460 F.2d 609, 613, 5th Cir. (1972).
King v. Saddleback, 445 F.2d 932 (1971).
Lane, K. E. & Stine, D. O. (1992). Dress codes and association. In W. Camp, J. Underwood, M. J. Connelly & K. E. Lane, (Ed.). *Principal's handbook for school law.* Topeka, KS: National Organization on Legal Problems of Education.
Ledger v. Stockton Unified School District, 202 Cal. App.3d 1448 (1988).
Massie v. Henry. 455 F.2d 779, 4th Cir. (1972)
Olesen v. Board of Education of School District No. 288, 676 F. Supp. 820 (N.D. Ill. 1987).
Olff v. Eastside Union, U.S. App.305 F. Supp. 557 (1969).
Piercy, D. (1992, November 20). The rap of gang clothes. *Inside Line,* p. 3 (Produced by the Public Affairs Department, Eugene Public Schools, District 4J).
Scott v. Board of Education, Union Free School District #17, 61 Misc.2d 333, 305 S.C. 601 (1969).
Thrasher, F. (1927). *The gang. A study of 13 gangs in Chicago.* Chicago: University of Chicago Press.
Tinker v. Des Moines Independent Community School District, 393 U.S. 503, 89 S.Ct. 733 (1969).
Totsiello v. Oakland Unified School District, 197 Cal. App.3d, 41, 45 (1972).
Wallace v. Ford, 346 F. Supp. Ark. (1972).

CHAPTER 7

Sexual Harassment in the Schools: A Safety and Liability Issue for All Administrators

SANDRA SIMPSON

IN California, a law made sexual harassment part of the school curriculum beginning in the 1993-1994 school year. Why are California, Massachusetts, Michigan, Florida and numerous other state legislatures mandating that all schools add a new subject to the traditional three R's?

INTRODUCTION

Sexual harassment is an issue of power, not sex. Sexual harassment is about intentional intimidation, coercion and discrimination. It involves the unethical abuse of one person by another.

Sexual harassment is a widespread problem within the schools at all levels. Studies at various universities have reported that anywhere from 25% to 70% of students have experienced sexual harassment over assignment of course grades (Carroll, 1993; Elza, 1992; Simpson, 1992). Only 3% to 17% of the male students surveyed indicate that they have been sexually harassed, so most of the incidents involve female students (Carroll, 1993; Riger, 1991). Institutions of higher education have had policies and complaint procedures which address the issue of sexual harassment for many years, yet less than an average of five cases per academic institution are filed each year (Elza, 1992; Riger, 1992).

Only recently has the pervasiveness of sexual harassment among adolescents been recognized as more than typical teasing behavior. During the spring of 1993, The American Association of University Women (AAUW) employed Lou Harris and Associates to conduct a series of studies on the problem within the public schools in grades eight through eleven. The results of the survey of more than 1600 students, released in June 1993, indicated that 81% of all students have experienced sexual harassment while at school. Eighty-five percent of the girls have been harassed and 76% of the boys. Twenty-three percent of the students responded that they had been harassed to such a degree that they did not want to attend school (Raney, 1993). Although the AAUW report defined sexual harassment liberally to include physical and nonphysical attacks, ranging from forced intercourse to being the object of sexual rumors, 65% of the girls and 42% of the boys reported having been touched, grabbed or pinched in a sexual manner. Most of these incidents involved only students, but 25% of the female students and 10% of the male students stated that they have been harassed by school personnel. Only 7% of the students who have been sexually harassed ever reported it to a teacher, and only 23% even mentioned it to a parent (Saltzman, 1993).

LEGAL BASIS: ESTABLISHING AND DEFINING THE ISSUE

During October of 1991, the nation listened to the compelling testimony of Anita Hill as she accused Clarence Thomas, a Supreme Court nominee, of sexual harassment before a Senate Judiciary Committee. Although the committee saw no grounds for withholding Thomas's confirmation, the nation as a whole responded to Professor Hill's emotional story. Revelation of her secret broke national silence on an ascendant issue.

Between 1976 and 1980, studies exposed that sexual harassment was a problem affecting 40% to 88% of the women employed within the United States. The nation, however, was not alarmed because sexually harassing behavior was considered "normative" (Riger, 1992; Shoop, 1992). Women accepted the intimidation as an occupational hazard. Even with the Civil Rights Act of 1964, less than 3% of working women filed a formal complaint (Riger, 1991). By 1990, however, attitudes began to change. The Equal Employment Opportunity Commission (EEOC) reported that it had received a total of 3,661 complaints of sexual harassment by 1981; 5,694 by 1990; 6,892 by 1991; and 12,537 by November of 1993 (Gage, 1993; Carroll, 1993).

At the end of 1991, the time was right for a new generation to vicariously commiserate with the quiet voice on Capital Hill. Women emotionally understood the media focus on Anita Hill's impassioned story, although the Senate Judiciary hearing committee's reaction served to demonstrate the disparity in gender sensitivity to the issue (Solomon, 1991). In the year following the Anita Hill hearing, female victims began to seek legal redress in ever-growing numbers and 3,329 complaints were recorded in that year alone. The EEOC filed lawsuits on behalf of sixty-six victims ("Sexual Harassment," 1992). Courts and legislatures across the country were forced to define sexual harassment and to establish legal procedures and precedents. Dialogue raised understandings between men and women. Corporations and employers directed their human resource administrators to develop policies, procedures and training programs (Solomon, 1991).

Title VII: Sexual Harassment during Employment

The basis for sexual harassment as a legal issue was established through Title VII of the Civil Rights Act of 1964, which prohibited employment discrimination on the basis of an ". . . individual's race, color, religion, sex or national origin" and established the Equal Employment Opportunity Commission as the regulatory agency. In 1977, *Barnes v. Costle* set a clear precedent for providing protection against sexual harassment under Title VII.

By 1980, the EEOC had enough direction from federal court decisions to formally add specific regulations prohibiting sexual harassment. These regulations became the first stated definition:

> Harassment on the basis of sex is a violation of Sec. 703 of Title VII. Unwelcome sexual advances, requests for sexual favors, and other verbal or physical conduct of a sexual nature constitute harassment when (1) submission to such conduct is made explicitly or implicitly a term or condition of an individual's employment, (2) submission to or rejection of such conduct by an individual is used as a basis for employment decisions affecting such individual, (3) such conduct has the purpose or effect of reasonably interfering with an individual's work performance or creating an intimidating, hostile, or offensive work environment. (1604.11(a))

This definition is broad enough to encompass a diversity of behaviors from verbal innuendo to invasive attack. Court cases are gradually circumscribing its parameters.

Meritor Savings Bank, FSB v. Vinson

The U.S. Supreme Court in *Meritor Savings Bank, FSB v. Vinson* (1986) supported the EEOC definition and confirmed Title VII protection against sexual harassment as a form of sex discrimination. The court set major legal precedents, including findings that:

(1) "Hostile environment" is a form of sexual discrimination which is actionable under Title VII, regardless of economic impact to the plaintiff.
(2) Employers are not automatically liable for sexual harassment by their supervisors, although mere existence of policies and procedures is not protection.
(3) Conduct must show that sexual advances were "unwelcome," even if sexual participation is voluntary.
(4) Speech and dress are relevant to the determination of consensual conduct.

The justices' conclusion that sexual harassment can be "sufficiently severe or pervasive" so as to create an abusive environment expanded the employee's right to be free from any form of discriminatory intimidation, insult or ridicule.

Two categories of sexual harassment complaints came out of the EEOC definition during the *Meritor* proceedings (Alexander & Alexander, 1992; Klein & Wilber, 1986). The quid pro quo category presumes a relationship of unequal status where one party uses power to coerce the other by holding sexual favors as a condition for benefit. Economic effect is usually connected to this type of sexual harassment. The non quid pro quo category focuses on the hostile environment which can create intimidation and distress, impairing the ability to work (Carroll, 1993). The courts have found it difficult to define what constitutes a reasonable environment versus an intolerable environment in the second category. A hostile environment includes a range of behaviors and materials such as: innuendos, gestures, sexual jokes, flirting, whistling, favoritism, cartoons, graffiti and pin-up posters (Carroll, 1993; Hayes, 1991). Culturally, there is some common standard for decency, but the interpretation of what is viewed as discriminatory against a particular sex is frequently subjective.

Harris v. Forklift Systems, Inc.

The Supreme Court granted *writ of certiorari* to *Teresa Harris v. Forklift Systems, Inc.* (1993) to address the conflicting opinions of the circuit courts of appeals on the necessity for a "hostile environment" to affect the psychological well-being of the employee. The decision reaffirmed *Meritor* and upheld *Ellison v. Brady,* rejecting the requirement for either severe psychological damage or a decline in job performance (Schimmel, 1994). Justice Sandra Day O'Connor, writing the unanimous opinion of the court, stated conclusively, "Title VII comes into play before the harassing conduct leads to a nervous breakdown" (p. 370). Recognizing that sexual harassment is often subjectively assessed in the eye of the beholder, the court set forth a standard that "takes the middle path between making actionable any conduct which is merely offensive and requiring the conduct to cause a tangible psychological injury" (p. 370). The court insisted that the sexual harassment be of a discriminatory nature and excludes individuals who are hypersensitive. In order to assess workplace equity, the court delineated five factors for determining a hostile environment: 1) the frequency of the discriminatory conduct; 2) its severity; 3) whether it is physically threatening or humiliating, or a mere offensive utterance; 4) whether it reasonably interferes with an employee's work performance; and 5) whether it has an effect on the employee's psychological well-being.

Originally, evaluations of what constituted sexual harassment were based on the "reasonable person" or "reasonable man" standard. But, in the case of *Ellison v. Brady* (1991), the Ninth Circuit Court of Appeals found that the "reasonable person" standard "tends to be male-biased and systematically ignores the experience of women" (Carroll, 1993, p. 23). The court proposed that a "reasonable woman" standard would be more sensitive to the effects of sexual harassment upon its female victims and would be better able to ascertain which behaviors are offensive. The "reasonable woman" has become the norm for determining which environments are hostile (Carroll, 1993; Elza 1992; Larson & Knee, 1991). The "reasonable man" or "reasonable person" standard is considered gender-biased and unfairly blind to the gender hierarchy of the workplace (Shoop, 1992). In *Harris,* however, Justice Ginsberg called for a return to the "reasonable person" standard. She stated that the main consideration is whether or not a hostile environment is discriminatory and concluded that a "reasonable person" should be able to recognize conduct that imposes disadvantageous conditions on one particular sex.

CIVIL RIGHTS ACT OF 1991: PUNITIVE DAMAGES FOR SEXUAL HARASSMENT

Remedies under Title VII of the Civil Rights Act of 1964 are limited to "equitable relief" such as back pay, job restoration or an injunction to cease the behavior which had prompted a complaint. Before 1991, only 5% to 10% of women who were sexually harassed filed a complaint (Larson & Knee, 1991).

Monetary awards became available when the Civil Rights Act of 1991 established guidelines for punitive damages in sex discrimination cases (Noah, 1991; Noah & Karr, 1991). Between 1991 and 1993, $18.6 million was paid as compensation for sexual harassment (Gage, 1993).

Punitive damages allowed under the Civil Rights Act of 1991 require a jury trial. Juries have the advantage of removing the stigma of gender bias for both the plaintiff and the defendant.

TITLE IX: SEXUAL HARASSMENT WITHIN THE SCHOOLS

Title IX of the Educational Amendments of 1972 extends the prohibition against sex discrimination to education. Interpretations of Title IX have paralleled Title VII. Case rulings under either piece of legislation become a common precedent to both. Sexual harassment has been found to be a form of sex discrimination under Title IX, just as it was under Title VII. Quid pro quo complaints of sexual harassment can be filed when one person holds the power of evaluation over the other. Non quid pro quo cases arise from student to student relationships and, until recently, have rarely been filed (Carroll, 1993).

Within the U.S. Department of Education, the Office of Civil Rights (OCR) is the regulatory agency for enforcement of Title IX. The OCR can recommend that federal funding be terminated for any educational institution that violates Title IX. If a civil suit is filed, remedies may also be awarded by the court (Klein & Wilber, 1986). The OCR published a memo to all Regional Civil Rights Directors on August 31, 1981 entitled "Title IX and Sexual Harassment Complaints." A definition of sexual harassment was given in the memo:

> Sexual harassment consists of verbal or physical conduct of a sexual nature, imposed on the basis of sex, by any employee or agent of a recipient that denies, limits, provides different, or conditions the provision of aid, benefits, services or treatment protected under Title IX.

The courts have firmly held that schools are to be a safe environment where students can learn and interact without fear or impediment (Carroll, 1993). Landmark cases have defined how the courts intend to ensure that educational institutions are havens from the coercion of sexual harassment.

LANDMARK CASES UNDER TITLE IX

Pfeiffer v. School Board

Arlene Pfeiffer was a student at Marion Center High School in western Pennsylvania. She became pregnant during the spring of 1983 and was, consequently, denied continued membership in the National Honor Society. She filed suit, alleging sex discrimination, under Title IX of the Educational Amendments of 1972. On an appeal, the court upheld the National Honor Society's right to set their own standards, but questioned their equitable application.

Although the Third Circuit Court of Appeals could find no direct causation for punitive damages in Arlene Pfeiffer's case, it did rule that compensatory damages were available under Title IX for intentional discrimination. The monetary damages ruling was in direct opposition to prior rulings by the Seventh and Eleventh Circuit Courts (Zirkel, 1991).

Franklin v. Gwinnett County Public Schools

The Supreme Court of the United States agreed to hear the case of *Franklin v. Gwinnett County Public Schools* (1992) by *writ of certiorari* due to the split of opinions in the circuit courts over whether compensatory damages could be awarded under Title IX (Zirkel, 1992). In their final ruling on February 26, 1992, the nine justices were unanimous in their support for punitive damages (Greenhouse, 1992). Justice White in writing for the majority opinion stated that a "traditional rule" of judicial construction is that a right to sue implies a right to "all necessary and appropriate remedies," including monetary compensation (Simpson, 1992). The court extended the Title IX private right of action beyond the limits of equitable relief (i.e., an injunction, prospective relief for lost benefits or back pay) to reflect the decision in *Cannon v. University of Chicago* (1979), giving victims the right to monetary tort damages (Valente, 1992).

The facts in *Franklin* were not disputed. Christine Franklin was a sophomore at North Gwinnett High School in the fall of 1986. Andrew Hill, her economics teacher, engaged her to grade papers for him and developed a "special" relationship with her. During the course of a year, he accorded her special privileges, arranged private meetings with her, engaged her in sexually oriented conversions, telephoned her at home and forcibly kissed her. Between October and December of 1987, he summoned her from class three times and coerced her into sexual intercourse on school grounds. Franklin's boyfriend told the band director about Hill's conduct and one of her friends told an assistant principal. She informed a guidance counselor and the principal of the sexual activity in February of 1988, but investigation of her allegations did not proceed until March. The school officials closed their investigation at the end of the school year when Hill agreed to resign. Franklin then filed a complaint with OCR in August of 1988. After the school district gave assurances that no more violations would occur, the OCR dropped its investigation. A civil suit for damages was filed in federal district court and appealed to the Eleventh Circuit Court. The Supreme Court finally overturned all prior dismissals (Greenhouse, 1992; Russo, Nordin & Leas, 1992; Zirkel, 1992).

The Supreme Court's decision made it clear that teachers, counselors and administrators have a greater level of responsibility to protect the school environment and to investigate complaints of sexual harassment than do employers. The age and vulnerability of students call for an increased degree of care. The school district was liable because it put its reputation and budgetary concerns above the need to protect the victim (Russo, Nordin & Leas, 1992).

Franklin v. Gwinnett extended the Civil Rights Act of 1991 and the *Meritor v. Vinson* case decision to education, making districts and administrators liable for the actions of their teachers. Has it opened a "Pandora's Box of educational liability" as many feared it would (Russo, Nordin & Leas, 1992, p. 741)? Several cases in the last few years have begun to set a pattern which indicates that districts are liable only when they are grossly negligent in their responsibility to investigate and give relief to students. The case must involve intentional injury by a district which receives federal financial assistance. What the Franklin decision does mean is that districts can no longer quietly ask a teacher to resign and pretend that an ugly incident never happened.

Despite studies which indicate large percentages of students are experiencing sexual harassment, only a few lawsuits have been filed and most have been settled before reaching trial. Katy Lyle of Duluth, Minnesota, settled for $15,000 in damages for "mental anguish" after a year and a half of complaints about male peers' restroom graffiti about her were ignored (Gross, 1992). Tawnya Brawdy settled for $20,000 in an out-of-court settlement after a U.S. Department of Education 211-page report found that the schools had failed to protect her during five years of continual harassment (Adler & Rosenberg, 1992). Cheltzie Hentz, a second grader, at the age of seven, is the youngest person to file a complaint with the U.S. Department of Education. She alleges that her male schoolmates use dirty language on the school bus to harass her and have not been stopped, despite twenty-two pages of letters sent to school officials by her mother. Her case has not become a lawsuit at this point and will probably never become one, if the school district remediates the situation (Adler & Rosenberg 1992; Will, 1992). Most lawsuits are avoidable, if complaints are handled quickly.

Patricia H. v. Berkeley Unified School District

The Supreme Court characterized Franklin's intentional injury as sexual harassment and sexual discrimination under Title IX, but did not distinguish its category as quid pro quo or non quid pro quo. *Patricia H. v. Berkeley Unified School District* was the first case to test whether a "hostile environment" claim could be filed under Title IX.

Patricia H., the mother of Jackie H. and Rebecca H., had a romantic relationship during 1987 and early 1988 with Charles Hamilton, the band teacher for several schools in the Berkeley Unified School District. While staying in Patricia H.'s home and on a trip to Lake Tahoe, Hamilton molested Jackie H., age twelve, and Rebecca H., age ten. The charges against Hamilton were not proven at the time Patricia H. filed under Title IX for monetary tort damages claiming that Hamilton's continued presence within the school district created a hostile environment.

District Court Judge Orrick remanded the case to a jury trial after making several important determinations. He cited the Supreme Court's direction to the federal courts in *North Haven Board of Education v. Bell* (1982) to interpret Title IX with a "sweep as broad as its language" (p. 1289). First, he ruled that a hostile environment claim could be filed under Title IX. Secondly, he allowed that it would take a jury's consideration of the material facts to determine whether or not a teacher's mere presence could create a hostile environment. Thirdly, he established that graduation did not render a claim invalid under Title IX. Finally, he upheld the findings of the state credentialing commission. He stated that the investigative hearing process involved in the revocation of a teaching certificate was fair and extensive. The commission's finding of sexual misconduct was considered proof of guilt in the absence of a completed criminal trial.

ELEVENTH AMENDMENT IMMUNITY

The Eleventh Amendment to the Constitution of the United States bars an individual from suing for state treasury funds. The amendment reads:

> The judicial power of the United States shall not be construed to extend to any suit in law or equity, commenced or prosecuted against one of the United States by Citizens of another state, or by Citizens or Subjects of any Foreign State.

Judiciary power is limited and can only be abrogated if a state consents to a suit in federal court or if Congress exercises its right through the Fourteenth Amendment (Alexander & Alexander, 1992). The legal question for educators has been whether school boards and school administrators are state agents protected by state immunity. The problematic question had no bearing on sexual harassment claims until Franklin opened the door for punitive damages.

Justice White, writing the majority opinion in *Franklin,* addressed the issue indirectly through a review of Congress's spending clause power. While he concurred that entities receiving federal funds are not liable for unintentional violations of Title IX, he found a precedent that required "state entities to pay monetary awards out of their treasuries for intentional violations of federal statutes" (p. 1038).

The distinction between unintentional and intentional violation is critical to the determination of a claim against a school district. It is incumbent upon the plaintiff to prove intentional discrimination on the basis of sex in order to meet the 1986 Congressional conditions for abrogation of state immunity under Title IX. *Franklin* was a suit against a school district which had power over Andrew Hill, an employed teacher. Intentional discrimination was shown because the school district, through its administrators, ignored the complaints and took no action to alleviate the situation. The district failed to use its power to supervise its employees and that was used as circumstantial evidence supporting the allegations of intentional discrimination.

Jane Doe v. Petaluma City School District (1993) was the first case to conclude that student to student sexual harassment is actionable under Title IX. The finding was in opposition to the Third Circuit Court of Appeals' disposition in an earlier case. The complaint alleged that a hostile environment was created by Jane Doe's peers through incessant sexual innuendos about hot dogs and threats to fight with her when she reported their slanders to the school counselor. The school district, principal, vice-principal and counselor were sued because the actions taken to stop the harassment were ineffective. It was alleged that under the Title VII employer's standard that they knew or should have known of the harassment and failed to take reasonable steps to stop it. The court upheld the Eleventh Amendment's immunity for school districts and school employees acting in their official capacity as arms of the state. Failure to take appropriate action was not equatable to intentional discrimination. The district had not ignored the complaints, although the actions taken did not have the desired effect of alleviating the harassing behavior. The case was dismissed with leave to amend the charges against the principal. When the amended charges were filed, the district settled out of court on behalf of the principal for $20,000 (Mentell, 1993).

Several cases of sexual harassment by peers are on the dockets. Administrative responsibility is not yet determinable, but it is certain that negligent inaction is culpable.

LIABILITY UNDER § 1983

The federal Civil Rights Act as amended by Title U.S.C. § 1983 is commonly referred to simply as § 1983. The relevant portion of the act permits anyone who is deprived of a right secured by the Constitution and the laws of the United States to bring legal action including monetary liability against the person who deprives the individual of that right. The Civil Rights Attorneys' Fees Awards Act of 1976 further allows the collection of all litigation costs for § 1983 claimants who prevail (Valente, 1990).

School districts and school administrators cannot be named in a § 1983 claim based upon the doctrine of *respondeat superior* which imposes vicarious liability on supervisors due to the actions of their subordinates (Horner, 1991; Valente, 1990). An individual who causes a § 1983 injury has personal liability, but the supervising administrator or the school district is liable only if there exists a policy or custom which denies a constitutional right (Horner, 1991). To be successful against a supervisor or a supervising agency, a Section 1983 claimant must allege and prove that 1) a constitutional right existed, 2) the right was denied and 3) either a special relationship implied a duty to protect the claimant or an official policy or custom existed to deprive the claimant of his or her constitutional rights (Valente, 1990). A policy is defined as any written rule, regulation, statement, by-law, ordinance or precedent. Custom is defined by a pattern of actions or an affirmative act performed by a policymaker. The definition of a custom may be further extended to include abusive practices which are condoned by the policymaker through his inaction to remediate a praxis of which he has knowledge (Horner, 1991; Valente, 1990). School districts are liable, as in *Franklin*, when a pattern of consistent inaction clearly permits the continuation of misconduct, as if the district had a custom of acceding to the sexually harassing behavior. School districts must not project a permissive policy through a custom of deliberate indifference.

The right of students to be free from sexual abuse by their teachers is established by the Fourteenth Amendment. The courts have upheld a constitutional right to bodily security. Section 1983 cases have sought to establish official liability through two theories. The first theory seeks to effect a "special relationship," which affirmatively obligates public school districts and administrators to protect students' constitutional right to bodily security. The second theory uses the standard of "deliberate or reckless indifference" when sexual abuse of a student is known or should have been reasonably known (Valente, 1990).

Testing the Theories

Stoneking v. Bradford Area School District (1987, 1988) in two successive appeals, referred to as *Stoneking I* and *Stoneking II*, tested both theories. *Stoneking I* adopted the special relationship theory which prevailed during September of 1988 in the Third Circuit Court of Appeals. However, the Supreme Court granted a *writ of certiorari* on March 6, 1989, and immediately remanded the case back to the Third Circuit in light of its ruling in *DeShaney v. Winnebago County Department of Social Services* (1989). *Stoneking II* acknowledged that the special relationship rationale had been delimited by *DeShaney,* and a new argument was heard based upon the deliberate indifference of authorities resulting in the deprivation of Stoneking's constitutional right.

The facts in the case can be summarized. Kathleen Stoneking was sexually harassed and abused by Edward Wright, the band director at

Bradford Area High School, during three of the years that she was a student and for two years after graduation. She filed a § 1983 personal injury claim against the school district, the superintendent, the high school principal and the vice-principal for failing to remedy the situation that violated her constitutional rights.

In *Stoneking I,* the Third Circuit found that the three elements for a personal injury claim under § 1983 did exist: Stoneking had a constitutional right; the right had been violated; and the defendants had a special relationship with her that established a duty to protect. The constitutional right was a "liberty interest" found in the Due Process and Equal Protection Clauses of the Fourteenth Amendment. Based on the Supreme Court ruling in *Ingraham v. Wright* (1977), that students have a substantive right to be free from bodily abuse, the Court found that Kathleen Stoneking had "the constitutional right to be free from state intrusions into the realm of personal privacy and bodily security. The acts of sexual abuse, sexual harassment and intimidation inflicted by Edward Wright "were a violation of that constitutional right" (p. 1095). The school officials' special relationship to Stoneking and their imposed duty to protect her rights was predicated upon the proportion of the day which was spent at school and the duty of the school officials to ensure that the school environment was safe for all students.

The Supreme Court in ruling for the dismissal of *DeShaney* held that no constitutional special relationship exists under the Fourteenth Amendment requiring a governmental agency to protect an individual from injury unless that person is in custodial care. A state or common law may exist to impose a special relationship duty, but the claim cannot be brought under § 1983 (Valente, 1990).

In light of *DeShaney, Stoneking II* applied the second theory for a § 1983 claim. Stoneking's claim was upheld "because she also alleged that the defendants, with deliberate indifference to the consequences, established and maintained a policy, practice or custom which directly caused her constitutional harm" (p. 725). It was proven during the proceedings that allegations of Wright's conduct had been summarily ignored for nearly ten years. *Stoneking II* was remanded for a jury trial, but was settled out of court.

The Special Relationship and Compulsory School Attendance Laws

Jane Doe v. Petaluma City School District (1993) argued for a special relationship claiming that compulsory attendance laws effect a custodial care situation during the daytime. The court found no Section 1983 claim existed because compulsory attendance laws for schools do not restrain personal liberty to the extent that students do not have other persons, including parents, to turn to for help on a daily basis. While the Third and Seventh Circuits are in agreement with the Ninth, the Fifth Circuit's application of *DeShaney* has allowed for a special relationship based on compulsory attendance.

Child abuse and *in loco parentis* statutes are being coupled with the common law duty of school officials to supervise. These state laws are also being tested as a means to construct the special relationship. The courts remain divided, despite the fact that several judgments have been vacated and remanded in light of *DeShaney*.

The Deliberate Indifference Standard

The Third Circuit Court of Appeals in the findings for *Stoneking I* stated that every school district official should know that it is a breach of duty to take no action to protect students from sexual abuse. It is a statement with which every parent would agree, especially a parent whose child has been sexually abused at school. The Supreme Court, however, does not agree that school officials have a constitutional duty to protect students. *Stoneking II,* upon remand, restated the case and labeled the pattern of inaction as a custom of "deliberate indifference" by policymakers that tolerated the sexual abuse of students by state employees. Deliberate or reckless indifference has become a standard used by the courts to litigate a cause of action and extend liability to an individual supervisor.

Jane Doe v. Taylor Independent School District (1994) illustrates the application of the deliberate indifference standard and demarcates appropriate and inappropriate behavior for school officials. Identifying the necessary components of a claim under Section 1983 of the federal civil rights statute, the Fifth Circuit Court of Appeals upheld Doe's liberty interest under the Fourteenth Amendment to bodily security and proceeded to conclude from the evidence that her right had been violated by Jesse Lynn Stroud, her biology teacher and coach at Taylor High. Coach Stroud sexually harassed and sexually molested Jane Doe over a two-year period. He finally resigned his teaching position and in a criminal trial pled guilty to the charges.

The principal of Taylor High, Eddy Lankford, was held personally liable due to his gross negligence in protecting the constitutional rights of a student in his charge. Using the standard of deliberate indifference, the court adopted a test to determine the personal liability of school officials in any physical abuse case:

> A supervisory school official can be held personally liable for a subordinate's violation of an elementary or secondary school student's constitutional right to bodily integrity in physical sexual abuse if the plaintiff establishes that:
>
> (1) the defendant learned of facts or a pattern of inappropriate sexual behavior by a subordinate pointing plainly toward a conclusion that the subordinate was sexually abusing the student; and
> (2) the defendant demonstrated deliberate indifference toward the constitutional rights of the student by failing to take action that was obviously necessary to prevent or stop the abuse; and
> (3) such failure caused a constitutional injury to the student. (p. 454)

By this test, it was held that a reasonable official would have understood that Lankford's inaction violated Doe's constitutional right. He excused the coach's behavior as just "Stroud's way of doing of things." Lankford chose to ignore and failed to document any incidents of inappropriate behavior by Stroud. Parents called, staff reported and students complained. Written evidence was brought to Lankford and, still, he refused to act over the course of several years. Coach Stroud's writing of love notes, gift-giving, kissing, touching and sexual abuse of freshman and sophomore girls remained unchecked until Jane Doe's parents went directly to the superintendent.

The superintendent, on the other hand, responded appropriately to Jane Doe's parents and was granted qualified immunity by the court. He retained the evidence brought by Doe's parents, questioned Jane, investigated allegations, warned Stroud about the consequences of future misconduct, checked Stroud's record with the credentialing commission and, eventually, asked for Stroud's resignation. The superintendent acted to resolve the complaint and documented every step.

TOLLING THE STATUTE OF LIMITATIONS

The courts have been very flexible and lenient when considering the statute of limitations for cases involving the sexual harassment of students (Mawdsley, 1993). The general rule is that tolling on the statute of limitations begins when the liability-creating injury occurs. In sexual harassment cases, however, the exception, known as the discovery rule, is often applied. The discovery rule permits the tolling of the statute of limitations to be postponed until the plaintiff actually discovers the injury and the cause of injury. The minority status of victims at the time crimes are committed is reason enough to delay tolling. The discovery rule was applied in *Patricia H. Stoneking,* and *Doe v. Petaluma.*

Stoneking provides an example as to how far the courts will extend the discovery rule. Kathleen Stoneking was molested at school from 1980 to 1983 and after graduation until 1985. Her personal injury claim was filed in 1987. The court set the tolling for the statute of limitations to March of 1986 when Edward Wright was asked to resign from the district, confessed and was convicted on ten counts for various sex crimes with minors.

LEGAL PROBLEMS FOR EDUCATION

Title IX and Section 1983 of the federal Civil Rights Act clearly protect students against sexual harassment. School officials can be held liable for punitive damages—but only if they ignore the problem and fail to act responsibly.

National Education Association (NEA) delegates to the 1988 Representatives Assembly adopted a resolution. The three main points called for

(1) Policies that define and prohibit sexual harassment
(2) Educational programs designed to help students and staff recognize, understand and prevent sexual harassment
(3) A grievance procedure that encourages the reporting of incidents of sexual harassment and investigates complaints efficiently, while protecting the rights of every individual involved (Simpson, 1992)

This simple outline of procedure has been repeatedly endorsed as a means for avoiding painful, damaging and expensive litigation (Carroll, 1993; Decker, 1988; Klein & Wilber, 1986; Strauss, 1988). With the recent *Franklin v. Gwinnett* ruling sanctioning monetary awards for injury, states and local educational agents are beginning to adopt these strategies and to act upon them.

The Supreme Court took away the administrative option of discounting complaints of sexual harassment as typical, harmless, adolescent exploration on the basis that "boys will be boys" (Adler & Rosenberg, 1992; Raney, 1993; Russo, Nordon & Leas, 1992; Smolowe, 1993). Districts can no longer shield themselves from costly lawsuits by keeping students and staff uninformed (Strauss, 1988). Following the NEA guidelines, however, poses some problems for administrators in actual implementation.

The first problem for administrators is in framing a definition of sexual harassment and specifically outlining for students and faculty what constitutes sexually harassing behavior in an educational setting. An existing legal definition can be adopted, but it must be clarified for students so that they can distinguish the forms of teasing, interactions, drawings, pictures and graffiti that create a hostile environment (Carroll, 1993; Hayes, 1991; Leo, 1990). It is quite obvious from studies on perceptions regarding sexually harassing behavior that men and women, boys and girls, do not perceive visual, physical or verbal social interactions in the same way (Bursik, 1992; Jaschik & Fretz, 1991; Marks & Nelson, 1993). Perceptions of what constitutes sexual harassment are gender specific; so, students and staff must be educated toward a common understanding of what behaviors are acceptable. Variations in reactions and feelings must be explored without intimidation so that an awareness of the effects of sexual harassment can be developed (Lozano, 1993; Raney, 1993; Smolowe, 1993). There is need for students and staff to understand the factors in their backgrounds which make them particularly susceptible to being victimized or culturally prone to being a harasser ("High School," 1992). It cannot be assumed that everyone knows what sexually harassing behavior is or what its effects are. Sexual harassment on campus can be diminished through education (Higginson, 1993; Saltzman, 1993).

The second problem for administrators is in the handling of complaints. Investigations must be conducted to comply with the law, but just the mere accusation can ruin a teacher's or an administrator's career (Brass, 1992). Accused students can become confused, and their self-esteem can be damaged by implications of sexual harassment. Victims may be adequately compensated by milder forms of discipline, such as apologies, written warnings, verbal reprimands, changes of class schedule or community service, but administrators need to keep records of their findings and consequent actions as protection against future liabilities (Russo, Nordin & Leas, 1992). Permanent records of alleged actions or minor offenses could be pernicious, but informal records kept without employee access or review are illegal (Elza, 1992). The legal requirements for documentation become entangling either way.

The third problem for school officials is the evaluation of offenses and the determination of correct restitution for the victim. The perpetrator, whether an employee or a student, must be disciplined and stopped. The victim must be compensated and, perhaps, medically treated for physical or emotional wounds. In quid pro quo cases of sexual harassment, *Franklin v. Gwinnett* set a precedent for monetary damages beyond termination of employment and many districts prefer to settle out of court (Russo, Nordin & Leas, 1992). Applying the standard to non quid pro quo complaints of a hostile environment caused by peers raises questions such as, "Who pays?" "Is suspension or expulsion sufficient relief?" There are no definite answers concerning sexual harassment by peers at this time. Future litigation will probably be necessary, but the courts have been consistent in regard to the responsibility of school officials in any sexual harassment situation involving one of their own employees.

THE RESPONSIBILITIES OF SCHOOL OFFICIALS

District Responsibilities

The school board and the superintendent have the ultimate responsibility for the establishment of policies, educational programs and procedures for investigation and enforcement of the law (Schimmel, 1994). The district should communicate written policies on sexual harassment and train all personnel within the district on the definitions, appropriate conduct and procedures. It should be made clear that sexual contact and sexual conversation, including sexual innuendo, are prohibited between school employees and students. Policies alone will not protect a district from liability, but understanding what constitutes sexual harassment and having established procedures can help prevent the fatal mistake of having an administrator insensitively disregard an incident.

Contractual indemnification of employees should be reviewed in light of state laws. Indemnification in many states is required only when employees are acting in good faith within the scope of employment. Sexual abuse is an intentional act of misconduct outside the professional scope of employment and teachers and other staff members should be personally liable for it (Mawdsley, 1993).

Districts are directly responsible for the hiring, supervison and firing of school employees. Investigations and documentation should be thorough in all personnel procedures. Hiring, supervision and retention of a teacher are not acts covered by state immunity, as ruled in *School Board of Orange County, Florida v. Coffey* (1988).

Hiring investigations can be tricky because they sometimes come into conflict with defamation or privacy laws. Districts often have to rely largely on information provided by the applicant. Sexually abusive teachers are often transferred or rehired for three reasons. First, teachers accused of sexual harassment or abuse are frequently allowed to resign before the allegations are investigated. Resignation saves embarrassment and legal hassle for all concerned. Since the issues are unsubstantiated, personnel records are cleanly silent. Secondly, former employers are reluctant to give detailed, documented information about a teacher's conduct for fear of a defamation suit. Finally, districts and administrators who are employing a teacher do not want to take the time or effort to investigate rumors of misconduct.

Districts should have consistent procedures for checking applicants. A district should require the applicant to provide letters of reference from all recent employers. Alleged personality conflicts or periods of unemployment should be further investigated. The applications should include a question regarding felony or misdemeanor convictions and, then, a criminal background or credential check should be done, especially for an administrator. Predetermined questions about moral conduct should be asked when checking references. Documentation should be maintained. When questioned about a former employee, the district is obligated to give factual knowledge. Truth is the defense against defamation (Mawdsley, 1993; Regotti, 1992).

At the district level, supervision requires that all complaints about a district employee alleging sexual harassment be investigated and resolved. The complaint, the nature of the investigation and the outcome should be placed into the employee's personnel file in order to protect the district, the accused and the accuser (Mawdsley, 1993; Regotti, 1992). If a warning is given or remediation is decided upon, a plan of supervision should include the name of the supervisor, actions expected, method of monitoring, timetable for supervision and date for evaluation of progress. Remediation opportunity is not required where the psychological damage to the student is extreme (Mawdsley & Hampton, 1992).

Dismissal of teachers for sexual misconduct is overwhelmingly upheld by the courts (Mawdsley & Hampton, 1992). The standard of proof necessary is the "preponderance of evidence" standard, not the "beyond a reasonable doubt" standard, as in criminal law (Mawdsley & Hampton, 1992; Zirkel, 1993). According to the ruling in *Sauter v. Mount Vernon School District* (1990), the district only has to show that the actions in question had no legitimate educational purpose and were harmful to the professional relationship between the student and the teacher. Sexual harassment of a student by persistent sexual innuendos or sexual intimidation does not have to be tolerated. A teacher may be disciplined by the imposition of a remediation plan, suspension, or termination. Sexual misconduct with a minor, whether within the school setting or not, is grounds for dismissal.

The Responsibility of Site Administrators

Site administrators have the greatest accountability because they are directly responsible for the safety of students and have direct control over teachers. School climate and toleration for misbehaviors are instilled by the principal. If the principal makes it a priority to abolish sexual harassment, policies will be articulated; educational programs will be set up for students, staff and parents; procedures will become known; and everyone will be encouraged to participate in the maintenance of a safe campus.

Students and parents should participate with staff in the formation of policies and behavioral expectations. Educational programs should teach students and staff to differentiate between teasing and sexual harassment while raising sensitivity to gender differences in perception. Everyone in the school community should know how to report sexual harassment complaints in order to safeguard the constitutional rights of all parties (Higginson, 1993; Mentell, 1993).

From the case law, it is clearly incumbent upon administrators to investigate, document and act upon sexual harassment complaints. Supervision should ensure the student's safety by taking all necessary steps to stop the sexual abuse. Suspected harassment between a teacher and a student should be reported to the district personnel director.

CONCLUSION

State legislators are reacting to the courts' decisions and many are passing laws to require school boards to enact policies and procedures on sexual harassment. Some are requiring that sexual harassment be added to the school curriculum.

The California law is a typical example of the legislation coming forth. In July of 1993, the legislation written by State Senator Gary Hart (D-Santa Barbara) went into effect. The new law requires that all schools adopt a policy for dealing with sexual harassment and teach all students to be more sensitive to the effects of sexually harassing behavior (Lozano, 1993; Raney, 1993). It proposes that sexual harassment be added to the school curriculum in grades 4–12. It allows students to be suspended or expelled for sexual harassment (Gross, 1992; Raney, 1993). It provides a new definition of sexual harassment which seeks to interpret student behaviors by the effects the behaviors have on another. The law defines sexual harassment as an act which is severe enough "to have a negative impact upon an individual's academic performance or create an intimidating educational environment" (Lozano, 1993). It requires all students to be accountable for their actions and it requires teachers to educate them as to what that means. The law leaves the adoption of policies, procedures, behavioral guidelines and curriculum up to the individual districts. All three components of the NEA 1988 resolution are included and districts will be forced to comply.

It should not be necessary for legislatures to regulate and police the school curriculum. School officials must take hold of school safety and act responsibly for the benefit and protection of students. Proactive policies and procedures can save administrators and school districts from costly liability.

REFERENCES

Adler, J. & Rosenberg, D. (1992). Must boys always be boys? *Newsweek,* 120(16):77.

Alexander, K. & Alexander, M. D. (1992). *American Public School Law* (3rd ed.). St. Paul: West Publishing Co.

American Association of University Women. (1993). Hostile Hallways: The AAUW survey on sexual harassment in America's schools, researched by Louis Harris and Associates. *Facts on File,* 53(2757):727.

Barnes v. Costle, 561 F.2d 893, D.C. Cir. (1977).

Brass, L. (1992). Till proven innocent. *Phi Delta Kappan,* 73(6):472–475.

Bursick, K. (1992). Perceptions of sexual harassment in an academic context. *Sex Roles,* 27:401–411.

Carroll, C. M. (1993). Sexual harassment on campuses: Enhancing awareness and promoting change. *Educational Record,* 74(4):21–28.

Decker, R. H. (1988). Can schools eliminate sexual harassment? *The American School Board Journal,* 175:28–29, 38.

Doe, Jane v. Petaluma City School District, 830 F.Supp. 1560, N.D. Cal. (1993).

Doe, Jane v. Taylor Independent School District, 15 F.3d 443, 5th Cir. (1994).

Elza, J. (1992). Liability and penalties for sexual harassment in higher education. *West's Education Law Reporter,* 78:631-642.

Franklin v. Gwinnett County Public Schools, 112 S.Ct. 1028 (1992).

Gage, R. (1993). The Supreme Court's quick turn. *U.S. News and World Report,* 115(20):11.

Greenhouse, L. (1992, February 27). Court opens path for student suits in sex-bias cases: Idea of damages upheld. *The New York Times,* 141(48889):A1, A16.

Gross, J. (1992, March 11). Schools are the newest arenas for sex-harassment issues. *The New York Times,* 141:B8.

Harris, Teresa v. Forklift Systems, Inc., 114 S.Ct. 367 (1993).

Hayes, A. S. (1991, October 11). How the courts define harassment. *The Wall Street Journal,* p. B1.

Higginson, N. M. (1993). Addressing sexual harassment in the hallways. *Educational Leadership,* 51(3):93-96.

High school girls face harassment. (1992). *U.S.A. Today,* 121(2567):12.

Horner, J. (1991). When is a school district liable under 42 U.S.C. 1983?—The evolution of the "policy or custom" requirement. *West's Education Law Reporter,* 64:339-348.

Jaschik, M. L. & Fretz, B. R. (1991). Women's perceptions and labeling of sexual harassment. *Sex Roles,* 25:19-23.

Klein, F. & Wilber, N. (1986). *Who's hurt and who's liable: Sexual harassment in Massachusetts schools. A curriculum and guide for school personnel.* (revised). Quincy, MA: Massachusetts State Department of Education (ERIC Document Reproduction Service No. ED 316 821).

Larson, J. E. & Knee, J. A. (1991, October 22). We can do something about sexual harassment. *The Washington Post,* p. A21.

Leo, J. (1990). What qualifies as sexual harassment? *U.S. News & World Report,* 109(7):17.

Lozano, C. V. (1993, January 18). Sex harassment law applies to students. *Los Angeles Times,* pp. A3, A27.

Marks, M. A. & Nelson, E. S. (1993). Sexual harassment on campus: Effects of professor gender on perception of sexually harassing behaviors. *Sex Roles,* 28:207-216.

Mawdsley, R. D. (1993). Compensation for the sexually abused student. *West's Education Law Reporter,* 84:13-30.

Mawdsley, R. D. & Hampton, F. M. (1992). Sexual misconduct by school employees involving students. *Education Law Reporter,* 73:883-895.

Mentell, E. J. (1993). What to do to stop sexual harassment at school. *Educational Leadership,* 51(3):96-97.

Meritor Savings Bank, FSB v. Vinson, 106 S.Ct. 2399 (1986).

Noah, T. (1991, October 28). Lawsuits by women, disabled are likely to be the main result of compromise civil rights bill. *The Wall Street Journal,* p. A18.

Noah, T. & Karr, A. R. (1991, November 4). What new civil rights law will mean: Charges of sex, disability bias will multiply. *The Wall Street Journal,* pp. B1, B10.

Patricia H. v. Berkeley Unified School District, 830 F.Supp. 1288, N.D. Cal. (1993).

Pfeiffer v. School Board, 917 F.2d 779, 3d Cir. (1990).

Raney, B. F. (1993, July 18). New law punishes kids for behavior. *The Sun,* pp. A1, A6.

Regotti, T. L. (1992). Negligent hiring and retaining of sexually abusive teachers. *West's Education Law Reporter,* 73:333-340.

Riger, S. (1991). Gender dilemmas in sexual harassment policies and procedures. *American Psychologist,* 46(5):497-505.

Russo, C. J., Nordin, V. D. & Leas, T. (1992). Sexual harassment and student rights: The Supreme Court expands Title IX remedies. *West's Education Law Reporter,* 75:733-744.

Saltzman, A. (1993). It's not just teasing. *U.S. News and World Report,* 115(22):73-77.

Sauter, Rocke J. v. Mount Vernon School District No. 320, Skagit County, 791 F.2d 549, Wash. App. (1990).

Schimmel, D. (1994). Sexual harassment in the workplace: When are hostile comments actionable? *West's Education Law Reporter,* 89:337-345.

School Board of Orange County, Florida v. Irma L. Coffey, 524 So.2d 1052, Fla. App. 5 Dist. (1988).

Sexual harassment, one year later. (1992). *U.S. News and World Report,* 113(16):18.

Shoop, R. J. (1992). The reasonable woman in a hostile work environment. *West's Education Law Reporter,* 72:703-716.

Simpson, M. D. (1992). Harass students and pay a stiff price. *NEA Today,* 11(1):28.

Smolowe, J. (1993, April 5). Sex with a scorecard. *Time,* 141(14):41.

Solomon, C. M. (1991). Sexual harassment after the Thomas hearings. *Personnel Journal,* 70(12):32-37.

Stoneking, Kathleen v. Bradford Area School District, 667 F.Supp. 1088 (W.D. Pa. 1987) 882 F.2d 688, 2nd Cir. (1989).

Strauss, S. (1988). Sexual harassment in the school: Legal implications for principals. *NASSP Bulletin,* 72:93-97.

Title VII of the Civil Rights Act of 1964, 701 et. seq., as amended 42 U.S.C.A. § 2000e.

U.S. Equal Employment Opportunity Commission. (1985). Guidelines on discrimination because of sex. 29 CFR 1604.

Valente, W. D. (1990). School district and official liabilty for teacher sexual abuse of students under 42 U.S.C. 1983. *West's Education Law Reporter,* 57:645-659.

Valente, W. D. (1992). Liability for teacher's sexual misconduct with students—Closing and opening vistas. *West's Education Law Reporter,* 74:1021-1031.

Will, G. F. (1992, December 14). Our expanding menu of rights. *Newsweek,* 120(24):90.

Zirkel, P. A. (1991). Honor rooted in dishonor. *Phi Delta Kappan,* 72(9):720-722.

Zirkel, P. A. (1992). Damages for sexual harassment. *Phi Delta Kappan,* 73(10):812-813.

Zirkel, P. A. (1993). Abuse of students by students? *Phi Delta Kappan,* 75(4):344-347.

CHAPTER 8

The Politics of "Zero Tolerance" Legislation in Michigan Public Schools: Origins, Implementation and Consequences

BEVERLEY B. GELTNER
JOHN S. GOODEN

THE large, bold headlines on the news releases from the State Senate Majority office and the Governor's office proclaimed the triumph:

> "Engler signs nation's toughest weapon-free school legislation" "Engler signs bill expelling gun-toting kids: toughest law in nation will help make students, teachers, and school safer"

Senate Bill 966, which was enacted as Michigan Public Act 328 on October 12, 1994, nine months after its introduction into the State Senate Education Committee, was praised by Republican Governor John Engler and sponsoring Republican Senator Joel Gougeon for heralding a new era of safe schools in Michigan. Filled with pride over its passage—its all too hurried passage, some critics would say—the Governor declared,

> The bill makes it possible for Michigan schools to expel permanently any student who brings a weapon onto school grounds . . . Across Michigan, too many teachers and students are being terrorized by young punks and thugs roaming the halls, classrooms, and school grounds. Our message to them is simple: Bring a gun, and you're done. . . . Expelled. No excuses. No exceptions. . . .
>
> Our schools must be sanctuaries—safe havens where teachers can teach and students can learn. . . . Now a weapon-toting punk can be permanently expelled from mainstream public schools in Michigan. . . .
>
> I've said it before and I will say it again: Guns in schools have got to go. And the punks who take guns to schools have got to go. (Governor's News Release, October 12, 1994)

NATIONAL CONTEXT FOR THE REFORM

The rhetoric during the months preceding the November 1994 elections gave voice to the national concern over violence in American society. In virtually every federal and state campaign waged that year—whether for U.S. Senate, for governor, for local state representative or local judge—the promise was made of new safety for law-abiding citizens in their homes, in their communities and in their schools. While on the one hand, new proposals urged the expansion of legal gun possession throughout American society at large, on the other hand, virtually all agreed that schools were to be protected as weapons-free sanctuaries with the highest penalties invoked for those who would dare bring guns to school.

The urgency of safe schools was proclaimed from the highest level of the land. President Clinton embraced the Goals 2000: Educate America Act, and on March 31, 1994, gained Congressional support for amendment of the Elementary and Secondary Education Act of 1965, with the addition of the new Gun-Free Schools Act. This new legislation stated that as a condition of receiving any assistance under the ESEA, a local educational agency had to have in effect a policy requiring the expulsion from school for a period of not less than one year of any student who brought a firearm to school. Latitude was offered to local districts in language stating that "the LEA's chief administering officer may modify the expulsion requirement on a case-by-case basis" (AASA, 1994, p. 6). Writing to his Education Secretary Richard Riley on November 1, 1994, President Clinton affirmed, "Enforcement should include termination of federal assistance" for states that fail to comply (p. 6).

BACKGROUND TO PUBLIC ACT 328

When the first steps were taken in the Michigan Senate to introduce statewide legislation on weapons in school, some local board members and district administrators questioned the rationale of these measures. Many of the state's 556 districts already had formal student codes of conduct and disciplinary policies as well as procedures for dealing with this issue. For more than a decade, some districts had enunciated specific violations and sanctions related to weapons in schools and had developed comprehensive suspension and expulsion procedures that complied with special education federal requirements (Southfield Public Schools, 1984).

In addition, Michigan had a long and cherished tradition of local control. Local school boards had jealously protected their autonomy and championed the special needs and values of their own communities. However, under the guise of school reform, the pendulum has within the last decade swung in the opposite direction. Barely a month would go by without some new mandate arriving from the state Capitol to improve schools. As is the case in other states, the Michigan legislature expanded its authority into areas that had been traditionally controlled by local school boards. Student assessment, core curriculum, "high-stakes" graduation diplomas, district accreditation—complete with financial rewards and penalties linked to local compliance or resistance—all were now defined and controlled by new state legislation.

Further, while local school districts did, in fact, *have the authority* to suspend students guilty of "gross misdemeanor or persistent disobedience," (in essence to pass stringent policies and punishments concerning weapons in school) and were by law required by the School Code to report all cases of weapons possession by a minor to police agents and parents, they were not *required* by current law to expel such students from school. Many districts remained silent on the issue, reluctant to acknowledge violence as a problem in their own schools: "those incidents" happened only "somewhere else"—in big urban centers—not in their own suburban or rural backyards (Horowitz & Boardman, 1994). Others chose to respond to such problems with leniency, either out of concern for the individual student believing that "the student did not really mean any harm" or out of fear of the wrath of local parents should their child be subject to expulsion. In some districts, the "school-to-school shuffle" was the order of the day with a student "expelled" from one school in the district and enrolled in another. In others, an expelled student simply left and enrolled in another district with no documentation required in the student's permanent record informing the new district of past behaviors.

As the national and state rhetoric on violence in schools became more inflamed, state legislators found themselves the target of conflicting demands. Some local board members appealed to their representatives. "Get us out of local politics," they urged. "Put the onus on *your* shoulders with statewide legislation forcing expulsion for weapons in school. That way," they argued, "we'll be protected from local pressures for favoritism for 'special' treatment of the children of 'special' families." For such boards, the cherished tradition of local autonomy was, in the case of guns in school, more a liability than an asset and one with enormous risks of front-page notoriety! Other boards of education questioned why the legislature would even get involved in this issue, unless they wished to fund new prevention measures or intervention services for students.

In the midst of these unfolding developments, a specific incident involving one middle school teacher, one middle school student and a gun served as the spark that ignited the entire statewide political debate. The official court record described the exact events that occurred in Carol Powell's classroom in the West Branch-Rose City Area Public Schools, in April, 1993:

> A junior-high-school-age minor . . . brought a loaded .22 caliber automatic handgun to school. During the course of the day, the student made statements to multiple students to the effect that he was "having problems" with a certain middle school teacher and that he had brought the handgun to school "in order to fix" the problems. Later that day, the student entered the classroom of the teacher with whom he disagreed and, while she was facing the blackboard with her back to the student, he brandished the handgun (which he had concealed in order to bring into the classroom), pointed the gun directly at the teacher's back, and spoke to her in a threatening fashion. Only after the teacher repeatedly directed him to put the gun down did the student finally drop the gun on the floor and run out of the room. The gun was later discovered to contain multiple live rounds in an ammunition clip, with a live round of ammunition in the chamber. The student's reason for his actions was that the teacher (acting on the request of the student's parents) had called the parents to tell them that the student was doing poorly in her class. (*Michigan Department of Social Services v. Tawas Area Schools*, 1993)

This incident was seized upon by the state's Republican administration as the catalyst and symbol for "zero tolerance" legislation. On January 12, 1994, Republican Senator Joel Gougeon with the enthusiastic support of the Governor's office introduced Senate Bill 966, a bill mandating automatic expulsion of any student bringing a weapon to school.

Powell, the West Branch teacher, joined forces with Gougeon and his Republican colleagues, telling her story over and over to all who would listen. "Children bringing guns to school has become a real, common and deadly occurrence," she said. "It changes innocent lives forever. It can destroy a child's or a teacher's sense of well-being and safety that schools have tried so hard to build" (Senate Majority News Release, May 25, 1994). Moreover, she asserted that she was not alone in being affected by this traumatic incident. "The student's classmates," she stated, "reported having nightmares, eating problems, and feelings of anger and frustration" (Senate Majority News Release, May 25, 1994).

It was in this context that Senator Gougeon introduced his bill. It would be, he touted, "the toughest weapon-free school legislation to be found anywhere in the nation." "Zero tolerance is our message," he continued. "We have to make sure kids know we are serious about this issue. Kids need to realize that drugs and weapons don't belong in public schools. If they disagree, then they're out" (Senate Majority News Release, January 12, 1994).

Republican Governor Engler led the "zero tolerance" campaign from the state Capitol. "Mrs. Powell was extremely fortunate," he stated, "but some teachers and students haven't been — and they've become grim statistics. That's why this bill is so urgent." He continued:

> The fact that there are some trying to hold up Senate Bill 966 is indicative of the confusion in the current crime debate. Some people object and focus on the one child who will be removed from school. I say: What about the one thousand children who have a right to learn in a safe environment?
>
> These same folks also express concern that the parents of the punk will sue. No! They've got it backwards. The punk and his parents should be afraid that the one thousand will sue . . . sue for their right to walk down safe halls, study in the library, play out on the school grounds. . . .
>
> This bill injects common sense in Michigan's criminal justice system and will make Michigan schools safe havens for teaching and learning. (Office of the Governor, press release, October 12, 1994)

SENATE BILL 966/PUBLIC ACT 328

Unanimously passed by the Senate (35–0) on May 25, 1994 (the last day of the session), and signed into law five months later, Senate Bill 966/Public Act 328 mandates the specific actions *required* of all public school districts in the state of Michigan in cases of students who possess a dangerous weapon in a weapon-free school zone or who commit arson or rape in a school building or on school grounds. (The latter two offenses were added to the original Senate bill during subsequent House debate.) The law became effective January 1, 1995.

Under PA 328, any student who knowingly possesses a dangerous weapon on or near school property must be expelled from *all* Michigan public schools. A "dangerous weapon" for purposes of the Act is defined as "a firearm, dagger, dirk, stiletto, knife with a blade over three inches in length, pocket knife opened by a mechanical device, iron bar, or brass knuckles" (School Code, 1994, 380.1313).

The Act mandates that students who violate the law must be expelled for ninety school days—or half a school year—for students in the fifth grade or lower. Students in the sixth grade or higher must be expelled for 180 school days—a full school year.

The student's parents or legal guardian in both cases were permitted to petition the expelling school board or the board of another public school district to reinstate the youngster at the completion of the mandatory expulsion period. The application can be made after sixty days for students in grades K–5 and after 150 days for students in grades 6–12. The preparation and submission of the reinstatement petition is set forth as the responsibility of the parents or legal guardian. The school board has no obligation to assist in the preparation of the petition other than making it available upon request. The form of the petition was to be developed by the Department of Education within ninety days of the Act's date of effectiveness.

The Act also mandates the procedures that are to be followed once a student submits a petition to be readmitted to school. A special review committee must be established by the board within ten days after the submission of the reinstatement petition. The committee will be comprised of two school board members, one school administrator, one teacher and one parent from the district. After their appointment, the committee is required to meet within ten days to review the petition and make a recommendation to the school board. It is the committee's responsibility to recommend that the student be fully reinstated, reinstated with conditions or not reinstated at all. They must utilize the following criteria to arrive at their recommendation:

- risk of harm to other pupils or school personnel
- risk to the school district or individual
- risk of liability to school board or school district personnel
- age and maturity of the student
- the student's record before expulsion
- the student's attitude concerning the expulsion incident
- the student's behavior since exclusion and the prospect for remediation
- the degree of cooperation and support by the parent or legal guardian

After receiving the recommendation from the committee, the school board would be required to act at the next regularly scheduled meeting.

To accommodate unique circumstances, school boards are given the latitude to choose not to expel an offending student if, in a "clear and convincing manner," the student established the following:

- The weapon was not intended for use as a weapon.
- The student did not know he or she possessed a dangerous weapon.
- The student did not know the weapon constituted a dangerous weapon.
- The student possessed the weapon at the suggestion, request, expressed permission or direction of school or police authorities.

PA 328 also mandates that students who violate the law are to be expelled from all public schools in the state; furthermore, no alternative placement, tutoring, educational plan or other services are required. If a school district operates an appropriate alternative education program for pupils expelled for weapons possession, rape or arson, the district may permit those students to enroll in the alternative program. However, the program must be operated in facilities and at times separate from those used for the general school population.

With regard to special education students, the statute is in compliance with federal law. PA 328 requires that expulsion procedures may not be used to diminish the due process enjoyed by special education students under federal law.

PA 328 requires that when a student is expelled for weapons possession, rape or arson in school, the expelling district must enter that fact on the student's permanent record. The district is also required to refer expelled students to the appropriate county social services agency or mental health agency and to inform the parents or, if eighteen or older, the student of the referral.

Finally, according to the Act, a school board or administrator who expels a pupil for weapons possession, rape or arson in compliance with the provisions of the new state law is not liable for damages. However, liability for school boards and administrators cannot be waived by the state for violations of federal civil rights claims.

REACTIONS TO "ZERO TOLERANCE" LAW PRIOR TO ITS IMPLEMENTATION

From its initial introduction into the Michigan Senate in January,

1994, Senate Bill 966 aroused both passionate support and vehement opposition. Virtually all major educational institutions, civil liberties and student rights organizations, legal bodies and concerned citizens-at-large expressed their points of view. The highlights of the debate are presented below.

Arguments in Favor of Senate Bill 966

Analysis of Senate Bill 966 conducted by the officials of the Department of Education highlighted some strengths of the proposed legislation (Michigan Department of Education, May 5, 1994). It was believed that the bill would send a strong statement that weapons in schools would not be tolerated and offer protection to both students and staff. It would eventually allow expelled students to return to school but would place the burden on the parents and student to convince the committee that reinstatement was merited.

A similar analysis of the bill by the Senate Democratic Office stated that the prime argument in its support was that guns in school posed a significant danger to students and school employees. Three major educational organizations: the Michigan Association of Secondary School Principals, the Michigan Association of School Administrators and the Michigan Association of School Boards supported a House substitute for the Senate bill. The substitute bill restored school district discretion within the limits of the four criteria described earlier, so long as they were presented by the student in a "clear and convincing manner" (Soffin, 1994). Finally, regarding costs, the initial state fiscal analysis anticipated that, "The bill would have no fiscal impact on state or local government" (Rich, 1994).

Arguments in Opposition to Senate Bill 966

Just as the Michigan Department of Education analyzed the arguments favoring the bill, so did it also examine the bill for its possible flaws (Michigan Department of Education, 1994). Three major concerns were cited: 1) The bill does not provide for an educational plan after expulsion. Even if the child is later reinstated, there may be long periods without school: a half year for grade 5 and under and a whole year for higher grades. 2) There is no provision in the legislation for a suspension period prior to an expulsion. 3) A school district is required to treat all students the same, whether the student had a history of violence or whether this was a first-time offender and a nonproblematic student. School boards, they argued, should be allowed to determine disciplinary or rehabilitative action on a case-by-case basis.

The Michigan Association of School Administrators also voiced some concerns. While supporting efforts to control school violence, "We had some problems with the political 'hard line' stance of this bill," said Ray Telman, Associate Executive Director. "Most educators," he continued, "already were expelling kids who brought guns to school. . . . I don't know that we really needed a law," he said. Further, it was essential that principals and administrators be allowed some exercise of discretion in deciding when to expel students, "for example, in the case of a 3rd-grader who brings his dad's hunting knife to school for show-and-tell" (AASA, 1994, p. 6).

The Middle Cities Education Association is an organization representing twenty-seven of the largest and mid-sized school districts in the state. In an April 19, 1994 letter addressed to every state senator, the Association voiced its opposition to SB 966. In the words of the Association's Executive Director, Michael Boulus, mandatory expulsion of any student found with a firearm or other dangerous weapon regardless of the circumstances is in reality "not only unworkable but . . . detrimental to the welfare of children in many instances." The proposed legislation was "draconian," precluding other alternatives short of expulsion and preventing school boards from determining "rehabilitative action on a case-by-case basis." It would force school districts to treat the normally nonproblematic student, the elementary student or the first time offender lacking criminal intent the same as the student with a history of violence and past offenses. "Where," the Association asked, "are the due process rights if all are equally expelled no matter what the board may find?" Rather, the Association recommended that districts be allowed the latitude to investigate circumstances, to use an assessment team approach (psychologist, social worker, educators) to refer expelled students to appropriate educational and rehabilitation programs, and that the reinstatement provisions should include a child study assessment team evaluation supplemented by evidence submitted by the family (Boulus, 1994).

These recommendations were followed by a study on school violence and weapons conducted by the Middle Cities Education Association and reported just prior to the passage of the bill in September 1994. Among its many findings, the study revealed the following:

- Increasingly, younger students were bringing weapons to school.
- More violence-related incidents and suspensions were occurring at the middle school level than at the high school or elementary levels.
- Students most frequently brought weapons to school for self-defense/concern about safety; neighborhood problems that were being carried over into the schools; and/or the need to show off, to be "cool," to have status and/or to be recognized.
- Districts were clearly stating and reinforcing a position that possession or use of weapons and violence in schools would not be tolerated.
- All districts (in the Association) had discipline policies addressing weapons, violence and related offenses with most allowing for discretion on a case-by-case basis.
- Possession or use of a firearm virtually always resulted in a recommendation for expulsion, with the exception of cases where expulsion was not deemed appropriate (i.e., a third-grade student found with a gun brought from home in his desk with no intent to inflict injury).

After reviewing a broad range of possible alternative educational programs, preventative strategies and collaboration models, the Association concluded this report with the following summary statement:

> Clearly, schools are responding to the violence problem and have or plan to implement a variety of measures and programs to create positive solutions. It is widely recognized, however, that whole communities must take responsibility for curbing and eventually eliminating violence. No one entity can do it alone. As there is no one identifiable cause for youth violence, there is no one solution. We need to focus on the root causes of the violence problem and steer clear of simple solution, quick fix approaches. (Middle Cities Education Association, 1994)

Testimony against the proposed legislation was also given by the American Civil Liberties Union of Michigan to the House Education Committee. Quoting the Michigan Constitution's provision for free public elementary and secondary education for all pupils "without discrimination as to religion, creed, race, color, or national origin," the statement concluded that such language led to the conclusion that free public education was a fundamental right of all children in the state. Further:

This bill only deals with half of the equation, i.e., removing potentially dangerous children from schools in order to protect the safety of other children. It completely ignores the second half of the equation, which is assuring that all children have educational opportunities available, even those children who have committed serious infractions.

By failing to address this second part of the equation, this bill may remove a problem from the schools, but, shortsightedly, place the very same problem on the streets.

Additionally, this bill would create the anomalous and unjustifiable result whereby children convicted of delinquency and committed to juvenile facilities would be entitled to continued educational opportunities, while children administratively punished by their schools for the same or a lesser offense would have no such educational opportunity. (American Civil Liberties Union, 1994)

Analysis of the bill conducted by the Senate Democratic Office documented opposition by seven additional organizations and professional associations on the grounds that the bill did not mandate alternative placement for the expelled students. Those organizations were the Michigan Federation of Private Child and Family Agencies, Michigan PTA, Michigan Legal Services, Association for Children's Mental Health, Student Advocacy Center, Greenville Board of Education, Michigan Association of School Psychologists and Michigan Federation of Teachers (Soffin, 1994).

It was noteworthy that the Michigan Education Association—the largest teachers' union in the state and the one that counted among its members middle school teacher Carol Powell—did not testify.

The tone of the opposition sounded by the above groups in reference to the bill may be sensed from the words of William E. Long, Executive Director of the Federation of Private Child and Family Agencies. Writing to the Co-Chair of the House Education Committee on September 19, he spoke on behalf of the more than fifty private non-profit member agencies of his Federation:

[We] serve between 15,000 to 20,000 youth in foster homes and private residential settings each year. . . . We agree that possessing a weapon in a school setting cannot be tolerated and recognize the Legislature is attempting to address the safety and security of the majority of our youth in the school environment.

We urge the Legislature, however, to also consider that unless more specific measures are required to address and support attention to the expelled youth, the risk to the community may not be lessened. . . . We think [the bill's] expulsion periods are far too long, unless the youth are involved in some constructive program. . . .

128 LEGAL ISSUES

> If we are truly going to address the problems . . . we also need to work with the parents and link the youth and families with other community support systems. This bill does not address how that will occur. . . . We note [the bill] relieves the school board of providing any assistance to a parent. . . . If these youth and parents are left to "drift" for 5 to 9 months after an incident involving a dangerous weapon, society may be more at risk, and we will have missed a possible opportunity for change to both protect society and save public dollars in the long term. . . .
>
> Our agencies are experienced and willing to assist, but there will need to be financial and policy support from the Legislature to permit (positive change) to happen. (Long, 1994)

Additional arguments from other presenters against the bill were cited in Soffin's analysis which included the following: (a) mandatory permanent expulsion from school is a drastic penalty for a pupil who probably already comes from a troubled home environment; (b) increasing the number of dropouts will not reduce community violence; (c) social service and mental health agencies have no affirmative duty to act; (d) the bill limits the discretion of local boards of education; and (e) the bill is likely to have heavy impact on children of color and poor children (Long, 1994).

Debate on the bill in the House of Representatives became more heated as November approached and both the educational and political stakes increased. Ten amendments were offered; one was adopted and nine were rejected (House of Representatives, 1994):

- Restore suspension authority to the superintendent and his or her designee. Adopted.
- Require local or intermediate school districts to provide alternative programs. Not adopted.
- Require the school district to confiscate any weapon found in a weapon-free school zone and deliver it to police authorities for prosecution. Not adopted.
- Exempt children below grade 6 and emancipated minors from the bill. Not adopted.
- Require the school social worker to assist the family with the reinstatement process. Not adopted.
- Expand the weapon-free zone. Not adopted.
- Allow the board to reinstate an individual on the discovery of new evidence. Not adopted.
- Allow the pupil's record to be expunged if he or she has a good record after one year. Not adopted.

- Change the effective date to April 1, 1994. Not adopted.
- Allow the enrollment of pupils in public school academies. Not adopted.

Fiscal Impact

In terms of the fiscal impact of the bill the initial state fiscal analysis predicted "no fiscal impact on state or local government" (Rich, 1994), a subsequent analysis completed three months later presented a more complex picture.

> The fiscal impact of the bill is indeterminate. The fiscal impact would depend on the number of students expelled pursuant to the bill and the nature and cost of the educational or social services programs used by an expelled student.
>
> In FY 1994–95, most school districts will be in-formula districts with state payments calculated on a per-pupil basis. A district expelling a student would lose the state payment for that pupil. An expelled student, however, possibly could become a student in another school district or in an institutional setting, requiring additional State support. (Pratt, 1994)

These concerns were expanded five days later by Pratt and a colleague at the Senate Fiscal Agency:

> The bill would have no fiscal impact on State government, but could affect local school districts required by the bill to expel certain students. . . .
>
> Depending on the timing of an expulsion with respect to the pupil count days, an expulsion could reduce a district's pupil count, causing the district to lose future State payments for that pupil. . . .
>
> There would be no expected additional costs to the Department of Social Services (DSS) and/or the Department of Mental Health (DMH), as a juvenile found in possession of an unlawful dangerous weapon would almost certainly come in contact with the DSS and/or DMH under existing child protection, juvenile justice, or probate laws. (Pratt & Walker, 1994)

After all the debate, all the heated rhetoric, all the impassioned presentations and all the political maneuverings – the bill was reported from Committee in violation of the notice provision of the Open Meetings Act, Senate rules and the Michigan Constitution and had to be returned to the Committee. On September 21, 1994, the bill passed the House and Senate and was ready for the Governor's signature.

Reactions Since Implementation

Since PA 328 became law, school districts, parents, teachers, students, legal advisers and other concerned citizens throughout Michigan have been attempting to understand and implement its provisions. After only one school semester, concerns have evolved that the legislation contains many complexities, contradictions, compromises and inadequacies. To what degree it is achieving its basic purpose of rendering Michigan's public schools safer remains to be seen and will require a longer timetable.

What is indisputable is that Michigan's "zero tolerance law" has become a central topic of discussion among virtually all constituents in the state. From informal coffee conversations in community kitchens to new legislative proposals in both the House and the Senate, citizens are pondering the impact and worth of PA 328.

Voices from the Community

Daniel Keck, superintendent of East Lansing schools, characterized the reaction of many members of the educational community to PA 328 when he stated that

> It's like an explosion. . . . If you throw kids off to the side without any type of training or any education or anything, you're going to get more bums, more hoodlums in the street and more crime. You can't just throw 13-year-olds away, that's an invitation to disaster. The kid I put out on the street without any services and, in essence, throw away is the kid who will take you out in the mall parking lot someday. (Andrejevic, 1995a)

John Pollard, director of Lansing's Black Child and Family Institute, who recently started a pilot program for expelled students concluded that the number of expelled students was increasing mainly because PA 328 does not give school districts discretion. "Whether it's a 9 mm or a cap gun that doesn't pull, everybody is treated the same," Pollard said. "The students I've seen are not the ones the lawmakers thought they were going to get. Most of the gangsters have too much savvy to get caught with guns in school. They leave them in their cars or hide them outside" (Andrejevic, 1995b, p. 4).

Expulsion, the total separation from the only stable environment that some troubled young people have in their lives, can be the final straw for a youth who already feels rejected. According to Carl Taylor, a criminologist and Michigan State University professor who studies gangs and youth violence, "It's like saying 'If you're not a criminal already, you might as well become one, because we don't give a damn'" (Andrejevic, 1995b, p. 4). To Carl Latona, director of Onondaga-based Highfields Inc., which has submitted a proposal to run an alternative program for students expelled by the Lansing School District, the law is "capital punishment of the mind for kids" (Andrejevic, 1995b, p. 4).

Local education officials and some lawmakers have complained that the bill's original get-tough approach has forced districts to expel six- and seven-year-olds who pose little danger but who have brought a weapon to school. Peggy Kusler, superintendent of the tiny Holton Schools in Muskegon County, commented after the expulsion of a first grader who brought a knife to school. She stated that "there was no wiggle room in the law in allowing boards of education to determine whether or not a student was a danger to himself or others."

Adam, a student who was recently expelled from school for bringing his father's police issued 9 mm Glock pistol and a fully loaded ammunition clip to his high school, found the pistol when his father was out of the country and took it to school to show his friends. He stated in his defense that he took the gun to school because "I thought I would be looked up to and thought of as cool. . . . If you ask anyone who knows me, they'll tell you I'm a nice guy who made a really huge mistake" (Andrejevic, 1995a, p. 4).

Problems Regarding Equity and Fairness

A problem critics cite is that the law allows broad discrepancies between districts by not requiring them to offer alternatives for expelled students. The Okemos School District, for example, does not provide any services to students expelled for weapons violations, whereas, the East Lansing School District offers in-home schooling services. The Lansing School District is implementing a new alternative education program for expelled students for which it will receive no state funding. As was anticipated in the earlier analysis of the Senate Fiscal Agency, the district will indeed receive no second-semester funding for the students it has expelled after the initial first-semester official student count.

Another criticism often cited is the law's special education loophole.

For instance in a recent case an Okemos student caught with a knife applied for and received special education status *after* the incident occurred. He was able to stay in school because of the federal provisions that if a student can show a weapon incident was the result of a diagnosed disability—such as an emotional disorder—the student is protected from expulsion. Ron Styka, Okemos School Board President, stated that "what's frustrating is a situation where someone is able, after the fact, to claim there's a problem and escape punishment" (Andrejevic, 1995c, p. 4). The special education protection means that the school board is not allowed to consider the case. Even if the expulsion is upheld, all special education students are guaranteed some form of educational services under federal law. According to Lynnwood Beekman, an Okemos attorney who specializes in special education law, "We have had districts contact us that almost want to find a way, with parent's cooperation, for the kid to be labeled handicapped so he won't be expelled." Tom White of the Michigan Association of School Baords commented that school board members are committed to treating all students fairly. He stated that "if we're going to deal with special ed students on a case-by-case basis, we should deal with all kids on an individual basis" (p. 4).

Political Response to Problems of Implementation

According to N. Wing, Student Issues Ombudsman with the Michigan Department of Education, while specific statewide figures on the impact of PA 328 are not yet available, "I think a lot more students are being put out of the public schools." Five months after its implementation, not only has the state Department of Education not gathered any data on the numbers and ages of students expelled under the new law, but it has also failed to develop any forms or data-gathering procedures from the state's 556 districts (Wing, 1995).

The absence of exact student expulsion figures has not, however, diminished the legislative debate on how Michigan schools should handle guns in school. To date, there have been two major legislative responses to PA 328. Democratic House Bill 4033 proposed giving school boards greater flexibility in setting the length of time for which students are expelled on a case-by-case basis, depending on the gravity of the offense. With critics charging the bill as a "gutting" of the law and with the Governor vowing to veto any dilution of PA 328, the House overwhelmingly passed the bill on March 29, 1995. Since then, the bill has moved to the Senate Education Committee where it has been tabled.

Senate Bill 527, introduced on May 11 by eight Republicans and one Democrat, sought the reinstatement of younger students following expulsion for ten school days in cases of weapon possession or threat of use. Opponents of the change blasted it as too soft. "It allows a lot of these liberal superintendents and liberal school boards in many instances to just expel the kids for a day," said Rep. Roland Jersevic, Republican, Saginaw (Andrejevic, 1995c, p. 4). Unsure of how far to modify the "get tough" message, Senate Republican leaders decided to refer the bill to a committee made up of representatives of constituent groups who would provide input for the bill's revision.

LESSONS TO BE LEARNED: QUESTIONS TO BE ASKED

What good has PA 328 done for Michigan schools? Are our schools safer? It is still too early to determine the long-term and short-term consequences of the Act. However, already it is clear that this legislation in its present form has much opposition because it strips local school districts of their decision-making authority over expulsions; it does not provide alternative educational opportunities for expelled youngsters; it lacks a therapeutic or counseling component; and it treats all children the same without consideration of their past record.

The Act does, however, highlight certain ironies. For instance, it is ironic that while national and state leaders are calling for more state and local control on many policy issues, the Michigan State Legislature has increasingly moved to eliminate discretion and decision-making authority at the local level. It is also ironic that while the Legislature is moving, on one hand, to counter the high cost of special education by supporting the "inclusion" model that integrates such students into the general classroom, its actions, on the other hand, are generating additional referrals to special education as parents and school officials seek ways to circumvent mandatory student expulsions.

Michigan's approach to school violence has been characterized by politicization, oversimplification, evasion and avoidance of deep consideration of effective prevention and intervention measures. Perhaps this is not so different from political behavior evident in other segments of American society. In the same way the public apparently seems to want a welfare state without picking up the tab for it, it wants safe schools without addressing any of the real issues and costs involved. In writing on some of the current dilemmas of the contemporary American political process, Stark (1995) asked:

> Is all this, in fact, what (historian) Daniel Boorstin called a "pseudo-event"—something in which the illusion of results becomes far more significant than the results themselves? . . . In crime bills that almost everyone privately admits will do next to nothing to reduce crime, the appearance and the drama of the action overshadow the importance of the action itself.

Violence is commonplace in American society; it will not disappear by building more prisons or by denying children the opportunity to be educated. The only way to combat the epidemic of violence in America's schools is through solid intervention and prevention strategies that also include no-nonsense zero-tolerance measures. However, we must remember that once we take our children to the woodshed, we need to help them learn and grow from their experiences and mistakes.

REFERENCES

American Association of School Administrators. (1994). Stateline: Michigan. *AASA Leadership News*, 147:6.

American Civil Liberties Union of Michigan. (1994). Statement before the House Education Committee on Senate Bill 966. Lansing, MI.

Andrejevic, M. (1995a, March 27). Expelled students in limbo. Kicked out under gun law, lose their shot at education. *Lansing State Journal*, pp. 1A, 4A.

Andrejevic, M. (1995b, March 28). Expulsion not whole answer: School officials seek alternatives for kids caught with weapons. *Lansing State Journal*, pp. 1A, 2A.

Andrejevic, M. (1995c, March 27). Special education "loophole" helps, hinder districts. *Lansing State Journal*, p. 4A.

Boulus, M. (1994, April 9). Personal communication.

Horowitz, S. V. & Boardman, S. K. (1994). Managing conflict: Policy and research implications. *Journal of Social Issues*, 50(1):197–211.

Legislative Service Bureau. (1994, October). *The School Code of 1976*. Lansing, MI: Legislative Council.

Long, W. E. (1994, September 19). Personal communication.

Michigan Association of School Administrators. (1995). What is House Bill 4541 (Alley)? Allows students expelled for possession of weapons on school property to petition for reinstatement in another school. *MASA: The Fortnighter*, 24(3).

Michigan Department of Social Services v. Tawas Area Schools, 930 AW, 23rd Cir. (1993).

Middle Cities Education Association. (1994). *School violence and weapons survey*. East Lansing, MI: Author.

Pratt, E. (1994, April 13). *Senate fiscal agency bill analysis*. Lansing, MI.

Pratt, E. & Walker, J. (1994, April 18). *State fiscal agency bill analysis.* Lansing, MI.
Rich, A. (1994). *State fiscal agency bill analysis.* Lansing, MI.
Soffin, M. F. (1994, September 30). *Senate democratic office bill analysis.* Lansing, MI.
Southfield Public Schools. (1984). *Board of education policy #5131: Student code of conduct.* Southfield, MI: Author.
Stark, S. (1995a). Stateline: Michigan. *ASSA: Leadership News,* 147:6.
Stark, S. (1995b, May). Too representative government. *The Atlantic Monthly,* pp. 92–106.
Wing, N. (1995). Personal communication.

CHAPTER 9

Creating Safe Schools: Policies and Practices

MARILYN L. GRADY

INTRODUCTION

PROVIDING a safe school environment is imperative. For many children, schools are the safest place in their lives. The concept that schools should be safe havens has found support in law throughout the history of public schools. For teachers to teach and children to learn, there must be a safe and inviting educational environment (Curcio & First, 1993).

However, as a society, we appear to have adopted a course of aiding and abetting troublemakers at school. In reviewing the literature concerning schools and violence as well as in interviews with school administrators, it is apparent that a minority of students may be causing excessive strain on the operation of schools.

A report of the National Association of State Boards of Education (NASBE), *Schools without Fear,* states that schools should be "advocates for all children." But the report focuses almost exclusively on the needs and "rights" of disruptive students. The kids who are forgotten are the vast majority of students that do not make any trouble. According to Shanker (1994–1995), the well-meaning people who believe that schools should put violent kids first must realize that they are helping to destroy public education.

Disruptive or violent students are not a new phenomena in schools. Even in the 1950s, student subcultures at school promoted misbehavior; in New York and other large cities, fights between members of street gangs from different neighborhoods sometimes broke out in secondary schools (Toby, 1993–1994). *West Side Story* captures the spirit of gangs and reminds us that gangs have been part of the American scene for a long time.

In the twentieth century, the promulgation and enforcement of compulsory attendance laws has exacerbated misbehavior in schools.

Higher ages for compulsory school attendance mean that some enrolled youngsters hate school and feel like prisoners. Compulsory education laws are successful only in keeping children *enrolled*. School is more pleasant and interesting than the streets in cold or rainy weather. Friends are visited, enemies attacked, sexual adventures begun, drugs bought and sold, and valuables stolen there (Toby, 1993-1994, p. 9).

Disruptions and violence in schools are occurrences that represent the acts of a minority of students. However, these acts have an impact on everyone associated with the school. Preventing these instances is a major challenge for all who have a role in the process.

Violence often results from a complex interaction of environmental, social and psychological factors. Among these factors are the learned behavior of responding to conflict with violence, the effects of drugs or alcohol, the presence of weapons and the absence of positive family relationships and adult supervision. Few violence prevention programs can muster the resources to affect all the possible causes. The key to providing students with the skills, knowledge and motivation they require to become healthy adults is a comprehensive program that responds to the new risks and pressures that arise with each developmental stage. Addressing these risks requires a sustained effort over the child's entire school career (Posner, 1994).

Finding a cure for violence is a serious challenge for schools, parents and communities. Like many health problems, those associated with violence are potentially contagious. Also: 1) for many the tendency to violence is learned; 2) violence is frequently enabled by the use of alcohol and other drugs, but most often alcohol; 3) the incidence of violence can be reduced through appropriate educational programs; and 4) for an educational program to reduce violence, it must involve and generate support from all levels of the community (Newman, Anderson & Perry-Hunnicutt, 1991).

DEMOGRAPHICS

Although a minority of students are responsible for the violent and disruptive acts that occur in school, the statistics concerning these instances are troubling. Reviewing the data concerning violence shows that life in schools may no longer be safe.

In 1989, a survey of inner-city sixth and eighth graders showed that more than 50% of them had had money and/or personal property stolen, some more than once; 32% had carried a weapon to school; and 15% had hit a teacher during the year (Curcio & First, 1993, pp. 2-3). Students admitted hitting teachers at least once, sometimes twice, during the year; *a small percentage of teachers said they were actually physically attacked or threatened with a weapon,* and a large percentage said their personal property had been damaged or stolen at school (Curcio & First, 1993).

Although young people between the ages of thirteen and nineteen comprise only 12% of the population, they account for 22.8% of the violent crime in the United States (FBI, 1987). The average age of arrest for a first offense is decreasing and is now below the age of thirteen (Strasburg, 1984). Homicide is the second leading cause of death for all fifteen- to twenty-four-year-olds and the leading cause of death for black males in this age group (Centers for Disease Control, 1983). Although juvenile males are delinquent more than juvenile females (4:1), females are closing the gap with aggravated assault being their most frequent crime (Committee for Children, 1992, p. 1). More than half of all the serious crime in the United States is committed by youths between the ages of ten and seventeen. One out of nine young people will appear in court before his or her eighteenth birthday (Cultrona & Guerin, 1994).

It is estimated that school violence is underreported by as much as 50%. Teachers feel the problem on many levels as they spend increasing amounts of time attending to students' disruptive and inappropriate behavior in the classroom, off-task behavior on assignments, and interpersonal conflicts both inside and outside of class. The prevalence of general behavior problems in school children approximates 25% (Cowen, Trost, Lorion, Door, Izzo & Isaacson, 1975). In a growing number of cases, teachers are threatened with violence by their own students (Committee for Children, 1992, p. 1).

By the time they reach high school, approximately 25% of the students in the United States fear victimization by their peers. It is estimated that 15% of school students are involved in bully-victim problems and 20% of students are regularly harassed or attacked by bullies (Committee for Children, 1992, p. 1).

Forty percent of the 250 judges surveyed in a *National Law Journal* poll said that there are circumstances in which juveniles should receive the death penalty. According to the U.S. Justice Department, violent crimes such as murder and assault committed by juveniles have increased nearly 70% from 1988 to 1992 (Bushweller, 1994, p. A9).

In November 1989 a survey on incidents reflecting racial hatred (i.e., hate crimes) in schools showed that such incidents had occurred in more than one-third of the Los Angeles public schools. The typical incidents were racial slurs, name-calling, graffiti, and physical confrontation; however, distribution of racist literature, fighting, waving of Confederate flags, and the use of guns, knives and other weapons also occurred (Curcio & First, 1993, pp. 31-32).

CAUSES

Among the causes of youth violence are family breakdown, drug abuse, economic issues and poor education. In the same survey of 250 judges, family breakdown was the number one contributor to violence by kids. Drug abuse was cited as the second greatest contributor, followed by unemployment, poor housing and poor education (Bushweller, 1994, p. A10).

Since 1981, the percentage of children not living with both biological parents has increased from 33% to 43% according to Child Trends, Inc., a Washington, D.C. organization that tracks the condition of American children (Bushweller, 1994, p. A10). Barely more than half of American children live in what many people think of as the traditional family, according to a Census Bureau report (Bushweller, 1994, p. A10). Consider how much moving around there is in the United States. Only 82% of persons were living in the same residential unit in 1990 as they were in 1989. Since cities have long been considered places to which people migrate from rural areas, from other cities and from foreign countries, it may come as no surprise that during a five-year period a majority of the residents of American central cities moved to a different house (Toby, 1993-1994).

Consider the following data about the usage of a variety of substances. The rate of daily smoking rose over the past year from 7% to 8% among eighth graders, from 12% to 14% for tenth graders, and from 17% to 19% for twelfth graders. Episodes of heavy drinking are a problem with 14% of eight graders, 23% of tenth graders, and 28% of twelfth graders saying they consume five or more drinks in one sitting at least once every two weeks. There has also been a rise in marijuana use at all three grade levels, as well as increases in the use of stimulants, LSD and inhalants (Bushweller, 1994, p. A9).

Between 1970 and 1991, the value of AFDC (Aid to Families with Dependent Children) benefits decreased by 41%. In spite of the proven success of Head Start, today only 28% of the eligible children are being served. The poverty rate among single-parent families with children under eighteen was 44%. Between 1980 and 1990, the rate of growth in the total federal budget was four times greater than the rate of growth in children's programs (Moynihan, 1993-1994).

Fear and lack of knowledge and skills precipitate violent student behaviors. Students who take guns or knives to school do so because they fear for their safety. "They feel they have no choice," says New York advocate Joan Harrington (Vail, 1995, p. 37).

Students who engage in violent behavior are those who:

- don't know what appropriate behavior is, due to a lack of modeling or guidance
- have the knowledge but lack the practice that comes with adequate reinforcement
- have emotional responses such as anger, fear or anxiety, which inhibit the performance of desirable behavior (Committee for Children, 1992, p. 2)

DEFINITIONS

Three factors often associated with discussions of school violence are weapons, gangs and behaviors. In the language of federal law, weapons are guns, bombs, grenades and poison gas. Knives, according to the federal law, are not weapons. States might choose to include knives in their own versions of the zero-tolerance requirement. In federal law, rifles used for recreation or sports, antique guns and fireworks are not considered weapons (Vail, 1995).

A standard for identifying a street gang is "any denotable group of adolescents or young adults who are (a) generally perceived as a distinct aggregation by others in their neighborhood, (b) recognize themselves as a denotable group, almost invariably with a group name, and (c) have been involved in a sufficient number of illegal activities to call forth a consistent response from neighborhood residents and/or law enforcement" (Takata, 1993, p. 95).

When members were asked why they had joined a gang the following responses were given: 1) had nothing else to do, 2) wanted to have more friends, 3) wanted people to look up to them, and 4) wanted to protect themselves from other gangs (Takata, 1993).

The behaviors that are associated with school violence are (Committee for Children, 1992, p. 1):

- aggressive behavior with peers
- negative and defiant behavior with adults and peers
- a tendency to rush into things without forethought
- high levels of attention-seeking behavior
- low levels of guilt feelings
- self-centered verbal responsiveness to others, exemplified by interrupting others, blurting out their thoughts and talk that is irrelevant to the ongoing conversation

Aggressive and violent behavior is correlated with social isolation and a lack of empathy, impulse control, decision-making skills, anger management and assertiveness (Committee for Children, 1992).

PROBLEMS AND RESPONSES

Newspaper articles offer graphic accounts of school violence. Interviews with young males are illustrative of the dimensions of the problem. TJ can tell you exactly when he turned to guns and drug distribution: It was when his mother turned herself over to cocaine. On the streets, getting a gun—any kind of gun—is no big deal: "It's as easy as buying a pair of shoes," TJ says. The least expensive one runs $100. The more military-like the gun, the higher the price. Gang members "were my family. We'd stick together. We'd kill and die for each other. They gave me love I never had before." He says a lot of the violence that goes on today is over money. "It's all money. Who's got the bigger car, who's got the best [clothes], who's got the best girl. Without money, you're nothing," he says. To stop the problem, "Stop the drugs from coming over here. Ain't nobody growing no cocaine bushes in the United States. It's all overseas." He says young people need more attention (Natale, 1994, p. 35).

Michael's story begins with his association with the wrong people, at about the same time his mother and stepfather separated. The people Michael started hanging with were older, into smoking marijuana and toting guns – a bad influence. The rationale behind having the guns, he said, was protection (Natale, 1994, p. 35).

Violent incidents occur in many school settings. However, athletic events provide a particularly attractive environment for violence. A Galveston, Texas, high school football player during a game in nearby Beaumont was wounded in a drive-by shooting. School officials were forced to stop the game and reschedule the event for the next day, but as a precautionary measure they barred any fans from attending. In Richmond, Virginia, a student was shot in a high school parking lot during a Friday night basketball game. As a result, school officials switched the remaining games that season to afternoon tipoff times (Riechers, 1995).

Two students were shot in September after a Friday night football game in Fairfax County, Virginia. In the wake of that shooting the superintendent considered canceling all Friday night athletic events, pep rallies and other nighttime activities. After the shooting in Beaumont, the school district fine-tuned its already good security program. More school security officers and city police officers were placed inside the stadium and around the perimeter during nighttime football games. Metal detectors were used to screen spectators at school basketball games.

Most stadiums in the Dade County schools are set up with one entrance for home-team fans and another for visitors with fences or barriers separating the two. For dances, schools typically sell tickets in advance to students and their guests only, and only ticket holders are allowed in (Riechers, 1995). The Indianapolis Public Schools, one of a handful of school systems across the United States to have its own certified police force, has also increased its vigilance at after-school events. The Indianapolis school board passed a resolution that allows the district's seventy-two school police officers to carry firearms for patrols and for emergency responses. In addition, the school system's chief of school police can approve the use of armed school police in special circumstances, with the superintendent's approval. The school board passed the resolution after somebody pulled a gun on an unarmed school police officer who was patrolling the school grounds at night. No shots were fired, but the officer's vulnerability left its mark on school board members (Riechers, 1995).

Many examples of violence in schools can be cited. Newspapers and television accounts of these incidents are abundant. Of greater utility are examples of school districts, programs, practices and plans that lead to the prevention of school violence.

ALTERNATIVE SCHOOLS

One response to violence by school districts is the development of alternative schools. Some examples of these alternative schools follow.

Baltimore's alternative middle school for violent and disruptive youth called the Woodbourne Academy is beginning its third year of operation. At Woodbourne students receive not only intensive academic support but psychological counseling, sessions in anger management and help with conflict resolution (Harrington-Lueker, 1994, p. 18).

"We have three goals," explains Woodbourne Vice President Patricia Cronin. "We want to help these kids get their behavior under control, we want to remediate their academic deficiencies, and we want to get them back into the regular setting." A full-time psychologist and a social worker round out Woodbournes's mental health staff; in addition, every teacher and aide is trained in crisis management, behavior modification and conflict resolution. Students are referred to the school once they have been suspended for a third time for violent or assaultive behavior and remain there from one semester to a year (Harrington-Lueker, 1994).

Several Virginia school districts—including the 139,000-student Fairfax County Public Schools—have contracts with the Woodbridge, Virginia-based Richard Milburn High School to provide off-campus instruction for students who have been expelled. According to company president Ken Underwood, the school prefers to have no more than fifteen students in a class and no more than thirty students at a site (Harrington-Lueker, 1994, p. 18).

When the Maryland Department of Education opens its school for disruptive middle school students in Prince George's County, the school will serve up to sixty students on an extended-day schedule. The program costs between $20,000 and $30,000 per student per year, according to preliminary estimates—over three times Maryland's average per-pupil expenditure of $6,502. Start-up costs for such programs are typically high (Harrington-Lueker, 1994).

Congress authorized $44 million for the program called the Youth Challenge Corps in 1992. Today, the corps, which uses National Guard facilities and staff in fifteen states, continues to help kids turn themselves around.

The first five months of the seventeen-month program mimics a military boot camp—long on structure and short on free time. Corps members live in barracks, devote time to physical training and perform community service. Days are long—the young men and women rise at 5:30 A.M. and lights go out at 10:45 P.M.—and time is intensively scheduled.

Youth Challenge has graduated 4,500 young people. Seventy-six percent of those who start the program graduate from the residential phase, and nearly 91% of those complete their GED. No graduate has gotten into trouble with the law (Harrington-Lueker, 1994).

By 1996, the state of Louisiana will require every parish to provide an alternative setting for students. At the Redirection Academy in Rapids Parish, Louisiana, drill instructors put students through parade paces at least once a day. In Corpus Christi, Texas, students carry charts with progress reports on their behavior everywhere they go. And in Colorado, public school systems are being asked to help plan and operate a statewide series of reform schools for students who have been expelled (Harrington-Lueker, 1994). New York City Schools' former chief, Ramon Cortines, proposed spending $8 million on four alternative schools to handle students expected to be expelled through a new zero-tolerance policy. Syracuse, with an enrollment of 23,000 students, received a $120,000 state grant this year to start its alternative program (Vail, 1995).

Issues of fairness, equity and race persist. There are very few educators anywhere in the country who want to administer schools for the incorrigible. "The history of alternative schools that separate kids is that the population has historically been poor and special education" (Harrington-Lueker, 1994, p. 20).

LEGISLATION

A number of states have enacted laws to address issues related to violence.

- Virginia last year passed several gun-related laws. One limits individual gun purchases to one per month, another bans possession of firearms by minors and a third bans possession of "street sweeper" assault weapons.
- Connecticut has passed a law that bans more than sixty types of assault weapons.
- Florida strengthened existing legislation, making it illegal for anyone under eighteen to possess a firearm.

- In Colorado, a law makes it a felony to provide handguns to juveniles for illegal reasons.
- Minnesota passed several gun control measures, including one that imposes a seven-day waiting period on the purchase of assault weapons (Natale, 1994, p. 38).

The Colorado legislature adopted a strict definition of *disruptive behavior* and required mandatory expulsion for students who caused more than five such disruptions during a school year (Harrington-Lueker, 1994, p. 17).

The result, say many in Colorado, is a marked increase in the number of expulsions statewide. In Jefferson County, the state's largest school district, the number of students expelled skyrocketed from five in the 1992-1993 school year to 109 in 1993-1994. In Denver, sixty-five students were expelled in 1994 compared to thirty-eight in 1993; in suburban Cherry Creek the number of students expelled rose from nine to thirty-three (Harrington-Lueker, 1994).

Illinois amended its School Code to require districts to provide violence prevention or conflict resolution education in grades 4-12. The Illinois Council for the Prevention of Violence has established a curriculum task force including representatives of a wide range of state and local groups. The task force is creating a framework for reviewing violence prevention curricula, identifying gaps and making recommendations for the use of such curricula in Illinois schools (Posner, 1994).

California has amended its constitution to read that schoolchildren and school staff members have an inalienable right to safe and peaceful schools, and its high court recognized a "heightened responsibility" for school officials in charge of children and their school environments (Curcio & First, 1993).

PROGRAMS

There are many programs available for implementation by schools. These programs include peer mediation, conflict resolution, anger control, predjudice reduction, interpersonal problem solving and behavioral skills training. Brief descriptions of these programs follow.

Peer Mediation

Peer mediation has been shown to 1) increase self-esteem, 2) reduce truancy, 3) decrease incidents of fighting and 4) offer an alternative to suspensions and expulsions. The skills and techniques learned include facilitating the mediation process, conflict analysis, active listening and paraphrasing, interviewing skills, brainstorming for options, evaluating options, bargaining, agreement writing and maintaining confidentiality and neutrality (Cultrona & Guerin, 1994).

The following guidelines (Miller, 1994, p. 8) are helpful for schools that want to set up effective peer mediation programs:

- Mediation should be just one aspect of a comprehensive schoolwide philosophy of nonviolent conflict resolution that is reflected in the school's curriculum and policies.
- Parents and other community members should be included in the program.
- Mediators should be chosen from all racial, ethnic and social groups in the school.
- High-risk students, in particular—not just the "goody-goodies"—should be trained and used as mediators.
- Mediators should deal with real problems and disputes, not just trivial ones.
- Adult supervisors should not intervene during the mediation unless invited to do so by the student mediators.
- Teachers should be willing to adapt their schedules to accommodate mediation sessions.
- Mediation should not be used as a form of discipline, and students should not be coerced into using it. The process should be completely voluntary.

Model Mugging

Model Mugging is a national self-defense and empowerment program. It teaches women and girls the physical skills to fight off an attacker using make-believe ("model") muggers in padded suits. Students are taught to focus on the goal of getting themselves to safety, but, if they need to fight, they are taught to use their strengths against the assailant's vulnerable spots. They aim for soft tissues such as the eyes, nose, mouth, and neck and for the top of the foot. The program fosters *nonvictim* attitudes, designed to deter potential attacks with verbal and body language and to build self-confidence. Tuition for the twenty-five-hour course is about $400 per student. Several private and public high schools in the Boston area are now offering or considering offering the course. Previous studies have shown that, when women do not fight back, almost all attempted assaults are completed, while women who employ three or more defensive techniques can usually stop an attacker (Amster, 1994).

Prejudice Reduction

At Wilson High School in Washington, D.C., a prejudice reduction workshop is held. Its purpose is to teach students, through discussion of their own experiences with prejudice as well as through other strategies, how to combat it in their school and improve race and ethnic relations. The majority of Wilson High School students are black, but there is also a percentage of white students and students from over sixty other countries represented in their student body (Curcio & First, 1993).

The workshop is run by the Center for Dispute Settlement. By focusing on the misunderstandings that young people have about race and ethnicity, they learn the harm that comes from racist jokes, ethnic slurs, snubbing, ridiculing and other demeaning behaviors, and they have an opportunity in a safe setting to empathize with each other (Curcio & First, 1993).

Many organizations, such as the Anti-Defamation League of B'Nai B'rith in New York and the National School Safety Center in California, have curriculum materials and other resources to help a school plan its program of prejudice reduction (Curcio & First, 1993).

Second Step

Second Step is a curriculum designed to reduce impulsive and aggressive behavior and increase social competence through empathy training, interpersonal cognitive problem solving, behavioral social skill training and anger management (Committee for Children, 1992).

Two strategies have shown promise when used with groups of impulsive and aggressive youths: *Interpersonal Cognitive Problem Solving* and *Behavioral Social Skills Training*. The former systematically teaches problem-solving strategies applied to social situations. The latter teaches a prescribed set of interpersonal behaviors which have a broad application to a variety of social situations. A study combining these two strategies found this approach was most effective in instilling prosocial behavior in fourth- and fifth-grade students when compared to the application of individual strategies (Committee for Children, 1992).

Second Step is a violence-prevention curriculum that is designed to help students learn prosocial skills and reduce impulsive-aggressive behavior. *Second Step* (Committee for Children, 1992, p. 5) has the following goals:

(1) To increase a student's ability to
- identify others' feelings
- take others' perspectives
- respond emphatically to others

(2) To decrease impulsive and aggressive behavior in students through
- recognizing anger warning signs and triggers
- using anger-reduction techniques
- applying a problem-solving strategy to social conflicts
- practicing behavioral social skills to deal with potentially violent situations

CAVEATS

Although there appears to be a plethora of programs available to educators, there are also a growing number of factors that need to be considered.

"Peer mediation," says Marvin Daniels, coordinator of the high school mediation program in Cambridge, Massachusetts, "has been misunderstood, misinterpreted, and transformed into something it was never meant to be. It is being used as a form of discipline, or as a prerequisite for suspension." Daniels sees mediation, used properly, as just one tool in a systematic campaign to begin changing the overall climate of violence in society (Miller, 1994, p. 8).

Few administrators under pressure to "do something" about violence have the resources or the expertise to assess the extent of their school's violence problem, to judge whether the program they have chosen is appropriate for their students or to find evidence that the program actually works. In fact, researchers are beginning to question whether the most commonly used school-based programs for violence prevention and conflict resolution actually do what they are supposed to do (Posner, 1994).

Most evaluations of these programs reveal little evidence of success. Daniel Webster of the Injury Prevention Center at Johns Hopkins

University reviewed evaluations of three widely used curricula—the Violence-Prevention Curriculum for Adolescents by Deborah Prothrow-Stith, the Washington (D.C.) Community Violence-Prevention Program and Positive Adolescent Choices Training—and found "no evidence that such programs produce long-term changes in violent behavior or risk of victimization" (Posner, 1994, p. 1).

Many programs have serious flaws that make them highly unlikely to overcome the inherent difficulties of changing complex human behavior. Too often, they lump together a broad range of behaviors and people ignoring the fact that different types of people turn to violence for very different reasons. Few school-based prevention programs target the relatively small group of young people who commit acts of serious violence. Violence is not like malnutrition or infectious diseases. A ten-session violence-prevention course cannot overcome the deprivations of a life of poverty or the pressures toward violence in the world outside school (Posner, 1994).

PREVENTION

Prevention of school violence requires the creation of a school culture that does not tolerate violence. Prevention of school violence requires administrators to take actions to limit opportunities for violent acts. Monhardt, Tillotson & Veronesi (1995) suggest the following seven principles.

(1) High expectations have a strong positive influence on behavior—and subsequently on school safety.
(2) Clearly stated rules and regulations are important. Especially unpopular with many students is a clothing policy than bans wearing caps in school. The wearing of caps is a characteristic of gang activity, and while not all students who wear caps are gang members, the message being sent is clear: Gang activity will not be tolerated in this school.
(3) Parental involvement is critical.
(4) The teacher's role is critical too. Teachers must be out in the halls between classes, helping to ensure a smooth transition to the next class. Students report that the presence of teachers is an important safety factor because the hallways are potential trouble spots—second, perhaps, only to school rest rooms. Parent and teachers agree that rest rooms should be monitored.

(5) Principals must exhibit a strong presence, establish a rapport with students, take quick decisive action in response to situations and administer justice equitably if school is to be a safe place.
(6) The best way to preserve a safe learning atmosphere is to have policies and procedures for dealing with problems before they occur. There are crisis intervention programs, gang task forces, police liaisons and other programs that stay one step ahead of potential trouble.
(7) Extracurricular activities—sports, band, various clubs—are the way to offer a positive experience and therefore, a safer environment. The more time students are involved with positive experiences, the less time is available for those that are negative.

Following is a list of actions and information items that should be incorporated in a prevention plan (Newman, Anderson & Perry-Hunnicutt, 1991, pp. 35-36):

(1) From the earliest grade levels, programs to prevent violence should encourage the development of a strong sense of personal worth and self-esteem.
(2) Opportunities to involve parents in all aspects of a youngster's education can potentially reduce the tendency to violence.
(3) Prevention programs should teach people the signs of high-risk individuals and suggest methods of early intervention.
(4) Prevention programs that identify early indicators of high risk must also identify easily activated referral patterns to assist and treat students identified as high risk.
(5) The establishment of easy referral patterns will involve increasing the general acceptance of using counseling and mental health services to reduce the stigma often attached to the use of these services.
(6) Effective ways should be developed to reintegrate young people who have been absent from school back into the school.
(7) Peer support groups at all levels of the community can be particularly effective in reducing risk, enabling access to treatment and providing continuing support for those who have received treatment.
(8) Any comprehensive program aimed at reducing the incidence of violence will need to establish meaningful relationships between schools, law enforcement and the judicial system.

(9) Much violence occurs in the home. Prevention programs need to ensure that individuals understand the state laws designed to prevent and intervene in instances of domestic violence and to understand how they can get help.
(10) Violence is often perpetrated by males upon females.
(11) Those most responsible for young people's education, school officials, should recognize that they alone cannot effectively reduce violence among young people. They can, however, be effective catalysts for involving others in the community in developing effective prevention programs.

Prevention must start when kids are very young. Schools play a crucial role in this endeavor, but they cannot do the job alone. Efforts must be made to eradicate poverty, to alleviate family stress, to improve the job outlook for young people, to reduce violence in the entertainment media and to control access to drugs and guns (Natale, 1994).

The key to success is knowing "which types of programs should be offered to whom, by whom, and at what age." Programs must take into account the age group targeted, the drugs being targeted, the selection and training of leaders and the influence of the community. Many of the most promising strategies are family interventions that teach parenting skills and improved family relationships. Schools that provide positive social attachments for youth can, at least in part, lessen the estrangement and hopelessness that lead kids to the alternative culture of gangs (Posner, 1994).

Curcio and First (1993) recommend five responses to school violence. The first response is *training*. The second is to support additional *policies and legislation that are protective* of the school employee. The third response is *the creation of a school culture and sense of community* in which those who work in a school take responsibility for each other and depend on each other. The fourth is to have *a plan for emergencies* with which every school employee is familiar. The final response is to understand that a school's responsibility to provide a safe setting where teaching and learning can occur means that *reasonable precautions must be taken regarding the safety of staff as well as that of students.*

Violence prevention should focus on three levels: teachers and students in schools, high-risk children's peer groups and children's families (Natale, 1994, p. 40).

Weak Administration

Weak administrators contribute to the increase in school violence. What would have been furtive larcenies in a well-ordered school become robberies when school authorities are not in control. Angry words turn into blows or stabbings. Under conditions of weak control, students are tempted to employ force or the threat of force to get property they would like or to hurt someone they dislike. Consequently, while student-on-student shakedowns (robberies) and attacks occur infrequently in most schools, they occur fairly often in some inner-city schools. School crime partly reflects weak control and is partly the cause of further disorder that in turn leads to more crime.

A school in which students wander the halls during times when they are supposed to be in class, where candy wrappers and empty soft-drink cans have been discarded in the corridors and where graffiti can be seen on most walls, invites youngsters to test further and further the limits of acceptable behavior. Students get the impression that the perpetrators of violent behavior will not be detected or, if detected, will not be punished. Some teachers, often the youngest and the most dynamic, consider leaving the profession or transferring to private or suburban schools. A disorderly atmosphere also demoralizes the most academically able students, and they seek escape to academically better, safer schools. For other students, a disorderly atmosphere presents a golden opportunity for class-cutting and absenteeism. The proportions of potentially violent students grow in the disorderly school, and, thus, the likelihood decreases that violence will meet with an effective response from justifiably fearful teachers. Disorder leads to violence partly because it prevents meaningful learning from taking place (Toby, 1993-1994).

Vandalism, called malicious mischief by the legal system, is a nuisance in most schools, not a major threat to the educational process. But vandalism of school property, especially major vandalism and arson, is a precursor of school violence because its existence suggests that school authorities are not in control and "anything goes" (Toby, 1993-1994).

Promising Practices

At the heart of all educational enterprises is the teacher. To address school violence we need star teachers whose basic decency is reflected by the following attributes (Haberman, 1994, p. 135):

- They tend to be nonjudgmental.
- They are not moralistic.
- They are not easily shocked even by horrific events.
- They not only listen, they hear. They not only hear, they seek to understand.
- They recognize they have feelings of hate, prejudice and bias and strive to overcome them.
- Teachers have a clear sense of their own ethnic and cultural identities.
- Teachers are culturally competent; they include diverse cultural perspectives in their classroom programs.
- They do not see themselves as saviors who have come to save their schools.
- They do not see themselves as being alone—they network.
- They see themselves as "winning" even though they know their influence on their students is much less than that of the total society, neighborhood and gang.
- They visit parents in their homes or in neighborhood places away from school.
- They think their primary impact on their students is that they've made them more humane or less frustrated, or raised their self-esteem.
- They derive all types of satisfactions and meet all kinds of needs by teaching children or youth in poverty.

As a profession we need to devote efforts to the *causes* of the problem, not to its symptoms (Hobbs, 1993b, p. 121). To put energy into achieving a violence-free school, people working in the school would have to accomplish the following (Curcio & First, 1993, pp. 48–49):

- Respect the school's youngsters as valuable and worth extraordinary effort.
- Value teaching and learning strongly.
- Have a student focus.
- Believe that risk factors with which children come to school can be mitigated.
- Have confidence that their efforts could make a difference.
- Trust each other to get the job done.

- Believe they are making a contribution that counts.
- Believe that they would be supported.
- Be willing to share, release turf and become interdependent.
- Be inclusive, not exclusive.
- Be willing to take risks.
- Be an integral part of the school community.
- Be committed to doing the right thing.

Involving students in the identification of potentially problematic situations is essential. Students should be encouraged to report incidents that they feel might be either leading to or already resulting in criminal behavior.

Athletics

Reducing the risk of violence at athletic events is essential. To reduce the risk, the following practices are useful (Riechers, 1995, p. 35):

- Size up the possibility for trouble.
- Have an adequate number of police or school security officers on hand.
- Make a strong statement about adult supervision.
- Keep home fans and visiting fans apart.
- Close off parking lots. Do not allow people to sit in a car or cruise in and out of the parking lot. Close off the lot during the event with police cars. Do not give anyone the opportunity to go to a car to get a weapon.
- Consider using metal detectors.
- Consider selling tickets to discourage nonstudents from attending. Some schools sell tickets throughout the entire game or dance. The reason: Troublemakers who come late—and whose real interest is not watching the game or dancing—might be discouraged if they have to pay full price. For dances, consider selling tickets in advance to students and their guests only. Admit only ticket holders.
- Remind students of their responsibilities.

Gangs

Reducing gang activity is important.

- Provide an after-school program and sports programs.

- Design a program to welcome and acclimate transfer students.
- Provide appropriate role models
- Develop a program of career counseling.

Learn to recognize gang symbols, colors, and insignia (Curcio & First, 1993, pp. 34-36).

Weapons

If an incident occurs involving a gun or weapon the following steps are important (Curcio & First, 1993, pp. 43-44):

- Follow the emergency plan.
- Arrange transportation for the students.
- Deal directly with the media and the parents.
- Offer counseling and outlets for grief.
- Upgrade security and keep school safety as the primary issue after the incident.
- Give ongoing assistance to the victim.

Every school must invest an adequate amount of time in the development, implementation and monitoring of a safety plan.

(1) Require the creation of comprehensive school safety plans at all public schools. An effective school safety plan includes the following elements:
- Establish an interagency safe-school team at each site. Each team should have an administrator, a teacher, a parent, two students, the head custodian, a local business-person and a police officer.
- Create a violence-prevention vision. This vision must be multi-disciplinary in the interrelated areas of suppression, intervention and prevention.
- Establish goals and objectives.
- Create a detailed plan of action.
- Train teachers.
- Educate parents.
- Develop student leadership.
- Adopt a violence-prevention curriculum. Include the teaching of responsible citizenship, the strength of cultural diversity, choices and consequences, and conflict resolution skills.
- Prepare for crises. This part of the plan should be directed by the team's law-enforcement representative.

- Offer after-school activities for students. Keep the school grounds open until 8 P.M.
- Create school-business partnerships.
- Build a strong interagency team structure.

(2) Remove a school's immunity if administrators fail to create a school safety plan.

Any plan will have the best chance of success when the folowing six building blocks are in place (Curcio & First, 1993, pp. 9-12):

(1) A shared system of beliefs and values
(2) A vision of respect
(3) Explicit policies
(4) A plan of staff development
(5) District statements of policy
(5) The use of learned strategies

RECOMMENDATIONS

In schools across the country, violent incidents occur daily. What appears to be violence in one setting is often dismissed as trivial or unimportant in another setting. School violence occurs along a continuum. At each point along the continuum there are actions an administrator should take.

Among the actions that need to be taken are the following: developing a closer working relationship between the juvenile justice system and the public schools (Harrington-Lueker, 1994, p. 21). Developing a family focus is essential. Helping teachers to continue teaching must be a priority. Smaller class sizes and professional-level salaries as well as teacher education on how to combat verbal and physical violence in the schools would represent indicators of this help (Violence on Campuses, 1993).

In each school, accurate naming and numbering of violent incidents must occur. Administrators need to ask the following questions (Cultrona & Guerin, 1994, p. 99).

- What kinds of conflict occur most frequently?
- Where do the conflicts originate in the school (e.g., bus, cafeteria, playground, hallways, classroom)?
- What percentage of the conflicts originates in the neighborhood and then spill over into the school?

- What percentage of the conflicts is related to cultural/racial differences?
- What percentage of school discipline problems is conflict-related?
- Who is responsible for handling school-related conflict between students?
- Who handles school-related conflicts between students and teachers?
- Who handles school-related conflicts between the school and the students' families?
- How much time is spent dealing with conflict-related matters?
- How well is the system for resolving conflicts working?
- Does the school collect statistical data about the disciplinary actions taken and their final disposition?

Finally, we need to get rid of guns. An almost universally accepted maxim in the public health community is that the most effective intervention for serious violence would be to outlaw the possession, manufacture and sale of these weapons (Posner, 1994).

REFERENCES

Amster, S. E. (1994). Model mugging teaches girls "nonvictim" attitudes—And how to kick men where it hurts. *Harvard Education Letter,* 10(3):6-7.

Bushweller, K. (1994, December). The face of childhood. *Education Vital Signs,* A8-A14.

Centers for Disease Control. (1983). Violent deaths among persons 15-24 years of age—United States, 1970-78. *Morbidity and Mortality Weekly Report,* 32(35):453-457.

Cole, J. (1993/1994, Winter). Moynihan is right: We must draw the line. *American Educator,* pp. 16-18.

Committee for Children. (1992). *Second step 6-8 teachers guide.*

Corporal punishment: Paddling against the stream. (1994). *Harvard Education Letter,* 10(3):5-6.

Cowen, E. L., Trost, M. A., Lorion, R. P., Door, D., Izzo, L. D. & Isaacson, R. V. (1975). *New ways in school mental health.* New York: Human Science Press.

Cultrona, C. & Guerin, D. (1994, Winter). Confronting conflict peacefully. *Educational Horizons,* pp. 95-104.

Curcio, J. L. & First, P. F. (1993). *Violence in the schools: How to proactively prevent and defuse it.* Newbury Park, CA: Corwin Press, Inc.

Donnermeyer, J. F. (1993). Crime and violence in rural communities. In Midwest Regional Center for Drug-Free Schools and Communities and The North Central Regional Educational Laboratory (Eds.), *Perspectives on violence and substance use in rural America* (pp. 27-63). NCREL.

Edwards, R. W. (1993). Alcohol, tobacco, and other drug use by youth in rural communities. In

Midwest Regional Center for Drug-Free Schools and Communities and the North Central Regional Educational Laboratory (Eds.), *Perspectives on violence and substance use in rural America* (pp. 65-86). NCREL.

Federal Bureau of Investigation. (1987). *Uniform crime reports.* Washington, D.C.: U.S. Department of Justice.

Frias, G. (1994). We need a national strategy for safe schools. *Harvard Education Letter,* 10(3):4-5.

Haberman, M. (1994, Spring). Gentle teaching in a violent society. *Educational Horizons,* pp. 131-135.

Harrington-Lueker, D. (1994, December). Hanging on to hope. *The American School Board Journal,* pp. 16-21.

Hazier, R. J. (1994, February). Bullying, breeds, violence: You can stop it! *Learning,* pp. 38-40.

Hobbs, D. (1993a). The rural context for education: Adjusting the images. In Midwest Regional Center for Drug-Free Schools and Communities and the North Central Regional Educational Laboratory (Eds.), *Perspective on violence and substance use in rural America* (pp. 5-26). NCREL.

Hobbs, D. (1993b). The context of rising rates of rural violence and substance abuse: The problems and potential of rural communities. In Midwest Regional Center for Drug-Free Schools and Communities and the North Central Regional Educational Laboratory (Eds.), *Perspectives on violence and substance use in rural America* (pp. 115-124). NCREL.

Hughes, T. (1993, April 30). Report of the task force on school violence. In Midwest Regional Center for Drug-Free Schools and Communities and the North Central Regional Educational Laboratory (Eds.), *Perspectives on violence and substance use in rural America.* NCREL.

Migliore, R. W. (1994, Winter). When the button clicks. *Educational Horizons,* pp. 64-66.

Miller, E. (1994). Peer meditation catches on, but some adults don't. *Harvard Education Letter,* 10(3):8.

Monhardt, B. M., Tillotson, J. & Veronesi, P. (1995, February). Safe by definition. *The American School Board Journal,* pp. 32-34.

Moynihan, D. P. (1993-1994, Winter). Defining deviancy down. *American Educator,* pp. 10-16.

Natale, J. (1994, March). Roots of violence. *The American School Board Journal,* pp. 33-40.

Newman, I. M., Anderson, C. S. & Perry-Hunnicutt, C. (1991). Violence, victims and suicide: Nebraska adolescents' attitudes and behaviors. Prevention Center Papers, Technical Report 23. Lincoln, NE: Nebraska Prevention Center for Alcohol and Drug Abuse, University of Nebraska-Lincoln.

News Update. Clinton seeks to save school gun ban (1995, June). *The American School Board Journal,* p. 15.

Posner, M. (1994). Research raises troubling questions about violence prevention programs. *The Harvard Education Letter,* 10(3):1-4.

Reissman, R. (1993, November/December). Creative solutions to discipline dilemmas. *Learning,* pp. 48-49.

Riechers, M. (1995, June). Friday night fights. *The American School Board Journal,* pp. 33-36.

Rozycki, E. G. (1994a, Winter). Wishful thinking versus reality: Dealing with violence in the schools. *Educational Horizons,* pp. 59-61.

Rozycki, E. G. (1994b, Winter). School violence, punishment, and justice. *Educational Horizons,* pp. 86-94.

Shanker, A. (1994-1995, Winter). Where we stand. Privileging violence: Too much focus on the needs and "rights" of disruptive students. *American Federation of Teachers,* p. 7.

Strasburg, P. A. (1984). Recent national trends in serious juvenile crime. In R. A. Mathias, P. DeMuro & R. S. Allenson (Eds.), *Violent juvenile offenders.* San Francisco: National Council on Crime and Delinquency.

Takata, S. R. (1993). A community comparison of "youth gang" prevention strategies. In Midwest Regional Center for Drug-Free Schools and Communities and the North Central Regional Educational Laboratory (Eds.), *Perspectives on violence and substance use in rural America* (pp. 95-114). NCREL.

Toby, J. (1993-1994). Everyday school violence: How disorder fuels it. *American Educator,* pp. 4-9, 44.

Vail, K. (1995, June). Ground zero. *The American School Board Journal,* pp. 36-38.

Violence on Campuses. (1993, April 30). Hearing. Senate Task Force on School Violence, California Legislature. Los Angeles, CA.

Wright, K. N. & Wright, K. E. (1994, May). *Family life, delinquency, and crime: A policymaker's guide.* Research Summary. Washington, D.C.: Office of Juvenile Justice and Delinquency Prevention.

PART III

STRATEGIES FOR MAKING SCHOOLS SAFE

CHAPTER 10

Creating and Keeping Safe Schools: The Roles of Parents and Community

CAROLYN L. WANAT

INTRODUCTION

CREATING and maintaining safe schools for the nation's children concerns parents, communities, educators and policy makers. While the popular press dramatizes shootings and hostage situations in schools, professional literature expresses the concerns of educators about the increase in violent behavior in schools (Boothe, Bradley, Flick, Keough & Kirk, 1993; McPartland & McDill, 1977; Rich, 1992; Stover, 1988). In an effort to maintain and create safe schools, policy makers at the local, state and national levels implement policies prohibiting unsafe school situations and provide resources for initiatives to create safer schools. Both communities generally and parents specifically play vital roles in those initiatives.

Over time, research has shown repeatedly that parental involvement improves the school behavior and academic performance of children (see the January 1991 *Phi Delta Kappan* special section for a summary of the benefits of parental involvement). Current popular and professional literature adds that parental and community involvement also are essential components of any policy or program effort to create and maintain safe schools. Many strategies to involve parents and communities in creating safe schools follow traditional models for involving parents in improving their children's academic performance. While traditional involvement strategies unquestionably are beneficial in helping children succeed academically, they are inadequate to maintain or create safe schools. Schools must devise more extensive strategies for involving parents and communities in the creation and maintenance of safe schools.

This chapter will provide a brief overview of research that examines the role of parental and community involvement in school safety and will describe programs that have successfully involved parents and communities in creating safe schools. Methods of parental and community involvement in these programs will be compared to academic involvement strategies. The chapter will conclude with a description of the essential components for successful parental and community involvement in creating safe schools.

RESEARCH ABOUT PARENTAL/ COMMUNITY INVOLVEMENT

While educators, parents and communities express heightened concern about school safety in the 1990s, researchers and policy makers have been studying school violence and its relationship to community characteristics for nearly twenty years.

Community Factors

During the last twenty years of research on school violence, it has become accepted knowledge that unsafe schools exist in unsafe communities (Hellman & Beaton, 1986). Indeed, violence in the schools is generally recognized as a reflection of violence in the community (Hill & Hill, 1994; Schriro, 1985; Stover, 1988; Wilson, 1977). Goldstein, Apter and Harootunian (1984) summarize contradictory studies that show school practices as contributors to school delinquency contrasted with those studies that show schools as victims of community violence. While Menacker, Welden and Hurwitz (1990) agree that ". . . the community context is critical to the level of school crime and violence" (p. 68), they feel that schools do not create unsafe situations and, in fact, are often safer than the communities in which they are set. Whether the school is perpetrator, victim or deterrent of violence, school and community violence are inseparable (McDermott, 1983), existing on a "circular continuum of causes" (Marvin, McCann, Connolly, Temkin & Henning, 1977).

Local and national surveys consistently have shown that school crime is widespread and not limited to a particular type of community. *Violent Schools–Safe Schools,* commissioned by the National Institute of Education (1978), reported widespread violence in schools throughout the nation. The National Association of School Security Directors reports yearly, its estimate of widespread physical and property violence (Rich, 1992). Stover (1988) documents the pervasiveness of school violence, noting that 32% of schools affected by serious crimes are not in urban areas. These and other reports (Baker, 1985; Pearson & Toby, 1991) show that teachers and students alike fear for their personal safety.

The link between school and community violence suggests that school safety is situational (Horowitz & Kraus, 1987). For example, Pearson and Toby (1991) found that teachers' and students' fears of attack are closely related to community factors including the presence of gangs and available modes of transportation to school. In their analysis of the NIE data from the *Safe Schools Study,* Gottfredson and Gottfredson (1985) assumed that both the communities where schools are located and the composition of the school population are important factors in explaining school disorder. Therefore, the situational factors in the local community must be examined to determine the local school's level of safety.

Home Factors

Specific community and home characteristics have been identified as having an effect on school crime. In a discussion of the *Safe Schools Study* (National Institute of Education, 1978), Schriro (1985) notes that schools in communities with rapid growth, poverty, minority families, working parents and unsupervised adolescents are more likely to be perceived as unsafe. Mitch Ginsburg, clinical child psychologist at Brooke Haven Psychiatric Center in Hagerstown, Maryland, attributes the cause of violent behavior in school children to the breakdown of the family. Specifically, he cites the fact that working and single parents lack time to teach their children values (Harrington-Lueker, 1991). Hellman and Beaton (1986) add that school crime is lower in communities with traditional, working class families. Harrington-Lueker (1992) summarizes the impact of home and community factors on schools by emphasizing that children must balance the cultures of the home, school and street. Often, she notes, the culture of the street may have a greater, though negative influence on children. Clearly, these experts agree that the rise in school violence is the result of changing family structure.

PROGRAM INITIATIVES RESPOND TO SCHOOL VIOLENCE

The increased occurrence and severity of school violence has led to local and national efforts to create safe schools. Exemplary programs have successfully replaced unsafe situations with safe school climates. For example, crime rates have dropped by one-half at Bassett High School in La Puente, California since parents began patrolling the cafeteria and hallways in 1981 (Gest, 1989). Similarly, discipline referrals have dropped by two-thirds and fighting has been virtually eliminated in Lake County Intermediate School in Leadville, Colorado since formal action teams of students, teachers, parents and administrators have developed and implemented action plans to deal with discipline problems (Malesich, 1994).

Programs have been developed at the school, district, community and state levels to tackle unhealthy local conditions existing in the family, school or community. The La Puente, California and Leadville, Colorado programs are examples of programs focusing on specific building problems that had a direct impact on the safe operation of the school and a proper climate for learning.

District Programs

Programs at the district level have focused on community conditions that permeate the school environment, making it unsafe for students to travel to school or to concentrate on learning once they arrive. In community-based programs, the districts of Tacoma, Washington (Nebgen, 1990); Portland, Oregon (Prophet, 1990); and Philadelphia, Pennsylvania (Nicholson, Stephens, Elder & Leavitt, 1985), have combined resources to correct unsafe neighborhood conditions. In Tacoma, community organizations including service clubs, block-watch organizations and the parent-teacher organization have worked together to report illegal drug activity, clean up neighborhoods and protest crack houses. The Portland school district has involved students, staff, parents and the greater community in developing a program to deal with gangs. The Philadelphia district created the Crisis Intervention Network, Inc. (CIN) to combat social conditions that foster potential and actual gang-related crises. CIN involved the school, law-enforcement agencies, neighborhood residents and other groups that dealt with youth. These groups formed mobile teams of street workers to discourage community violence. Each of these programs has relied on all segments of the community to identify local problems and to suggest and operationalize strategies to correct them.

Other programs at both local and state levels have devised methods to help families with problems that may affect the well-being and safety of children. A pilot project in the Chicago Public Schools consisted of an intervention program of family assistance to develop problem-solving and parenting skills (Harrington-Lueker, 1991). The nationally recognized Missouri Parents as Teachers program is an exemplary program in which communities provide activities that offer experiences of self-efficacy for both parents and their children (Garbarino, Dubrow, Kostelny & Pardo, 1992).

National Policy Efforts

National policy makers and funding institutions have supported local community initiatives to combat unsafe school conditions. With the creation of the Safe Schools Act of 1993, the federal government recognized the necessity of involving all segments of the community in creating safe schools. According to Madeleine Kunin, Deputy Secretary of the U.S. Department of Education, "Creating [a safe school environment] will require a new partnership between the federal government and our nation's schools and between the schools and the communities in which they are located" (U.S. Senate Subcommittee on Education, Arts and Humanities, 1993). She adds that, "Every segment of the community—schools, law enforcement, social services, businesses, clergy, parents, and students—has a role to play."

The Robert Wood Johnson Foundation has used a community-based approach in funding strategies to create safe conditions for youth. Fourteen communities—San Antonio, Texas; Columbia, South Carolina; Little Rock, Arkansas; Kansas City, Missouri; northwest New Mexico; Oakland, Vallejo and Santa Barbara, California; Milwaukee, Wisconsin; Washington, D.C.; Worcester, Massachusetts; New Haven, Connecticut; Charlotte, North Carolina; and Newark, New Jersey— have received five-year implementation grants in the National Fighting Back Program (U.S. Senate Subcommittee, 1993).

The National Fighting Back Program is based on the premise that diverse community groups can collaborate to develop a common vision to solve community problems. From that vision, communities may develop creative solutions to problems of substance abuse, youth violence, crime, economic development, deterioration of neighborhoods, inadequate educational systems and health care costs. Though it is too early to predict program success, the National Fighting Back program reports impressive early results through the integration of human services, education, basic services (i.e., community policing, neighborhood revitalization, economic development) and resident action at both community and neighborhood levels (U.S. Senate Subcommittee, 1993).

DIFFERENCES IN PARENTAL INVOLVEMENT IN ACADEMICS AND SAFE SCHOOLS PROGRAMS

The programs described in the previous section dealt with problems that ranged from specific issues such as school discipline to general conditions such as deteriorating communities. Despite the fact that the scope of these programs ranges from building level to national efforts, all of them have characteristics in common. Many of these characteristics also are a part of traditional efforts to involve parents in the educational aspects of schooling. Yet other components of these programs to create safe schools either are extensions of traditional parental involvement practices or are departures from more traditional practice. The characteristics of traditional parental involvement practices will be described and compared to the approaches used in programs to create safe schools.

Academic Parental Involvement Models

In parental involvement programs that address academic concerns, the roles of parents and schools are collaborative, but dichotomous. The parent is required to meet certain obligations at home and deliver the child to the schoolhouse door. The school then takes over and lets the parent know what happened while the child was at school. If both sides have met their obligations and if they communicate effectively with one another, the parent and school then can work together to help the child be successful in his or her academic work.

The parent's role includes specific ways in which they should send children to school ready to learn. For example, parents should see to it that their children are well fed, clothed, rested and have a place and the opportunity to complete their homework. Most importantly, they also should convey the value of an education to their children.

Schools, on the other hand, are obligated to communicate with parents about their children's school performance and to alert them to any difficulties that the children may be experiencing. If necessary, the school also is responsible for educating parents about child development, parenting skills or any other areas necessary to help them fulfill their responsibilities as parents.

An important component of all traditional parental involvement programs is volunteering. Parents assist the school with a variety of projects. In the earliest parental involvement programs, parents came to the school to volunteer in the classroom. They might tutor children who needed extra instruction, prepare materials for the teacher or share their expertise by talking with the students. Parents also may be asked to help out with larger projects such as the building of a new playground. As families have become more diverse and often are unable to come to the school, they may work at home preparing materials or working with their children on assignments that need their input. Volunteering activities ideally utilize parents' strengths to supplement the existing school program and curriculum. When parents help out, teachers are better able to teach. By helping out, parents can see the educational program and routines of the school. The communication that takes place will help parents and teachers work together in helping children.

Another specific aspect in most models of parental involvement is assistance with homework. As with volunteering, parents are asked by the teacher to perform prescribed tasks so that their children complete their homework: helping with basic skills, providing necessary materials or perhaps actually participating in the assignment. The teacher is responsible for providing the parent with any information to assist the child.

Attendance at school activities is a popular component of parental involvement. Parents are asked to attend events at the school directly pertaining to their children's performance (i.e., parent-teacher conferences, concerts, plays, fun nights). Some schools hold events that allow children and parents to participate in activities together. One school at which this author has studied parental involvement has sponsored math nights and reading nights at which parents and children complete math games or reading activities together. In most schools, parents also are encouraged to attend activities related to the general operation of the school. The common activity is parent-teacher organization meetings. As with the previous involvement activities, the school's role is to invite parents to preplanned activities.

Finally, the highest level of parental involvement is governance. At this level, parents hold positions on advisory committees and provide input for decisions to guide the operation of the school. For example, in one district in which the author researched parental involvement, parent representatives had served on a task force that made recommendations to the principal for improving school attendance. The principal took these recommendations into consideration when drafting a new attendance policy. Both parents and the principal were comfortable with this arrangement, sharing the belief that the final decision was "up to the principal." In another local district that recently opened a new building, parents were asked to sign up for committees to deal with facility issues. Two popular committees for parental involvement were the landscaping and playground equipment committees.

The traditional components of academic parental involvement programs—parent responsibilities, school responsibilities, volunteering, assistance with homework, attendance at school events and governance—have different degrees of parental presence and influence in school affairs. Yet all components have kept parental and school roles separate though complementary. This arrangement suggests that the combination of these separate tasks will help children.

Safe Schools Parental Involvement Programs

Programs that have successfully involved parents and community members in creating safe schools share many of the characteristics of academic parental involvement models that were described in the previous section. Yet many of those characteristics have been modified to deal specifically with the school safety issue. Looking at differences in traditional involvement models and successful safe schools programs will suggest essential characteristics of safe schools initiatives.

In the programs described above, roles and responsibilities of parents and schools have been redefined. The roles were not predetermined with separate criteria for schools and parents. Rather, the criteria were developed locally based on specific problems and available resources. The National Fighting Back Program (U.S. Senate Subcommittee, 1993) specifically recommends that duties and responsibilities be clearly defined according to local situations. Duties and responsibilities of school personnel and parents in these exemplary programs respond to local unsafe situations. For example, in the Tacoma, Washington schools; all members of the school, parent and community groups shared responsibility for reporting illegal and unsafe activities in the community. In Portland, Oregon, a similar partnership was created in which students, school staff, parent and community groups learned together how to deal with gangs. Training sessions were provided at the school and through neighborhood workshops so that all school and community groups would be prepared to cooperate with local authorities in eliminating the gang problems.

School and parental roles were not the only ones that changed. Students also shared central roles in many programs. For example, in Leadville, Colorado, intermediate school students were not simply the passive recipients of disciplinary actions. They helped determine consequences for the inappropriate behavior of their peers in a youth court. Community members also fulfilled a key role. In Leadville, Colorado, and in two urban middle schools in the northeastern United States (*Urban Middle Schools,* 1992), representatives of the entire community contributed input and resources. Students and community members worked with school personnel and parents to initiate, implement and evaluate the program's success. Community donations in Leadville helped establish a Saturday School and made it possible to substitute community service in place of suspensions from school. The schools in these and other projects have shared the goal of defining roles and responsibilities for creating safe schools with all community groups. Blurring the lines between areas of responsibility has fostered "a universal buy-in" for safe schools projects (Malesich, 1994).

While lines of distinction have disappeared between roles in most safe schools programs, specific needs of individuals and groups are respected and addressed. To create safe schools, programs first must meet participants' needs and interests (Harrington-Lueker, 1991; Marvin, McCann, Connolly, Temkin & Henning, 1977). An intervention project to deal with violence in the Chicago Public Schools includes family assistance for families who need help with problem-solving and parenting skills. Similarly, schools that provide breakfast programs, health services, scouting, after-school care and emergency hot lines are responding to the basic needs of individuals as the basis for schoolwide and communitywide safe schools projects (Menacker, Welden & Hurwitz, 1990).

The delivery of parental education also has changed in safe schools projects. In traditional parental involvement models, the school gives and the parent receives education. Parental education usually deals with how to help children complete homework, how to discipline or parent a child, and other specific activities that relate to school performance. In the safe schools projects, school personnel, parents and community members are all both providers and recipients of education. Knowledgeable individuals provide information and training about local unsafe circumstances and approaches to deal with them. Gang awareness training is a typical example.

The importance and extent of volunteering have intensified in safe schools projects. Typical volunteer activities for parental involvement can be summarized as strategies to enrich the classroom experience. Parents provide additional tutoring for children who need it or assist teachers with routine tasks to give teachers more time to spend with students. Parents with special expertise may share their knowledge in presentations. While these types of activities are important, they are not essential to the operation of the classroom and school. Volunteer activities in safe schools programs often are central to the basic operation of the school because they address unsafe conditions that prohibit learning. While volunteer activities usually are not related directly to the curriculum in safe schools projects, they are designed to create a safe learning environment for children. Whether parents are patrolling the hallways or school cafeteria, reporting illegal drug activity in the community or attending a disciplinary hearing for their children, they actively contribute to improving the safety of the school.

As the extent of volunteering has increased, the involvement of parents in homework assistance and, especially, school activities has taken on an intensified role. The focus of these two activities is not only on ways in which parents may have a distinct part to play in helping their children experience academic success. Rather, the role of parents in safe schools projects is to perform an activity either in the school or community that has a direct effect on the safety of the school climate. Parents in safe schools do not merely observe activities; they report unsafe ones. They come into the school to serve as a visible presence with the authority to take action against inappropriate activities.

Parental authority extends beyond monitoring and reporting unsafe activities, however. Parents and community members in safe schools projects also have a central role to play in school governance. While parental involvement in academic models is largely in an advisory capacity, parents in safe schools have a direct impact on decision making. Not only professional literature, but also popular magazines, stress the fact that parents should take an assertive role in deciding how to make schools safer. For example, the November, 1994 issue of *Better Homes and Gardens* recommends specific actions for parents to take (Atkins, 1994). Not only should parents advise or approve policies created by school officials; parents also should participate in identifying unsafe conditions and in creating policies and carrying out procedures to correct them. In other words, parents and communities do not simply do as the schools ask; they too ask what needs to be done.

Communication embodies the key difference in the involvement of parents in academics and safe schools. Parents who are involved in academic aspects of schooling primarily are the recipients of communication. They are informed of their children's progress and given suggestions of ways to help their children. Schools may ask parents to provide specific types of information to the teacher or to ask questions about children's classroom performance and achievement. In safe schools, parent communication takes on a more active role. Indeed, parents may provide critical information about the community's culture and activities that is needed to eliminate undesirable conditions. Parents may have an understanding of the community's history, values and ethics that school personnel do not share. In essence, parents become instructors so that teachers and administrators may learn about the community's foundation. This key communication role gives parents real decision-making authority.

A PROCESS FOR PARENTAL AND COMMUNITY INVOLVEMENT

The examples of successful programs illustrate the importance of involving both parents and communities in creating strategies for safe schools. Parental and community involvement does more than help create safe schools. Many authorities feel that, "A lack of parental involvement contributes strongly to school violence" (Boothe, Bradley, Flick, Keough & Kirk, 1993). In fact, an absence of parental involvement is a more important factor in school violence that social class, racial or ethnic tension, gangs, alcohol and drug abuse or student transiency (Marvin, McCann, Connolly, Temkin & Henning, 1977). One fifth grader speaking about safe schools stated his feelings on the role of parents very strongly: "Parents are responsible for making schools safe. They should pay attention to what their kids have to say. They should tell kids — not just their own — to stop doing something they shouldn't do."

The community shares with parents the central role in creating safe schools. As has been previously stated, the roles of parents and community should be interrelated with the school since, as research has shown repeatedly, safe schools exist in safe communities. One teacher emphasized, "If the community at large doesn't take care of its members, the parents are not going to take care of their children, and the children aren't going to take care of their school. A healthy school breeds a healthy community."

The roles of parents and communities are multidimensional in safe schools. Parent and community groups form a symbiotic relationship with the school in which the specific role of one group is an extension of another group's role. Based on the local community, each group can play an active role in identifying and correcting unsafe situations. It is essential that all local parent and community groups be included in safe schools initiatives. More parent and community groups must be involved than ever before. Stronger linkages must be forged with law-enforcement and the legal system while more common ties must be maintained with business, social services and recreational organizations. Parents from all circumstances must be given greater responsibility to help solve problems.

The interrelationship of home, school and community suggests a type of involvement that varies even from the successful programs described earlier in this chapter. While specific programs and practices may be successful in one area, they simply may not work with a different issue in another locality. Therefore, to successfully involve parents and communities in creating safe schools, the development of a process is more important than the nature of the specific programs. This section will list and describe the essential components of a process to successfully involve parents and communities in creating safe schools.

All of the successful programs previously described shared the necessary components of an effective process orientation. These components are modifications of process components of effective school–community relations identified by literally hundreds of respondents in earlier research at the University of Wisconsin-Madison Research and Development Center (Wanat & Bowles, 1993). The components are: communication, involvement, participation and resolution.

Communication

Effective communication with parents and the community is basic to any safe schools project. Research has shown that effective communication has identifiable characteristics. Though communication may be written or verbal, it must allow for two-way interaction between the school and other groups. Indeed, two-way communication gives the schools' attempts to create safety legitimacy in the eyes of the community and instills in parents and community members a willingness to help out. While communication is important for all community groups, it had a greater impact in the Wisconsin studies on urban, low-income minority communities. Therefore, it is especially important in communicating with the public about school safety to respond to the community's diversity, reach all parent and community groups and ensure that all groups have an equal opportunity to express themselves.

Involvement

While this chapter has talked about "involvement" of parents and community, involvement meant something different than the current use of the term in the Wisconsin research. This author feels that the distinction is important. Respondents in the Wisconsin study defined involvement as contributing time, energy, money, expertise and other resources to the school. Examples of traditional involvement activities include academic parental involvement programs and school-business partnerships. While there are many examples of such contributions to safe schools endeavors, involvement in this sense alone is not sufficient to gain the total support of parents and the community. Also needed is participation, which was defined in the Wisconsin research as a separate activity.

Participation

Participation is a decision-making activity at both the district policy-making level and at the individual school practices level. Examples include serving on advisory boards and governing councils. Participatory activities have become more frequent as schools have reorganized through a site-based management approach. One of the more highly publicized examples of parental participation has occurred in the New Haven, Connecticut schools as parents, professional staff and members of the Yale Child Study Center have developed a curriculum and hired a staff to provide educational services demanded by the community (Comer, 1980).

Safe schools initiatives must allow parents and community members to actively participate in the decision-making process. While this role includes serving on formal advisory councils and task forces, it also means having real input and authority to help make decisions about whatever needs to be done to create safe schools. In one district, it may be setting up a block-parent program to protect children walking home from school; in another, it may mean coordinating a program in which parents monitor hallways and playgrounds. The key point is that parents must not only be involved as block parents and hall monitors; they must participate in deciding that there need to be block parents and hall monitors.

Resolution

Resolution is a problem-solving activity to reduce or eliminate actual or potential conflict between the school and community groups. In the Wisconsin research, conflict resolution focused on disputed disciplinary actions, special education placements and questionable instructional practices. With the increase in unsafe school conditions, conflict resolution now includes more basic issues of physical safety from verbal or physical harassment and harm in both the school and community. Conflict resolution in a safe schools project must deal with eliminating the unsafe conditions and, more importantly, it must provide a procedure for all school, parent and community groups to resolve differences in values about what constitutes a safe school.

OTHER BASIC REQUIREMENTS IN A SAFE SCHOOLS PROCESS

While the general components described above are necessary for any effective school–community relations program, the following requirements are specific to safe schools processes.

Shared Values

Obviously, parents, community and the school must share the same philosophy about what constitutes safety. However, determining what a safe school is can be a complex process. The definition of a safe school is specific to the community and reflects the values of the people who live there. For example, in one major metropolitan high school where school safety was studied, students had brought guns to school on previous occasions. Therefore, a student who reported that an unloaded gun had been brought to school the previous week felt that an unloaded gun was safe in that particular school. In another school where there had never been a gun in the school, an unloaded gun would constitute an unsafe situation. This example illustrates the necessity of all members of the school and community working together to define what they consider to be a safe school. Effective communication will formulate that definition.

Including values of *all* special interest groups in the community is a challenging task, particularly in the types of communities that may be plagued most by unsafe conditions. As previously cited research has shown, communities with the greatest diversity in mobility, socioeconomic status and family structure are usually less safe than the more stable, homogeneous communities. Logically, the heterogeneous groups in a less safe community may not share basic values beyond that of the desire for school safety. Extra time and effort may be required to integrate different social, cultural and personal values into a generally acceptable definition of what constitutes a safe school and how best to attain school safety.

Decision-Making Procedures

In addition to respecting individual and group differences, schools must ensure that those individuals and groups have influence in any efforts to achieve school safety. Advisory committees and task forces should include members of parent and community groups connected with the school. Representation should reflect the social, economic and family demographics of the community as well as established parent and community groups.

To work effectively together, parent, school and community groups need to be trained in group process. Basic rules need to be established about how the group will work together to accomplish its task. For example, decisions need to be made about how to identify unsafe situations, collect information to help solve problems, select strategies for policy and program development and implement and evaluate the effectiveness of the final selection. If necessary, parent, school and community teams should receive training in the processes they have selected to function as a group. For example, if they have decided on a consensus-building approach, they may need to be trained in this particular strategy. The point is, to be successful, representation and decision-making processes must be developed to fit the local community's demographics and values.

Support

In addition to financial support, a safe schools initiative requires other types of support. While moral support, or sharing of values, obviously is important, the commitment to those values needs to be translated into practical approaches. All community agencies need to share the responsibility for creating and implementing programs. Cooperation between the school and all parent and community agencies is essential. The law-enforcement and legal systems in particular must help to solve safe schools problems, not simply serve in an enforcement role. For example, police officers in schools may serve as liaisons with the community and provide positive role models for students. Social service agencies of all types also may lend their expertise to work with students and families needing their assistance with violent or otherwise unhealthy behaviors.

Program Format

To eliminate unsafe situations, safe schools policies and programs must attack specific problems directly. The relationship between the problem and the solution must be clear to student, parent and community groups. The format must be socially and culturally acceptable as well. Similarly, indicators of the program's success must be measurable and easy to document. This information must be available to parent and community groups to maintain their interest and involvement.

Education/Training

Relevant education and/or training must be provided to all school, parent and community participants. Examples include training in gang awareness, abuse and harassment and conflict resolution. Education needs to be made available at times and locations that encourage participation by all of these groups.

Use of School Facilities for Community Programs

Many popular programs to create safe school climates house other social services within the school building. Services may include health care, social services, child care and various types of counseling. Providing these services during extended hours makes the school the hub of the community, thereby naturally involving parents and the community in maintaining a positive school climate. This arrangement can be ideal in fostering an ongoing positive relationship among those providing a stable environment for children.

CONCLUSION

This chapter has presented some examples of successful involvement of parents and community in turning unsafe schools into safe ones. None of these programs is a cure-all solution for this increasingly prevalent situation. However, all of these programs do share the common characteristic of looking at *how* to involve these groups in schools. By attending to the process, rather than trying to create a specific type of program, schools may achieve similar success in working with their parents and communities to maintain schools that are safe for their children to attend.

REFERENCES

Atkins, A. (1994). Violent hallway. *Better Homes and Gardens*, 72(11):36, 38.

Baker, K. (1985). Research evidence of a school discipline problem. *Phi Delta Kappan*, 66(7):482–488.

Boothe, J. W., Bradley, L. H., Flick, T. M., Keough, K. E. & Kirk, S. P. (1993). The violence at your door. *The Executive Educator*, 15(1):16–22.

Comer, J. P. (1980). *School power.* New York: The Free Press.

Epstein, J. (Ed.). (1991). Parent involvement: A special section. *Phi Delta Kappan*, 72(5):344–388.

Garbarino, J., Dubrow, N., Kostelny, K. & Pardo, C. (1992). *Children in danger: Coping with the consequences of community violence.* San Francisco: Jossey-Bass.

Gest, T. (1989). These perilous halls of learning. *U.S. News and World Report*, 106(10):68–69.

Goldstein, A. P., Apter, S. J. & Harootunian, B. (1984). *School violence.* Englewood Cliffs, NJ: Prentice-Hall.

Gottfredson, G. D. & Gottfredson, D. C. (1985). *Victimization in schools.* New York: Plenum.

Harrington-Lueker, D. (1991). A fifth grader is accused of trying to poison her principal. *The Executive Educator*, 13(6):25–26.

Harrington-Lueker, D. (1992). "Blown away: The expectation of safety in schools is dying of gunshot wounds. *American School Board Journal*, 179(5):20–26.

Hellman, D. A. & Beaton, S. (1986). The pattern of violence in urban public schools: The influence of school and community. *Journal of Research in Crime and Delinquency,* 23(2):102–127.

Hill, M. S. & Hill, F. W. (1994). *Creating safe schools: What principals can do.* Thousand Oaks, CA: Corwin.

Horowitz, T. R. & Kraus, V. (1987). Violence at school: Situational factors or societal input. *School Psychology International,* 8(2–3):141–147.

Malesich, R. F. (1994). Making schools safe for students: Solutions to discipline problems. *Schools in the Middle,* 3(3):38–40.

Marvin, M., McCann, R., Connolly, J., Temkin, S. & Henning, P. (1977). Current activities in schools. In J. M. McPartland & E. L. McDill (Eds.), *Violence in schools* (pp. 53–70). Lexington, MA: Lexington Books.

McDermott, J. (1983). Crime in the school and in the community: Offenders, victims, and fearful youths. *Crime and Delinquency,* 29(2):270–282.

McPartland, J. M. & McDill, E. L. (Eds.). (1977). *Violence in schools.* Lexington, MA: Lexington Books.

Menacker, J., Welden, W. & Hurwitz, E. (1990). Community influences on school crime and violence. *Urban Education,* 25(1):68–80.

National Institute of Education. (1978). *Violent schools–safe schools: The safe school study report to congress.* Washington, D.C.: Author.

Nebgen, M. (1990). Safe streets in Tacoma. *American School Board Journal,* 177(10):26–27.

Nicholson, G., Stephens, R., Elder, R. & Leavitt, V. (1985). Safe schools: You can't do it alone. *Phi Delta Kappan,* 66(7):491–496.

Pearson, F. S. & Toby, J. (1991). Fear of school-related predatory crime. *Sociology and Social Research,* 75(3):117–125.

Prophet, M. (1990). Safe schools in Portland. *American School Board Journal,* 177(10):28–30.

Rich, J. M. (1992). Predicting and controlling school violence. *Contemporary Education,* 64(1):35–39.

Schriro, D. (1985). Safe schools, sound schools: Learning in a non-disruptive environment. Columbia, NY: Teachers College (ERIC Clearinghouse on Urban Education Reproduction Service No. ED 253 602).

Stover, D. (1988). School violence is rising, and your staff is the target. *The Executive Educator,* 10(10):15–21, 33.

U.S. Senate Subcommittee on Education, Arts and Humanities. (1993). *Recess from violence: Making our schools safe.* Washington, D.C.: U.S. Government Printing Office.

Urban middle schools become safer, more effective. (1992). *Schools in the Middle,* 2(1):45–46.

Wanat, C. L. & Bowles, B. D. 1993. School–community relations: A process paradigm. *Community Education Journal,* 20(2):3–7.

Wilson, J. Q. 1977. Crime in society and schools. In J. M. McPartland & E. L. McDill (Eds.), *Violence in schools* (pp. 43–49). Lexington, MA: Lexington Books.

CHAPTER 11

The Involvement of Community Agencies in the Development of Safe Schools

HARBISON POOL
DOUGLAS W. POOL

SPEAKING from the perspectives of professional educator and law-enforcement officer, respectively, we both recognize the critical importance of the relationship between the schools and agencies normally outside the domain of the local school district. Words like cooperation, network, partnership, teamwork and collaboration come to mind. Communication must be genuinely open and two-way.

Physiologists explain that the body of a healthy human being performs as it is supposed to only if the nerves, blood, muscles and organs all do their jobs in synchronization with one another. So it is with a community; it too is the sum of its parts. Like the brain to the human body, a community's governing entities are supposed to provide a unity of action, but effective government is dependent on various public agencies, as well as schools, churches, businesses and individual citizens.

Unfortunately, even though it is in the self-interest of each of these "parts" of the "grand system" that schools function properly, we find that other agencies often work at cross-purposes with one another, leaving needed services unperformed or causing wasteful duplication of effort. At best this is inefficient; at times, it is counterproductive or even self-destructive. When the parts are not working together for the common good with at least some measure of logic and harmony, the entire community suffers, its youngest members perhaps most of all.

SAFE SCHOOLS—PERCEPTION, REALITY, RESPONSE

California's Crime Prevention Center (1989) defines safe schools as "orderly and purposeful places where students and staff are free to learn and teach without the threat of physical and psychological harm" (p. 2). Of course, every community wants such schools. Many, however, are short of the mark at this time. To approach this lofty goal, we must first bring perceptions in line with reality. We must realize and acknowledge where we are, and how far we are from where we want to be. Then, of course, we must decide what we must do, both incrementally and more dramatically, to begin to achieve that to which we aspire.

We must also recognize and debunk myths. For example, as Quarles (1993) points out, dangerous schools are not necessarily located in high-crime areas. Indeed, Schriro's impressive research (1985) turned up instances of safe schools in poor, inner-city areas and of unsafe schools in upper middle class suburbs; she also located "sound schools" (schools where students perform well) that were unsafe and safe schools that were "unsound" (where little, if anything, was accomplished academically). Obviously, parents would like to have their children in schools that are both safe and sound.

Happily, this is attainable—and not just in neighborhoods where students are "advantaged." This is not to say that it will come easily. As the National Institute of Education (1978) found in its flagship report on school crime and violence, *Violent Schools–Safe Schools,* risks to youth during their teenage years are often greater *in* school than out! Quarles (1993) reminds us that young people between the ages of twelve and nineteen account for more than one-half of all arrests in the United States. In other words, middle and high school "teachers are working with the primary crime-age population" (p. 5).

To begin with, effective educators must—and will—face conditions in their schools as they really are. Then, with all the help they can command, they must—and will—pursue ambitious, aggressive agendas for developing more positive "realities." Some ideas will be original, some borrowed. Some solutions will be partial, some more complete. Some measures will provide temporary relief, while others will offer more long-lasting benefits. Above all, no challenge can be perceived as too overwhelming, no setback too discouraging. Very simply, the stakes are too high for the faint of heart. The quest for safe, sound schools must be persistent, resolute, tenacious, unrelenting and persevering.

ADDRESSING THE PROBLEM: BEFORE, DURING, AND AFTER

Following the recognition that there is a problem or at least a need and a commitment to do something about it, solid security steps must be taken that respond to local needs (Mancuso, 1983). School officials must engage in both policy (strategic) planning and operational (tactical) planning (Crime Prevention Center, 1989; Vestermark & Blauvelt, 1978). In our view, we must speak about both prevention *and* intervention, "proactivity" *and* reactivity. Even where major problems already exist, we believe the emphasis can be on positive, forward-looking (i.e., "proactive") steps toward finding solutions. We think that research, awareness, knowledge of one's own community, involvement of all interested parties and especially anticipation are in order. It is important to understand, we argue, that those considered "interested parties" should include many outside governmental and private agencies, school teachers and administrators, parents and other members of the lay public, the students themselves and any other individual or group of people who has the potential to contribute to the search for—and identification of—answers. There are times, of course, particularly when first assuming the mantle of leadership in entrenched, out-of-control, unsuccessful schools, when even the most progressive principals must 1) *re*act, perhaps forcefully, 2) be visible and 3) put out a few fires.

Capable school administrators will undertake safe school audits. They will not stop with the discovery of existing deficiencies. What, they will want to know, can be done in the way of prevention and thinking ahead? Nor will this evaluation of conditions and needs be confined to the obvious. They will consider too what salutary steps might be taken 1) in schoolwide and classroom reorganization (e.g., inter-age grouping, team teaching, differentiated staffing); 2) in curriculum modification (e.g., real-world content, interdisciplinary and problem-centered treatments, nontraditional curricular structures); and 3) in the revision of instruction and assessment (e.g., increased student participation and initiation, mentorships and fieldwork, discovery and inquiry approaches, simulations, student creation of computer software, portfolios, student goal-setting and personalized assignments, cooperative learning strategies).

Good principals know that selected programmatic, structural and environmental changes will contribute to a safer school (Curwin, 1990; Hensel, 1991; Post, 1991; Schriro, 1985). Even in the toughest schools, an engaging curriculum (in some cases with content that directly confronts safe school issues), heterogeneous small group activity, good instructional practices and a caring school climate can significantly reduce the need for overt discipline (Burns, 1981; Carducci & Carducci, 1984; Dreyfuss, 1990; Ellis, 1989).

When problems do occur, however infrequently, regardless of what may have been done by way of anticipation, prevention and proactivity, effective principals do not just throw up their hands and hide in their offices; neither do they devote much time or energy to the largely unrewarding exercise of assessing blame. When possible, they contribute to—and, when necessary, initiate—such correctives as improving the teaching and learning environment; developing reasonable, humane and enforceable rules; and implementing sound security measures. They establish disciplinary approaches that are dignified, empowering and motivating; that build toward and encourage self-discipline; and that use student mediation and positive social pressure. Firm, fair actions—as appropriate to the situation—are taken to eradicate or at least curb unacceptable behavior and teach and promote thoughtful and enlightened alternatives.

INVOLVEMENT

If safe schools are to remain safe and unsafe schools are to become safe, the buck cannot be passed: all school personnel and "outsiders" of goodwill have to contribute. Without doubt, there are tasks and jobs enough to go around. And, as Duke and Meckel (1980) stress, no-one—student, teacher, administrator or lay citizen—benefits from the performance of disciplinary functions "so onerous and unrewarding that talented and sensitive educators avoid them whenever possible" (p. 113).

School Personnel

The role of the teacher in achieving safe schools is perhaps obvious, but it must not be taken for granted (Quarles, 1993). Teachers must both instruct and act as disciplinarians. Often, the same individual—especially true of the elementary teacher and the secondary assistant principal—will serve as lawmaker, accuser and judge. Inconsistent discipline, the loss of student respect for the school as a just organization, educator frustration, low-morale and other role-related problems can be minimized, according to Duke and Meckel (1980), if certain organizational changes are undertaken. "Greater coordination of activities among individuals performing disciplinary functions; clearer behavioral expectations for teachers as well as students; shared responsibility for discipline (between teachers and students); and greater incentives for school personnel who deal with student behavior problems" (p. 113) are some of the changes. Duke and Meckel (1980) would pay special attention to improving the jobs of those—like deans and vice principals—who spend most of their time each day reacting to student misbehavior.

Foremost among those who can make a positive difference in creating and maintaining safe schools, according to much of the professional literature, are school principals. Brodinsky (1981), who calls principals "key figures in maintaining school safety" (p. 33), specifies a number of related duties and reporting responsibilities, including establishing a committee on school safety that will include a broad range of individuals in the school community, and developing cooperative relationships with the school's student council, parent-teacher group, community organizations and social agencies that are concerned with youth and school safety.

"Regardless of school responsibilities," Furtwengler and Konnert (1982) assert, the principal "is almost always held accountable for the behavior of the students" (p. 155) and, they continue, the quality of school discipline in a school has much to do with a principal's overall success. "The role of the principal," as Schriro (1985) expresses it, "is uniquely suited to reducing school disruptions" (p. 46). Able principals, Schriro (1985) finds, provide competent leadership in curriculum and instruction and act much like master or head teachers. They know how to encourage their teachers to participate in decision making without relinquishing administrative prerogatives, such as "the authority to set expectations for staff and students and to reward good behavior" (p. 48). They recognize that meaningful change occurs at the building level and that they must provide the leadership to bring it to fruition (Goodlad, 1983).

Principals must also adapt to their situations. Secondary principals in schools studied by Schwartz (1988) had to adjust their leadership style according to the social context of their schools; those whose schools were in "hostile" (e.g., gang-impacted) areas displayed significantly more control orientation, whereas principals in "safe" schools were more concerned with administrative tasks. Each principal's predominant choice of leadership behavior was that which related most positively to the student climate in his or her type of school.

There are many other school personnel—certificated and classified—who contribute to the well-being of a school and to whether it is a safe and disciplined place or not. Hyman et al. (1982), for example, document the importance of the school psychologist's role in achieving good student discipline. Effective principals realize that the fortunes of their schools are in the hands of many; they solicit and support the best efforts and goodwill of all.

School personnel, as we see it, have another important role. They should accept primary responsibility for working with their students to build their school into a model of community—*community* viewed as a vital, compelling, interdependent entity. When more and more parents, agencies, business people, lay leaders and others accept the educators' invitation to become partners in such an enterprise, both the school-as-community and the greater neighborhood it serves are strengthened and better able to resist negative social, cultural and economic forces that might undermine a more fragile, less well-established and less dynamic undertaking.

VOLUNTEERS

It is almost axiomatic that the finest schools and school programs utilize the services of volunteers. Leaders in such schools invite, cherish and show appreciation of the work of their volunteers (Fletcher, 1987; O'Connell & O'Connell, 1989). They have a well-designed volunteer network with good parent and teacher coordination. While there is virtually no potential problem in the use of school volunteers which cannot be overcome, the benefits, particularly when parents serve directly in their children's classrooms, are numerous, substantive and demonstrable—indeed, as Henderson's impressive review of research (1987) shows, virtually indisputable!

Volunteers can improve the lives of children and youth and help create better, safer schools by serving in school programs, neighborhood watch organizations and civic groups or by being part of community education projects (Andrews & Linden, 1984; Decker & Decker, 1988; Decker, Grimsey & Horyna, 1990; Scrimger & Elder, 1981). In one troubled Indianapolis high school, a group of fathers calling themselves "Security Dads" became the catalyst in a remarkable change; this school, once "notorious for its atmosphere of danger, has become a peaceful place of high-spirited teamwork and eager learning" (Whittemore, 1992, p. 12). These "small miracles" can and do occur in urban, suburban and rural settings, but they are all too infrequent.

A potentially useful twist on the "traditional" adult volunteer model involves secondary and postsecondary students in school and community service. Many aspects of such programs have not yet been fully evaluated, but the examples of student service that have been studied—such as same-age and older-to-younger student tutoring—have yielded significant educational and personal benefits for both givers and receivers (Conrad & Hedin, 1991).

Bringing the "Outsiders" In

Volunteers who spend many hours in schools may be accepted by teachers and staff members as part of the school family. Others, however, are traditionally viewed as outsiders. We believe this to be a giant—but fortunately correctable—mistake. Most working parents, a growing percentage of whom are single, are unable to serve in or even visit the school on a regular basis, at least during standard school hours. Many think of the school as an intimidating, perhaps even inhospitable, place. We maintain that a concerted, deliberate effort to accommodate these "outsiders" is clearly in the interest of parents, educators and students. As Ryan (1976) remarks, "All too seldom do parents presume to suggest, or teachers admit, that 'we share a common concern' " (p. 120). Good parenting is not easy and schools can help if they will (Israeloff, 1992; Montgomery, 1992).

Social agencies are often thought of with the same disdain and they know it. They too should be brought into partnership with the schools. This notion is a largely unrealized legacy of "progressive" education (Sedlak & Schlossman, 1985). Whether the motive is to create safe schools or just good schools, *educators cannot do it alone* (Nicholson, Stephens, Elder & Leavitt, 1985). There are many examples in the professional literature of successful school-community and school-agency collaborations (e.g., Dryfoos, 1993; Higbee, 1991; Levy & Copple, 1989; Liontos, 1990; Melaville & Blank, 1993; Stone, 1993). That educators and officials from other agencies concerned with the health and welfare of children and youth should get along and work collegially seems apparent to us. Indeed, can there by any doubt?

But the obstacles are many and in some cases downright daunting, so much so that only the stout of heart, the most persistent and the extremely dedicated will endure. As Levy and Copple (1989) note,

> The barriers to successful collaboration between education and human services are many and imposing—restrictive laws, regulations, and policies; categorical funding streams; large and complex organizational

structures; very different jurisdictional boundaries and lack of comparability between governance structures; differing professional orientations, training, and vocabulary; competing pressures and priorities; "turfism"; the difficulty of establishing intersystem accountability; and the time and resources the collaborative process itself absorbs. (p. 15)

Robinson and Mastny (1989) decry a dominating leadership approach which tends to discourage group decision making, a failure to listen, top-down and expedient forms of administration and other inhibitors to collaboration. Firestone and Drews (1987) speak to the concern for institutional survival, regulations and personal qualities of administrators as factors that can get in the way of harmonious interaction and sharing between or among agencies; they found that both interagency conflicts and service blockages were major problems. It is clear, however, that none of these barriers is insurmountable (Levy & Copple, 1989).

Interagency Cooperation

Even better than schools just working with individual agencies is the prospect of true multiagency or interagency interaction on behalf of students (Davies, Burch & Palanki, 1993; Dryfoos, 1991, 1993; Elder, 1980; Robinson & Mastny, 1989; Ringers, 1976). Illustrative of the agencies with which a school staff might work to help reduce violence and other threats to a safe school are those listed by Kadel and Follman (1993): social service providers, early childhood specialists, mental health/family counselors, medical practitioners, court judges and probation officers, parks and recreation department representatives and staff of state departments of education, health and human resources. A level of trust, equality and balance are among the elements of a successful interagency collaboration (Fertman, 1993).

Banding together to address gang violence and other problems yielded positive results as two cities in the Pacific Northwest—Portland and Tacoma—found (Gaustad, 1991; Nebgen, 1990). In Tacoma, for example, various community organizations (service clubs, block-watch groups and PTAs), public schools, businesses, government agencies, labor unions, secondary students, religious organizations and prevention and treatment agencies all united in a safe schools campaign (Nebgen, 1990).

One of the duties of a grand jury, which is empaneled as a citizens' group with investigative powers, is to study the integrity and efficiency of county government (Beale & Bryson, 1992; Coalition to End Grand Jury Abuse, 1977; Grout, 1970). In the end-of-year grand jury reports we have seen, one of the problems that turns up consistently is a lack of interagency cooperation. It is perhaps not surprising that this is a difficulty common to many communities across the nation. That it cries out for attention is apparent. It may be equally evident that this is a problem that seems to elude an easy solution.

Law Enforcement and Schools

In the Tacoma case and in several others documented in the professional literature, DARE (Drug Abuse Resistance Education) officers worked with students, beginning at the elementary level, to teach them about illegal drugs and the value of substance abuse prevention (Alcohol and Drug Defense Program, 1990; Green, Wooldridge & Bowman, 1992; Kadel & Follman, 1993; Nebgen, 1990). Kadel and Follman (1993) call the use of DARE and other school resource officers (SROs) a "dynamite idea," indicating that SROs provide a variety of other services to students and staff members too, tailored to a particular school and its needs, including classes on law, drug and alcohol prevention and life skills; many will teach the DARE certification course or a similar program.

SROs do not, in fact, like to be thought of as security guards because "guard" does not accurately describe what they do (Hackle, 1994). Rather, having undergone a specific training course, they are specialized peace officers who interact with teenagers and build trust between youth and law enforcement. They serve "as a visible and positive image for law enforcement" (Kadel & Follman, 1993, p. 42), offer student counseling and provide law enforcement on school campuses.

Do SRO programs work? Kadel and Follman (1993) indicate that both participating schools and law enforcement officials have found these programs *are* successful in reducing school violence, enhancing the collaborative efforts between schools and law enforcement and, perhaps, of greatest importance, improving perceptions and relations between law enforcement and students. Rubel (1986) dicusses police liaison programs beginning back in the 1960s. Positive relations between schools and police are most likely to be achieved, he finds, when schools initiate the contacts, placing police and educators on the same team.

In a 1992 National Center for Education Statistics report (Mansfield

& Farris), sixty-nine percent of public school principals stated that "police provided assistance or educational support to a great or moderate extent in promoting safe, disciplined, and drug-free schools" (p. iii). About half of these principals received the same level of support from social services agencies and parent groups. Some years back, Ringers (1976) spoke of how many communities used "law enforcement personnel to establish youth resource sections to provide counseling for problem youth and to develop a spirit of trust between youth and the authorities" (p. 81). This

> . . . resource unit attends athletic contests, holds rap sessions, arranges rumor clinics, provides instructional program units, sponsors clubs or other activities, and in general strives to develop confidence in law and order as well as good safety habits. They [members of the resource unit] are particularly effective in calming down difficult situations. While the initial period of such a program may be viewed with suspicion, youth resource officers tend to become respected members of the Community/ School adjunctive team. (p. 81)

In the 1960s and 1970s, according to Blauvelt (1984), the general national opinion developed that most educators were soft on crime and most police officers were "poorly trained sadists who were more interested in 'busting heads' than in assisting a school principal plan for and engage in crime prevention. Fortunately, for both sides," he avers, "this climate has now changed; both police and school officials recognize the many advantages gained through cooperation" (p. 1).

Blauvelt (1984) calls for effective communication and the establishment of a partnership between the schools and all three elements of the criminal justice system—police, courts and corrections. Once such communication recognizes that both partners—the school system and the criminal justice system—have different clients and different needs, he says, we can begin "to break the cycle of frustration and mutual distrust that seems to have been the byword for decades" (p. 3).

The Media

Educational leaders must also not forget the part played by the print and electronic media when a community is attempting to establish safe and productive schools. The media can be of enormous help in such an endeavor or, as is so often the case, serve in a more adversarial role. Clearly, there is much educational leaders can—and probably should—do to improve and take advantage of the school-media relationship (Bagin, Gallagher & Kindred, 1994; Kadel & Follman, 1993; Lober, 1993; Warren, 1994). McQuaid issued an alarm in 1989 that press reporting regarding schools and education in general was typically mediocre, inappropriately selective and frequently superficial; moreover, many educational beat reporters have a fairly limited understanding of the field. Fearing "a backlash of negative coverage" (p. K8) if they criticize the quality of press handling of educational issues, most institutions will not, he says, complain too loudly.

The fact is that the press tends to be very self-critical. Hence, it makes good sense, McQuaid (1989) counsels, for educators to demand better. We are uncertain of the extent to which school leaders have followed McQuaid's advice or how he would assess the caliber of media coverage today. Our experience in working with the media, especially newspapers, is that most reporters and editors do care about covering the news that people want to know about and, we find, probably no area of local interest exceeds that of how well the community's children and youth are being served.

On any given day in most newspapers, there will be both national press service reports and local stories regarding the educational profession, how politicians are currying the favor of the electorate with their version of better-education initiatives and changes or happenings in the field. It is not naive in our view to believe that the media can be enlisted to support good-faith efforts to make and keep the community's schools safe, particularly when part of the strategy involves a strengthening of curricula and of instructional practices. The media do not have to abdicate their responsibility to provide fair, comprehensive and impartial coverage to serve a legitimate role in forging a better community.

THE REAL WORLD AS IT IS NOW

There are countless situations involving elementary, middle school and high school children and youths, their families, the schools and other agencies. Most practicing administrators and teachers can recount instances when school-agency and interagency cooperation saved the day and perhaps even more when a lack of it led to unresolved problems or even disasters. Four situations come immediately to mind.[3]

---

[3]The names of people and schools in the four scenarios have been changed.

The Fruit That Falls from This Tree

Davey, a fifth grader, and his sister Molly, in the third grade, attend Oakbrook School, a K–5 serving a wide variety of socioeconomic levels. Both children frequently wear dirty clothes and are usually in need of a bath. School officials' talks with their mother about the children's hygiene on a number of occasions have been unproductive. Contacted several times, Child Welfare Service views this "problem" to be of low priority and takes no action.

While Molly works below grade level, she is quiet and not considered a discipline problem. Davey gets some special help, but he is mainstreamed for most of the day. Both children receive free breakfasts and lunches at school. Davey is teased by other children who call him "Stinky." Efforts by teachers and administrators have reduced but not eliminated this behavior.

Davey brought a very realistic model of a gun to the school playground one Saturday morning and waved it at other children in an aggressive manner. The police were called; they confiscated the model gun and cited Davey. The school decided not to take action since the incident occurred outside normal school hours.

Several students say that Davey has now threatened to bring a real gun to school and "get them." When his teacher and principal confront him with this allegation, Davey is sullen and denies he has made such a statement. The police are summoned but indicate that, unless an actual gun is involved, there has been no crime and, anyway, they do not have adequate personnel to send an officer to the school. They suggest calling Child Welfare Services (CWS). Because of a poor response in the past, school officials are reluctant, but believe the threat to be real and call. CWS says it does not become involved unless there is a danger to the child in the home and recommends calling the police.

Frustrated, the principal finally phones his school's DARE officer. Though such problems are not normally the function of the DARE program, it is not uncommon for the DARE officer to be contacted when the school is unable to solve them. Upon checking, the DARE officer eventually learns that the home is known to police. It seems the father has been out of the home for about two years because of domestic violence toward the mother. However, despite restraining orders, he regularly shows up at the house. He is often drunk and sometimes beats the children's mother in their presence. He has been arrested numerous times, but the mother will not prosecute. She is on welfare and periodically lets the father move back in, accepting support from him in addition to her regular welfare payments. Most of the neighbors are aware that the mother has a drug problem, routinely see the children alone and often provide them with food. This has been informally reported to the police and CWS, but the neighbors will not go on the record so no action has been taken.

Davey was sexually molested when he was in the first grade by one of his mother's friends. Currently, there is another man in the house who has been staying there off and on. Further investigation reveals that this man is on probation for child molestation, and, even though he is not supposed to be in the vicinity of children, the mother has covered for him with probation, saying that there are no children in the house when she is asked. In fact, the mother has on several occasions let this molester watch her children while she has gone shopping.

Based on this information, a raid was made on the home. Drugs were found, and evidence of molestation of both children was uncovered. The molester went back to prison, the children were placed with the grandmother and the mother was forced to confront her drug problem. Two guns were removed from the home. Both children improved in school, and the hygiene problem was corrected. The threat of the child bringing a gun to school was dealt with and a possible catastrophe averted.

At least for now, the situation appears to have been defused. Still, one must wonder how much better and faster an answer could have been found had the agencies cooperated and shared information. And, of course, it is a little scary to think what would have happened had there been no DARE officer to turn to.

Guilt by Association

There is the case of two brothers, sixth-grade Jeff and second-grade Bill, who are intradistrict transfers to a basically upper middle class, K–8 Merrytimes Elementary School. Facing declining enrollment and a possible resultant loss of teachers, the school has sought other students to boost its ADA. The boys have difficulty adjusting to the new school, get into trouble, and show little remorse when caught. Teachers and other school officials work hard to help the students and both show signs of improvement, but their progress is not sustained.

A new custodian is suspected in a rash of school thefts from classrooms and teachers' purses and cars. As in the case of Davey, eventually the school's DARE officer is asked for help. Aware of similar thefts at other schools, he checks with his department's detectives who indicate they are working on an active case regarding the mother and aunt of the two boys. The investigation and a search of the house reveals that the aunt and mother were using the children to divert attention while they stole money and property from various schools and hospitals in the area.

Child welfare had an ongoing case for neglect. Both the aunt and mother were on probation. The father was on parole for grand theft and knowledge of these burglaries sent him back to prison. The aunt was committing welfare fraud. Jeff and Bill were frequently left at their maternal grandfather's home while their mother and aunt were away for long periods of time. The grandfather was beaten when he objected and was himself the victim of various thefts. Because of elder abuse, this case also involved the Ombudsman Services.

It is, of course, important for schools to have good community involvement and interaction, but this case also makes it apparent how critical it is to establish effective networking among schools and school districts, especially in this era of frequent relocation of families from school to school, county to county and even state to state. Both academic records *and* special considerations that a student brings to a new school community must be shared.

This Should Be a Time for Living!

The product of a loving, happy home, Tom did well in school until he reached Edgeton Middle School. Initially well-liked by his teachers, Tom's only brushes with trouble at school came when he followed someone else's lead. This propensity to follow concerned his teachers and parents. At Edgeton, he met another boy, Pete, who had lived an entirely different life. Though previously removed from his drug-addicted parents' home twice and placed in foster care, by the time he was in middle school, there was no one to report neglect in his home and Pete was able to come and go as he wished. He got some food at home, some from friends and some by stealing. He was on probation for theft and had completed several stints in juvenile hall. Forced to attend Edgeton to obtain release from juvenile hall, Pete, a bright boy, does well in school despite attendance and discipline problems.

Many were troubled by the friendship between Tom and Pete. Probation was approached, but did not intercede. Tom's parents were unsuccessful in their attempts to break up the contact. Tom was arrested for shoplifting and released to his parents. Had police been aware of the association, they may have caught Pete at the same time. Had this happened, the contact would have been severed by probation. Seeing the effect on his parents and having experienced the scare of juvenile probation, Tom did break off the friendship for a while.

Some weeks later, though, Pete talked Tom into going with him to "see something special." The boys were observed conversing after school by teachers and others who did not think they could take any action. Pete persuaded Tom to try some marijuana and drink some beer. Now intoxicated, Pete showed Tom a handgun he had stolen in a burglary, and in handling the gun it went off and struck Tom in the chest, killing him instantly. This took place less than a quarter mile from the school. Had all the agencies involved worked together and used a common strategy, they might well have prevented a tragedy and helped both boys.

Of course, this also raises questions regarding the inability of authorities to consider appropriately the needs of a child without caring or capable parents, and with an overburdened and less-than-adequate foster care program. As we see it, we essentially throw these young people away.

Ricky of the Streets

Ricky was placed with his aunt when he was in the sixth grade. His mother is on drugs and is no longer able to care for him or his sister who lives with another relative. Ricky is the victim of child molestation and does not perform very well in school. By the time he reaches Morningmont High School, he is on probation for shoplifting and is far behind most of his classmates in his academics.

Ricky's aunt favors her own children and makes it clear to Ricky that what he does is of little concern as long as it does not cause her a problem. After repeated probation violations, the aunt threatens to send him back to his mother to a life that Ricky recalls with horror: being abandoned, living in a car and not having enough to eat. The living conditions at the aunt's house are not appreciably better. Several reports by neighbors to Child Protective Services have yielded little beyond some half-hearted counseling attempts that have produced no discernible change in the family.

In high school Ricky does poorly, frequently cuts class, and is often in trouble. He is approached by a gang that offers Ricky the first people in his memory who really seem to care about him. In trade for this,

Ricky is soon selling drugs at school and is involved in violence toward other students that the gang wishes to intimidate. Before long, Ricky has participated in a gang rape, a drive-by shooting and numerous burglaries. Now caught, he can expect some time in a maximum-security youth detention facility.

Teachers who had Ricky in elementary and middle school and, for that matter, in his first years of high school remember him as a likable, quiet and extremely unhappy child. Again and again, they said that something should have been done by someone. Efforts to obtain agency intervention met with disinterest, apathy and sometimes even anger on the part of overworked government officials. Everyone seems to agree that, had all those who were or logically might have been "involved" worked together with a common strategy, this story might—indeed, probably would—have had a very different and decidedly happier conclusion.

AN ALTERNATIVE PARADIGM

We envision a real world that we earnestly believe could be. Our experience, our review of the literature, and our involvement and discussion with principals in schools at every level in all sorts of settings lead us to the conclusion that any school can legitimately expect to provide an atmosphere for teaching and learning that is productive, stimulating and, yes, in the very best sense of this word, *safe*.

To do so, though, we are not talking about business as usual. In most schools, a substantial metamorphosis will need to occur—different orientations, expectations, ways of thinking, academic programs, instructional strategies and classroom and school organization. Private and public institutions and agencies, families (however we may find them), and individuals (including, certainly, educators, students and lay citizens) will all have to contribute. No school or community should be written off. What we have in mind can be—and, at least to some extent, has been—achieved in the most unlikely of neighborhoods.

Prognosis: Decline or Renaissance?

It seems to us that schools will get better or worse. However much many might want it to be different, in the dynamic age in which we live, schools—perhaps even more than most other societal institutions—cannot opt for the status quo. In any case, most existing situations appear to us to have little to recommend them; and, we suspect, any fleeting loyalty they command will be due only to the comfort of the familiar and fear of the unknown. Neither, we believe, can schools choose to return to a time gone by.

There are ways in which most schools are probably not as bad as they are frequently portrayed, maintains Gerald Bracey, in his third annual report on the condition of public education in October 1993. Indeed, as he shows, at least in some respects, American education is significantly better than it was thirty years ago.

Still, he acknowledges, as he did in the two previous years, that "American schools face many challenges, some of them horrific" (Bracey, 1993, p. 116). He chronicles some of the monumental predicaments of city schools and alludes "to the even more intractable problems in impoverished rural areas. Schools," he goes on to say, "in poor districts need resources that they are neither getting now nor are likely to get soon." He then gets to the heart of the matter, something not openly observed or owned up to by many in education, when he writes: "I am certain that in the U.S. there are unspecified numbers of incompetent teachers, corrupt administrators, and inept board members. Why," with a touch of cynicism, he asks, "should education be different from other institutions?" (p. 116).

It hardly seems possible that it has been more than ten years since *A Nation at Risk* warned that the United States was drowning in a tide of mediocrity (National Commission on Excellence in Education, 1983). This stern pronouncement and the findings of other, more research-based reports (e.g., Goodlad, 1983) prompted a decade of reform activity. Improvements have occurred, especially in the area of curriculum (e.g., National Council of Teachers of Mathematics, 1989). And, we are keeping at the task; though, as Terrel Bell (1993), Secretary of Education when *A Nation at Risk* was published, observed, we probably should have made greater progress. Clearly, the job *is* far from done; and, in fact, there are numerous instances at the district and site levels in which any reform that has occurred has been superficial or unsustained.

People's ideas as to what, if anything, ought to happen are legion. By no means are all the ideas compatible. As Berliner (1993) points out, some are structured from false premises. Others appear to be responsive to one or another political agenda more so than to answer a demonstrated need or to overcome an existing problem; neither do all "reformers" construct their new visions on the basis of educational excellence. Some proposals are a mixed bag, with some features which are very attractive and some of more questionable value. And, finally, there are those ideas which seem to have great promise, especially in particular circumstances. We believe, even where resources are extremely limited, that imaginative, dedicated, forward-thinking people can generate a positive outcome—persons of all stripes working together to create and nourish safe, sound schools.

The Goal, the Task

What are we looking for? We—the members of a community of teachers and learners—must first give definition to what we are aiming for; then decide how this goal can best be achieved; and, finally, pursue our site-appropriate, logically formulated plan with every ounce of vigor, discipline and determination we can muster. We want schools which are genuinely excellent—academically and otherwise—with a built-in dynamic to adjust appropriately to changing conditions and demographics. Where the starting point is less than ideal, we want schools which are as good as they can possibly be under the circumstances. Where there are obstacles in the path of the optimal realization of this goal, we must take every feasible step to remove, neutralize, circumvent or minimize them.

Part of being an excellent school or even a good school is in our view also being a safe school. Schools that are now unsafe can reasonably aspire to becoming safe schools; though, certainly, we recognize this is a bigger undertaking for some schools than others. We have already examined some of the "dimensions of the undertaking." What, then, in sum, is the task facing those who seek to establish and preserve safe schools? At the very least, as stated at the outset of this chapter, safe schools are those which provide a productive, healthy atmosphere and victimize neither teachers nor students with physical or psychological injury or abuse. According to this perspective, safe schools

> ... are characterized by sensitivity and respect for all individuals (including those of other cultural and ethnic backgrounds), an environment of nonviolence, clear behavioral expectations, disciplinary policies that are consistently and fairly administered, students' affiliation and bonding to the school, support and recognition for positive behavior, and a sense of community on the school campus. Safe schools also are characterized by proactive security procedures, established emergency response plans, timely maintenance, cleanliness, and a nice appearance of the campus and classrooms. (Crime Prevention Center, 1989, p. 2)

A Sense of Community

Where must we begin? Where crime, drug abuse, unemployment, homelessness, pollution and other painful manifestations of societal dysfunction flourish, the fallout from a lack of community sharing and cooperation are particularly apparent. And, as we indicated before, oftentimes it seems that our youngest citizens must suffer most from the negative effects of this inability to communicate, interact and collaborate. While this is generally attributed to the breakdown of the family, we believe that the deterioration of the community is more at fault. In fact, we find that one reason for a failure of the family is a lack of support in the community.

In the past, communities in our country helped raise children. Most citizens realized the importance of all the community's children; in them were the community's only hope for a robust future. We must recapture this concept of community, we contend, if we are going to turn around the problems facing our children and youth today. Indeed, we find that the escape to gangs by many of our young people is prompted not so much by a search for family, as has often been reported; but rather a desperate exploration of the sense of community that they feel is lacking.

We believe the logical starting place to regain this sense of community is in the schools. The school is where all our children come to learn and it is a natural hub of community activity. As all educators know, the school has of necessity assumed certain family responsibilities. In many cases, this includes providing breakfast and lunch and even teaching basic hygiene. Perhaps the best way to handle this increased role in family life is to embrace it. When we work with children, we have a much greater opportunity to bring about positive change than we do when we work with adults. If we make the school our focus as a community, we increase the potential that the changes we seek as a society will be realized.

A SOMEWHAT IMMODEST PROPOSAL

We propose a cooperative safe schools model. Dryfoos (1991) states that "the marriage between the school and 'everything else' is [already] taking place" (p. 135) in some places, at least as regards social and health services for so-called "at-risk students." This is a marriage born of necessity, not mere convenience, she asserts. However, such instances of sharing the role of "surrogate parents" to the large and growing "disadvantaged family" is largely limited to "places with individual charismatic leaders and sophisticated grant-getters" (p. 135).

Toward a Community School

Instead, Dryfoos's (1991) idea of what needs to occur

> . . . calls for a "community school"—a vital collaborative venture with open doors for the whole family and an array of community services: a satellite health clinic, mental health services, infant and child care center, outreach home-visiting services, after-school recreation and cultural events, adult education, drug treatment, life skills, and community service programs. This vision includes the location of a public assistance office on school grounds, so that young welfare parents are assured a role—a beautiful picture, and one that demonstrates the complexity of collaborative ventures, because at least ten different categorically funded and operated programs would have to be involved as well as the school's educational function. (p. 135)

Judging that a marriage broker would be required to realize her fantasy within the existing institutional and ideological climate, Dryfoos recommends the creation of a central youth development agency. She also believes that financial and other "incentives have to be offered to integrate programs and bridge the distance between schools and agencies" (p. 136).

Much of this vision makes sense to us. We like the idea of community schools. In fact, with Wilensky and Kline (1989), we advocate community renewal and recognize the reorganization of schools as models of community to be a step in this direction. We also agree with Dryfoos (1991) that it makes sense to concentrate services in the school. We realize, of course, that such a holistic view of the nature and mission of the school is a bold departure from the status quo in most schools. It is, perhaps, obvious that there will be a need for new functions to be defined and new relationships to be forged. We think the potential benefits of such an undertaking will certainly merit the considerable effort essential to get such an undertaking off the ground.

Who Will Do It and What Will They Do?

The key player is the principal; but not so much, we think, in negotiating between the school and public agencies as in serving as a "primary gatekeeper" (p. 556), as Dryfoos (1993) suggests, but in articulating meaning and a sense of urgency, in bringing possible partners together, and in providing leadership and energy to the enterprise. With regard to the creation of safe schools, we do not see the need for either a new layer of bureaucracy or substantial additional funding. We believe almost any competent and conscientious—though not necessarily charismatic—principal with persistence and a strong sense of purpose could pull this off. Of course, the execution of the vision would need to be localized to fit any given school situation.

The principal would enlist the support of officials in all agencies and entities working with the school on a regular basis to assign caseloads primarily by school attendance areas. Cases would be allocated to one person who deals with all incidents that are generated from that school. When that person is unavailable (due to illness or other reason), a case would have an initial responder but would be routed back to the assigned individual for record-keeping and any follow-up required.

These workers would meet with the principal at the school periodically (maybe weekly or biweekly) to share information and to determine if they can help each other in the interests of the children with whom they are working and the school. Contact can be maintained between meetings by a secure e-mail system that could often be provided by a local database at little or no cost. When multiple agencies are involved, a coordinating council of interested parties could devise a strategy to organize efforts and to make the best use of resources. This should cost very little to implement and should result in a cost savings after the plan is fully activated because it will reduce duplication of services by two or more agencies. Agencies involved might include police, probation, welfare, child welfare, public health, mental health, parole, the courts, the district attorney and the housing authority.

Private participants could include businesses, neighborhood watch, health services, foundations, Scouting, 4-H, service clubs, the Chamber of Commerce, the media and others with an interest in the school and its students. For some purposes (such as confidentiality concerns), at least initially, the private and public sides might need to be kept separate with the principal acting as liaison. When the organizations need to be linked, the principal can bring them together.

First Steps

At the outset, the principal should share the plan with his or her superintendent (who in turn may wish to speak with the board of education). The principal would probably next approach the community's governing body (e.g., a city council or board of supervisors) and obtain its member's support for the concept. Once secured, the coordinating council would issue a press release or make personal contact with the local print and electronic media. Ideally, the information given to the press will make clear the need for this coordinated effort and the direction the school is planning to take to implement this rough blueprint for action. We have recently taken this idea to two elementary principals and one superintendent; all are excited about the possibilities and will pursue the idea with their boards of education with no anticipated opposition.

The next step is to contact the department heads of public agencies, one by one, and ask each "to buy in" individually. This does not have to be accomplished all at once. Once a department assigns a worker to one's school, the project is up and running. The principal should work at making this a good relationship and publicize its success, using this to gain the cooperation of other participants. The private side will usually be very easy to get on board, especially with the success of the public side.

The initial setup will no doubt take some time, but probably not as much as one might imagine. The principal would make appointments with the various agency heads, giving in each instance a brief and informal—but thorough—presentation of what he or she is trying to accomplish and the rationale behind it. Eventually, this should mean the principal has to devote less time to the matters the agencies are working with. As the school begins getting the support it needs, we expect discipline problems to be less frequent. The principal will then have more time to devote to educational program improvement, the area almost all principals judge to be of greatest importance (Smith & Andrews, 1989). This should also have a salutary effect on both the school's safety and its soundness.

Principals should get these agency participants to the school site to meet the children. They should make it personal. When people are making decisions that affect people's lives, in our opinion, they should know the people involved.

A good initial step for many principals is to get a DARE program, a school resource officer or a campus police officer. As we indicated previously, having a uniformed presence at the school site does not have to be viewed in a negative way. One high school principal told us that he thought he would never have a police officer on campus. When some serious gang problems started up, however, he found he needed a police officer to protect his students from negative outside influences. He now says he would never again wish to be without a police officer assigned to his school. He notes that the youth attending his school love "their" policeman (in this instance the officer is male) and generally feel safer when he is around. With a police officer in the school, nonstudents rarely come on campus anymore. The many problems associated in the past with nonstudents in his school building and on the school grounds have been virtually eliminated.

What to Expect

With the evidence we have seen and read about, we are convinced that, in time, what we envision will create a transformation. Agency workers will no longer see themselves — or be seen by others — as frustrated, unappreciated bureaucrats with over-heavy caseloads who confront problems myopically and sometimes indifferently. They will be indispensable parts of a community team. Because the workload will be divided by school site and they will be working with their colleagues from other agencies and the school, they will have an improved understanding of each individual situation and its environmental context. They will contribute to the decision about what they and their partners should do to help improve or cope with each case.

Local businesses and industries will learn how they can be involved. With encouragement, they will give donations of time and money. This will be good for businesses and for the school. Business people will come to school and talk to students about how business and commerce fit into the community. They will know these students personally, mentor student apprentices and arrange part-time and summer jobs. Students and faculty members will learn what skills and experiences students need to succeed in the jobs that will be available in local factories and businesses. Personal involvement of business owners and employees will give students a more intimate connection and will bring down considerably the level of such crimes as vandalism and shoplifting.

People in the neighborhood around the school will hear and read about what is going on. Many will realize the importance of their involvement, wish to be a part of this effort, and be welcomed with open arms. Beyond membership in the school's parent-teacher group, they will be asked and will agree to reach out to other members of the neighborhood to promote the safety of the school. This will be done through the local neighborhood-watch organization. The school will become an institutional member and tap into this resource as one more helpmate in the goal of a safer school and community. (If a community has no neighborhood watch, the school can be instrumental in getting one started.)

More and more local citizens will feel comfortable at *their* school, join the neighborhood watch and volunteer, on rotation, to patrol the perimeter of the school in the mornings and afternoons. They will no longer be reluctant to make activities at the school their "business" and they will thus report, with the expressed gratitude of school personnel, any possibly suspicious happenings in or around the school. Reported cases will be fully investigated by the appropriate authorities.

In many instances, local and regional foundations will provide help in upgrading security measures at the school. These will be mostly inexpensive projects, approached one a time; they might include locks, alarms, lights, two-way radios and fences. Where required, matching funds may be obtained through school fund-raisers and business support. Foundation grants will be acknowledged at formal ceremonies attended by the media, putting further emphasis on the community aspect. Help and involvement will also be solicited from local service clubs. These are both an important source of funds and of additional persons to assist in school activities.

Administrators will get acquainted with the members of the media who cover their schools—reporters from radio, television, newspapers and local magazines. The media, used to being frozen out, will probably be flattered to be included in the school's plans. It will be recognized as an important conduit in getting information out to the general public.

Principals will solicit the active participation of private groups and individuals interested in promoting the school as the focus of the community. The school will be a hub of activity in the evening and on weekends. Adults and children alike will see the school as theirs. It will be—and be viewed as—a place where community education classes and meetings of community organizations are held. It will be a center for before- and after-school daycare for working parents (if public funds are unavailable for this, a combination of grants and volunteer support staff will help make this a reality; secondary schools can also provide daycare for teenage parents). This will attract parents to the school, and, where there is declining enrollment, raise the average daily attendance. Preschool children will also be seen as valuable members of the community. Exciting after-school programs will attract children who would otherwise be left to their own devices ("latchkey children"); this reduces both academic and safety problems.

CONCLUSION

We do not pretend that the ideas discussed and proposed here will be easy to implement. We know, however, that they are viable. And, even if there were no statistics to back up these recommendations, which in most cases there are, we believe it should be self-evident that the recommended steps are worth the effort. We think doing nothing is unacceptable. If we are right, and one must do something, he or she might as well choose a comprehensive plan which brings in help from many sources and promises to make a positive difference. Moreover, it is becoming painfully evident that schools cannot, even if they wish to, succeed in teaching students effectively or within a safe environment without the support of other community agencies and institutions.

Aleem et al. (1993) document the finding that drug/alcohol use, violence or at least discipline problems confront educators in almost every school almost every day. Hence, they join many others in insisting that we take most seriously the national goal that calls for providing a safe-schools environment for all students by the year 2000. They indicate that this goal is achievable if we do the "right" things.

On the other hand, we find merit in the reasoning of Kamii, Clark and Dominick (1994) that "schools cannot *offer* a disciplined environment"; rather, they argue, "a disciplined environment has to be *created from within* by students and teachers—together" (p. 676). They seek classroom practices which help develop autonomy in children. They would, for example, have educators 1) encourage students to make decisions and enforce their own rules, 2) foster intrinsic motivation and 3) promote the exchange among children of various points of view. We concur; indeed, children must be active participants in their own education and we certainly want them to grow up to be independent thinkers, capable of informed and logically reached decisions. We cannot do it for them. What we can do is help them. Along with parents, business people, agency workers and a host of others, educators can *help* students create a comparatively drug-free, violence-free, safe and disciplined teaching and learning environment. We believe all the ideas we have recommended in this chapter are compatible with the current research on how children grow and develop.

We agree with Doyle (1993), too, that there is much that is right with education and that the prospects for the future of American education are bright, *provided* we pay attention to constructive criticism, recognize that principals should be facilitators rather than autocrats, value the role of effort over innate ability, realize that all students can experience success and hold our schools to the standards of not only the best schools but the best among high-performance organizations of all kinds. Such school reform will be true reform. It *will* make a difference. Do not the most successful businesses, public agencies and schools today operate according to the principles of 1) full development of each individual to be an autonomous, competent human being; 2) the worth of the contributions of each person and organization involved in any venture; and 3) the efficient, prudent use of all resources?

Finally, we observe that most parents, it seems, have a natural inclination toward protecting their children. The school, acting *in loco parentis*, also wishes for children to be safe. Safe from what, protected from what? At least as far as we are concerned: Not from the consequences of their actions. Not from either physical or mental growth spurts. Not from the opportunity to be exposed to diverse multicultural ways of perceiving the world. Not from the pretty and even ugly lessons of history. Not from stimulating and powerful and happy and ecstatic and uplifting and stirring ideas. Nor, at least not completely, from those things that are boring and outrageous and derelict and discredited and depressing and even, when students are old enough to evaluate them intelligently, the heinous. Not from discovery or creativity or test tubes or pushups. Not from politics or polygons or iambic pentameter or the Pentagon or Emily Dickinson or Charles Dickens or Eric Dickerson. Or, for that matter, ten thousand or maybe ten million or probably even more thoughts, methodologies and opportunities.

From what then? The answer is really fairly simple. We want to save our children and our students from—for them to be safe from—that which will keep them from spreading their wings, from learning all that they can, all that they are able to. From that which would stop them from approaching—or even fail to encourage them to approach—their intellectual, physical, emotional, social and spiritual potential. From artificially imposed fear, from physical violence, from sexual abuse, from abject poverty, from psychological mistreatment. This seems reasonable enough. Would that it were easier. Caring parents make a difference. Unfortunately, though, even with the support of the most "advantaged" home, the schools cannot do all this for any child.

We have said that most schools will benefit from substantial—not superficial—changes programmatically and organizationally and that such changes will make a difference in terms of their relative safety. However, our primary purpose in this chapter was to attempt to show that *any* school, led by a capable principal, can develop a thoroughgoing collaboration with enlightened representatives of law enforcement, the media, social agencies, private institutions, foundations and school and neighborhood groups to achieve much safer schools—by our definition—than the schools by themselves would be able to accomplish. We close with this admonition: Perhaps in a given situation, a principal will need to obtain a waiver or seek for his school to become a charter school. Whatever hurdles must be jumped, whatever impediments must be overcome, we think a safe-schools network similar to the one proposed here, but adapted to meet local needs and accommodate local conditions, should be built in every school as soon as humanly possible.

REFERENCES

Alcohol and Drug Defense Program. (1990). *Drug Abuse Resistance Program: Administrative orientation* (rev. ed.). Raleigh: North Carolina Department of Public Instruction.

Aleem, D., Moles, O., Veltri, V., Rowan, B., Doyle, W., Cavanaugh, N., Chandler, K. & Grymes, J. (1993). *Review of research on ways to attain Goal Six: Creating safe, disciplined, and drug-free schools*. Washington, D.C.: U.S. Department of Education, Office of Educational Research and Improvement.

Andrews, D. D. & Linden, R. R. (1984, July). The role of volunteers in preventing rural child abuse. Paper presented at the annual conference of the National Institute on Social Work in Rural Areas, Orono, ME (ERIC Document Reproduction No. ED 257 794).

Beale, S. S. & Bryson, W. C. (1992). *Grand jury law and police* (2 vols.). New York: Clark Boardman Callaghan.

Bagin, D., Gallagher, D. R. & Kindred, L. W. (1994). *The school and community relations* (5th ed.). Boston: Allyn & Bacon.

Bell, T. H. (1993). Reflections one decade after *A nation at risk*. *Phi Delta Kappan*, 74:592–597.

Berliner, D. C. (1993). Mythology and the American system of education. *Phi Delta Kappan*, 74:632, 634–640.

Blauvelt, P. D. (1984). *Interface: Schools and police cooperation*. Bethesda, MD: National Alliance for Safe Schools.

Bracey, G. W. (1993). The third Bracey report on the condition of public education. *Phi Delta Kappan*, 75:104–112, 114–117.

Brodinsky, M. (1981). *Reporting: Violence, vandalism and other incidents in schools.* Arlington, VA: American Association of School Administrators.

Burns, M. (1981). Groups of four: Solving the management problem. *Learning,* 10(2):46-51.

Carducci, D. J. & Carducci, J. B. (1984). *The caring classroom: A guide for teachers troubled by the difficult student and classroom disruption.* Palo Alto, CA: Bull Publishing.

Coalition to End Grand Jury Abuse. (1977). *So you're going to be a "grand juror?: A guide for more effective citizen participation in the grand jury system.* Washington, D.C.: Author.

Conrad, D. & Hedin, D. (1991). School-based community service: What we know from research and theory. *Phi Delta Kappan,* 72:743-749.

Crime Prevention Center. (1989). *Safe schools: A planning guide for action.* Sacramento: California Department of Education and California Office of the Attorney General.

Curwin, R. L. (1990). *Entering adulthood: Developing responsibility and self-discipline—A curriculum for grades 9-12.* Santa Cruz, CA: Network Publications.

Davies, D., Burch, P. & Palanki, A. (1993). *Fitting policy to family needs: Delivering comprehensive services through collaboration and family empowerment.* Boston: Center on Families, Communities, Schools, and Children's Learning.

Decker, L. E. & Decker, V. A. (1988). *Home/school/community involvement.* Arlington, VA: American Association of School Administrators.

Decker, L. E., Grimsey, R. P. & Horyna, L. L. (1990). *Community education: Building learning communities.* Alexandria, VA: National Community Education Association.

Doyle, D. P. (1993). American schools: Good, bad, or indifferent? *Phi Delta Kappan,* 74:626-631.

Dreyfuss, E. T. (1990). Learning ethics in school-based mediation programs. *Update on Law-Related Education,* 14(2):22-27.

Dryfoos, J. G. (1991). School-based social and health services for at-risk students. *Urban Education,* 26(1):118-137.

Dryfoos, J. G. (1993). Schools as places for health, mental health, and social services. *Teachers College Record,* 94:540-567.

Duke, D. L. & Meckel, A. M. (1980). Disciplinary roles in American schools. In K. Baker & R. J. Rubel (Eds.), *Violence and crime in the schools* (pp. 101-113). Lexington, MA: Lexington Books.

Elder, J. O. (1980). Essential components of interagency collaboration. In J. O. Elder & P. R. Magrab (Eds.), *Coordinating services to handicapped children: A handbook for interagency collaboration* (pp. 181-201). Baltimore: Paul H. Brookes.

Ellis, T. R. (1989). Good teachers don't worry about discipline. *Principal,* 69(4):16-18, 20.

Fertman, C. (1993). Creating successful collaborations and community agencies. *Children Today,* 22(2):32-34.

Firestone, W. A. & Drews, D. H. (1987). *The coordination of education and social services: Implications from three programs.* Philadelphia: Research for Better Schools.

Fletcher, K. B. (1987). *The nine keys to successful volunteer programs.* Washington, D.C.: Taft Group.

Furtwengler, W. J. & Konnert, W. (1982). *Improving school discipline: An administrator's guide.* Boston: Allyn & Bacon.

Gaustad, J. (1991). Schools respond to gangs and violence [Issue]. *OSSC Bulletin,* 34(9).

Goodlad, J. I. (1979). *What schools are for.* Bloomington, IN: Phi Delta Kappa Educational Foundation.

Goodlad, J. I. (1983). *A place called school: Prospects for the future.* New York: McGraw-Hill.

Green, C. R., Wooldridge, B. & Bowman, D. (1992). *Qualitative analysis of teaching strategies in the DARE program.* Knoxville: City of Knoxville Police Department (ERIC Document Reproduction No. ED 358 065).

Grout, L. J. (1970). *Handbook for grand jurors of Georgia.* Athens: University of Georgia, Institute of Government.

Hackle, A. (1994, September 25). High school cop is the real thing. *Statesboro Herald,* p. 3A.

Henderson, A. (1987). *The evidence continues to grow: Parent involvement improves student achievement.* Columbia, MD: National Committee for Citizens in Education.

Hensel, J. (1991). Making choices: Lowell Elementary turns tradition upside down and creates something that works. *Currents in One,* 12(1):4–5.

Higbee, P. S. (1991). *How rural schools can build alliances for at-risk youth.* Spearfish, SD: Black Hills Special Services Cooperative.

Hyman, I., Stern, A., Lally, D., Kreutter, K., Berlinghof, M. & Prior, J. (1982). Discipline in the high school: Organizational factors and roles for the school psychologist. *School Psychology Review,* 11:409–416.

Israeloff, R. (1992, October). How to talk to your child's school. *Parents,* pp. 115–120.

Kadel, S. & Follman, J. (1993). *Reducing school violence in Florida.* Palatka, FL: SouthEastern Regional Vision for Education (SERVE).

Kamii, C., Clark, F. B. & Dominick, A. (1994). The six national goals: A road to disappointment. *Phi Delta Kappan,* 75:672–677.

Levy, J. E. & Copple, C. (1989). *Joining forces: A report from the first year.* Alexandria, VA: National Association of State Boards of Education.

Liontos, L. B. (1990). *Collaboration between schools and social services.* Eugene, OR: ERIC Clearinghouse on Educational Management (ERIC Document Reproduction No. ED 320 197).

Lober, I. (1993). *Promoting your school: A public relations handbook.* Lancaster, PA: Technomic Publishing Co., Inc.

Mancuso, W. A. (1983). Take these steps to keep schools safe and secure. *Executive Educator,* 5(7):24–25, 27.

Mansfield, W. & Farris, E. (1992). *Public school principal survey on safe, disciplined, and drug-free schools: Contractor report* (National Center for Education Statistics rep.). Washington, D.C.: U.S. Department of Education, Office of Educational Research and Improvement.

McQuaid, E. P. (1989). A story at risk: The rising tide of mediocre education coverage [*Kappan* special rep.]. *Phi Delta Kappan,* 70(5):K1–K8.

Melaville, A. I. & Blank, M. J. (1993). *Together we can: A guide for crafting a profamily system of education and human services.* Washington, D.C.: Center for the Study of Social Policy.

Montgomery, D. (1992). EPIC: Helping school life and family support each other. *Schools in the Middle,* 1(3):3–5.

National Commission on Excellence in Education. (1983). *A nation at risk: The imperative for educational reform.* Washington, D.C.: U.S. Government Printing Office.

National Council of Teachers of Mathematics, Commission on Standards for School Mathematics. (1989). *Curriculum and evaluation standards for school mathematics.* Reston, VA: Author.

National Institute of Education. (1978). *Violent schools–safe schools: The safe school study report to Congress.* Washington, D.C.: Author.

Nebgen, M. (1990). Safe streets in Tacoma. *The American School Board Journal,* 177(10):26–27.

Nicholson, G., Stephens, R., Elder, R. & Leavitt, V. (1985). Safe schools: You can't do it alone. *Phi Delta Kappan,* 66:491–496.

O'Connell, B. & O'Connell, A. B. (1989). *Volunteers in action.* New York: Foundation Center.

Post, J. (1991). *Into adolescence: Stopping violence—A curriculum for grades 5-8.* Santa Cruz, CA: Network Publications.

Quarles, C. L. (1993). *Staying safe at school.* Thousand Oaks, CA: Corwin.

Ringers, J., Jr. (1976). *Community/schools and interagency programs: A guide.* Midland, MI: Pendell.

Robinson, E. R. & Mastny, A. Y. (1989). *Linking schools and community services: A practical guide.* Morristown, NJ: Geraldine R. Dodge Foundation.

Rubel, R. J. (1986, November). Student discipline strategies: School system and police response to high risk and disruptive youth. Paper presented at the Working Meeting on Student Discipline Strategies Analysis, Office of Educational Research and Improvement, U.S. Department of Education, Washington, D.C. (ERIC Document Reproduction No. ED 315 906).

Ryan, C. (1976). *The open partnership: Equality in running the schools.* New York: McGraw-Hill.

Schriro, D. (1985). *Safe schools, sound schools: Learning in a non-disruptive environment.* New York: ERIC Clearinghouse on Urban Education (ERIC Document Reproduction No. ED 253 602).

Schwartz, A. J. (1988, April). Principals' leadership behaviors in gang-impacted high schools and their effects on pupil climate. Paper presented at the annual meeting of the American Educational Research Association, New Orleans (ERIC Document Reproduction No. ED 296 451).

Scrimger, G. C. & Elder, R. (1981). *Alternatives to vandalism: "Cooperation or wreakreation."* Sacramento: Office of the Attorney General, School Safety Center.

Sedlak, M. W. & Schlossman, S. (1985). The public school and social services: Reassessing the progressive legacy. *Educational Theory,* 35:371–383.

Smith, W. & Andrews, R. L. (1989). *Instructional leadership: How principals make a difference.* Alexandria, VA: Association for Supervision and Curriculum Development.

Stone, C. R. (1993). *School-community collaboration: Comparing three initiatives.* Madison, WI: Center on Organization and Restructuring of Schools.

Vestermark, S. D., Jr. & Blauvelt, P. D. (1978). *Controlling crime in the school: A complete security handbook for administrators.* West Nyack, NY: Parker.

Warren, C. (1994). *Promoting your school: Going beyond PR.* Thousand Oaks, CA: Corwin.

Whittemore, H. (1992, September 27). Dads who shaped up a school. *Parade Magazine,* pp. 12–13.

Wilensky, R. & Kline, D. M., III. (1989). School reform and community renewal. *Equity and Choice,* 5(2):13–18.

CHAPTER 12

School-Based Intervention: The Tucson, Arizona, Model

GAIL BORNFIELD
ROGER PFEUFFER

INTRODUCTION

TUCSON Unified School District (TUSD) lies within the Pima County boundaries in southern Arizona, sixty miles north of the Mexican border. TUSD serves approximately 61,000 students from diverse cultural heritages. Within the district's boundaries, there are 104 school sites.

To understand the needs of TUSD, it is necessary to look at a profile of the city of Tucson and Pima County. A Tucson/Pima County community profile was developed by a diversity project that brought people together from all walks of life—from government and business, from health centers and neighborhood centers, from schools and human resource agencies, from homes and places of cultural and spiritual enrichment. This group worked for two years to identify the strengths, trends and needs of the Tucson/Pima County community in the hopes of developing creative ways to enhance the quality of life (Southern Arizona Committee, 1991).

There are approximately 100,000 students enrolled in 123 elementary schools, thirty-two middle schools, five junior high schools, twenty high schools and four alternative schools. Nearly 61,000 of those students are enrolled in Tucson Unified School District. Enrollment is expected to increase steadily, particularly in areas with large Latino populations.

Arizona ranked forty-sixth nationally in high school graduates in 1990, a decline from the thirty-sixth position in 1985. The dropout rate for American Indian students reached 55% in 1993. Enrollment in adult education programs has increased by 71% in the past six years. Enrollment figures reflect a large number of people who cannot read, write or communicate at a level adequate to fulfill their personal and professional goals. Some are learning disabled; others are not proficient in English. Many require assistance in academic development and job training.

Bilingualism has become increasingly important to personal and professional success within the the community. However, there is also a great need for multicultural fluency. Multicultural fluency means a strong working knowledge of various cultures. The total community needs to have a better understanding of the different cultures within it.

Security is important to the people of Tucson. Fundamental to the security of a community is the requirement of meeting the basic needs of its people. The community offers a wide variety of services, but poverty continues to be present. In Pima County, 23% of all children under the age of eighteen years live in poverty. For children under the age of five years residing in female-headed households, the figures rise to 57.8%. There is also a shortage of affordable housing in Pima County. More than 10,000 people experience homelessness in Tucson each year.

When people suffer constant stress because of poverty, high unemployment, poor housing or homelessness and hunger, they are at increased risk for behavioral health problems such as alcohol and other drug abuse, violence and suicide. Crime by juveniles, especially crime of a violent nature, has increased dramatically. Between 1991 and 1992 there was a 340% increase (from five to twenty-two) in number of juveniles arrested for charges of homicide and attempted homicide.

Another problem facing the community is the high rate of pregnancy among unwed mothers. At this point, 32.5% of all births in Pima County are to unwed mothers. Teen pregnancy is also a great concern with 13.4% of all births to women under twenty years of age.

Life expectancy is often related to gender or ethnicity. Anglo-American females and males in Pima County, on the average, live longer than other population groups. American Indian males in Pima County have the lowest life expectancy (forty-nine years).

Homicides, most often the result of fatal assaults with firearms or stabbing, are the fourth leading cause of death for children between one and fourteen years of age in Pima County. Homicide is the fifth leading cause of death in the fifteen- to forty-four-year age group in Pima County.

Women receiving late or no prenatal care in Pima County represent 36.1% of all pregnancies. This contributes to the 6.3% of all infants entering the world with low birth weight. Reports of child abuse and neglect total 5.3% of all children under the age of eighteen years.

Pima County has a large population of students with limited English proficiency, totaling 8.4%. The high school dropout rate is 10.5%.

Juvenile arrest rate for teens eight to eighteen years old in Pima County is 11.3%. Juveniles sentenced to county detention centers represent 3.4% of all teens. Those sentenced to state correction facilities total .17%. Juvenile arrests are rising in Pima County. A 25% increase between 1985 and 1990 has resulted in an arrest rate of one out of every nine children ages eight to eighteen years. Arrests for violent crimes (armed robbery, rape, aggravated assault, murder, manslaughter) increased 56% between 1985 and 1990. These statistics are also reflected in suspension and arrest rates on campuses in the district. The records on suspension rates from schools across grade levels reflect increases over a three-year period.

As exemplified by the community profile, many students in TUSD come to school with needs beyond gaining academic skills. TUSD has made great efforts toward addressing these needs through the implementation of numerous programs throughout the district.

The district received the 1993 Golden Bell Award from the Arizona School Boards Association. This award is given to exemplary programs in school safety within the state of Arizona. TUSD's efforts toward safe schools have also been recognized by the Council of Great City Schools (Newkumet & Casserly, 1994). Safety programs implemented districtwide were recognized as a standard-setting program.

SCHOOL-BASED INTERVENTION PROGRAMS

Strategies for intervention used by the Tucson Unified School District are divided into categories: prevention, intervention and safety. Several of the strategies used by the district are applicable across all three categories. The prevention component includes the articulation of school-based programs as well as district policies aimed at reducing and eliminating violence on campuses.

Prevention

There are two facets to prevention. The first is early prevention or activities designed to keep students out of gangs. The second facet of prevention refers to preventing violence on school campuses.

TUSD approaches prevention from both of these perspectives and has developed strategies in both areas. Strategies designed to prevent students from joining gangs encompass several levels. The first level is the policy level. The school board has formulated a diversity policy that has led to 1) increased emphasis on culture, 2) modification of the curriculum to enhance cultural relevancy and 3) emphasis on the value of cultural diversity. At this point, a new social studies curriculum has been written and adopted by the district for K–12. The motivation for the development and adoption of the new curriculum was the Diversity Appreciation Policy adopted in November, 1991. The second outcome of this policy has been a revision in the required books for high school literature courses. The new selections contain material or content that reflect the culture of the city and state. The literature books also reflect the focus of the social studies curriculum, thereby allowing for the integration of two subject areas.

School District Programs

TUSD has also adopted curricula for use with students in K–8 that encourages the use of alternatives to violence. These include "Peacebuilders" and "Path of the Warrior" developed by Heartspring, Inc., Tucson, Arizona.

Prevention activities assist elementary and middle school students to develop skills that will ultimately reduce youth violence. Peacebuilders is a curriculum designed to provide teachers with tools to help children begin to make healthy, safe choices when it doesn't seem possible to them. This curriculum advocates six active core steps for children and adults.

- noticing and praising prosocial behavior in others who do something positive for you
- reducing the use of putdowns and demonstrating respect
- noticing and speaking up about hurts caused by oneself to others and offering ways to right the wrong
- using wise people and resources as mentors
- picturing the good that can be and actions that can bring it about
- avoiding situations that produce victimization

In order to implement these steps and to reduce the chances of violence, Peacebuilders advocate the use of four behaviors:

- modeling prosocial behaviors

- providing rationales for such prosocial behaviors
- prompting these behaviors in many contexts
- rewarding and recognizing the use of prosocial behaviors in many difficult situations

Peacebuilders is designed for grades K-5. It is integrated into daily actions in classrooms and schools. Peacebuilding activities do not take extra classroom time. It uses daily rituals to increase signals of cooperation and reduce signals of threat.

The middle school curriculum is called Path of the Warrior. This curriculum advocates and trains in the use of positive coping strategies that address the impact of behavior on oneself and others as well as its real-life consequences. Social coping strategies are presented through the vehicle of challenges to the warrior:

- Show respect when faced with disrespect.
- Seek wise people as advisors and friends.
- Picture the good that can be, then act to bring it about.
- Look for the good in others and acknowledge it.
- Watch for danger and act to make yourself and others safe.
- Speak up about wrongs you have done and offer ways to make them right.
- Increase the peace.

These challenges can be brainstormed in classrooms with students and/or teachers providing real-life examples for which solutions using one of the challenges can be generated. The idea, of course, is to get students to buy into the Path of the Warrior and change their behavior to live the warrior ideal.

The aforementioned policy and programs are designed to prevent young children from becoming involved with gangs by providing strategies that promote behaviors which are inconsistent with behaviors required for gang membership.

The other prevention component is concerned with current violence on campuses. A primary piece of this prevention component is the district "Guidelines for Rights and Responsibilities in Grades K through 12" (*Rights and Responsibilities Handbook*), which is a handbook designed to achieve a quality education for all students by presenting guidelines for student behavior. This is reviewed with all students enrolled, and copies are given to all parents. It is intended to create a positive and safe teaching and learning environment in the schools. This guide has replaced a board-adopted Code of Conduct. The guide was a collaborative effort of students, parents, teachers and principals.

School District Policies

The TUSD Governing Board has taken a public position on gang behavior and activity, which is stated very clearly in the handbook. "The behaviors that have become associated with gang activity or membership, especially violence, intimidation, and disrespect will not be tolerated on or near school property or in activities associated with school. In accordance with this zero-tolerance policy, any students engaging in gang activities will be disciplined and prosecuted, if applicable, to the fullest extent of district policies, local ordinances, and state and federal laws."

This is a very clear message to students and parents that gang activity will not be tolerated, and severe consequences can be expected for those who choose to participate in such activities. This serves as a prevention strategy in the sense that it is a clear warning to students of the consequences of gang activity, providing them the opportunity to engage in appropriate behavior.

An activity packet has been developed to accompany the *Rights and Responsibilities Handbook*. Teachers are instructed by principals on the handbook prior to school opening each fall. Posters with information on rules and consequences are placed in every classroom in the district. These are in the shape of a heart and referenced as the "Consequence Heart."

Another key to prevention is community collaboration that includes representatives from schools, juvenile authorities, families, business interests and other organizations. In Tucson, this occurs in part through a mayor's task force on violence.

Within the district, there is a Violence-Prevention Team, which is comprised of five violence-prevention specialists. This team is responsible for prevention as well as intervention and safety activities. As a part of prevention, they provide staff instruction on gang identification and related issues. They also provide awareness presentations for parents and community organizations. In addition, they have developed videotapes that can be used for informational meetings.

Many of the activities described in the intervention section have preventive components to them. Prevention is the most effective way to reduce youth violence.

Intervention

Intervention can be thought of as a means of interfering with attempts to proceed with gang activities on school campuses by students. The area of intervention can be divided into school district practices and school district programs.

School District Practices

Intervention can first be addressed by looking at current district practices related to violence on campuses. A ground level attempt at intervention is to look at basic security needs of a campus. TUSD employees are requested to protect their campuses by performing a few simple tasks:

- Secure all doors and windows.
- Keep keys on their person or in a secure area.
- Keep valuable items away from windows.
- Report broken windows and doors that cannot be secured to maintenance immediately.
- Report all broken inoperative security lights to maintenance as soon as possible.

TUSD also equips all of their facilities with intrusion alarm systems to detect unauthorized entry.

Each school site has established a site safety committee. Each safety committee is asked to conduct a safety needs assessment at their school sites. These needs assessments are presented to the assistant superintendent's office where they are reviewed and considered for implementation in the next year's budget building process. In order to facilitate the process of identifying safety needs, a school safety assessment checklist was developed. The checklist addresses a number of areas (e.g., perimeter, grounds, building entrances, hallways, bathrooms and stairwells).

For the perimeter of school grounds, safety issues relate to adequate fencing to limit unauthorized campus access, monitoring of entrances and the immediate removal of graffiti when observed. On the grounds, issues relate to blind spots, coverage in the event of an absence, knowledge of emergency-use procedures by monitors, and immediate observance and removal of graffiti. The immediate observation and removal of graffiti is important because it symbolizes territory for a particular gang and serves as a communication board for members. Immediate graffiti removal is a vital intervention strategy.

All indoor areas are monitored during heavy traffic times as well as off-times. Graffiti is constantly checked for and removed. Meetings are held with monitors daily to ensure that administrators are aware of all activities on their campuses, as well as to reinforce the importance of the monitoring activities. An "all is well" message is what we all want to hear every day!

At the elementary level, the checklist was expanded to include additional protections. These included ensuring that children are aware of recommended routes to and from school, keeping children away from easy-access parking lots, instruction in stranger-danger and providing badges to adults while they are on campus for easy identification. At the elementary level, it was recommended that crisis procedures be developed in the event of a hostage situation, drive-by shooting or bomb threat.

School District Programs

One program that has been successfully implemented is "School-Watch." This was modeled after the "Neighborhood-Watch" program. TUSD sent letters to neighbors within visual contact of district schools (104 sites) requesting their help. TUSD requested that they report any suspicious activities on the campus within their view to a twenty-four-hour phone number. Callers were told that they need *not* give either their name nor their address. There was a small reminder regarding tax dollars.

Within other schools, a program referred to as "TUSD Safe-T-Zone" was implemented. This program solicits commitment from staff, students and parents to support school safety proclaiming, "All schools must be safe: All staff and students are responsible for seeing that they are."

Within the Safe-T-Zone, violent or potentially violent situations cannot be ignored. Action must be taken when a confrontation is observed. This action can be direct interaction or reporting of the incident, but the key is *taking action*. Students as well as staff are asked to report incidents and to become involved in conflict resolution programs.

The Safe-T-Zone program asks staff and students to watch for potential problems. Things to look for include weapons, confrontations, large groups, clusters of rival groups, unusual movement of a group from its normal area, gang-related graffiti, nonstudents on campus, and rumors of any of the above. They are asked to report this information anonymously to a hotline number within the district.

Yet another program is that of "Parents on Patrol" (POP). This is a program designed to involve parents in the safety and security of schools. The program encourages parents, grandparents and other relatives to volunteer their time to assist school personnel. The volunteers become the eyes and ears of school staff, in addition to being highly visible on campus. They are not there to take any action other than to inform the school's staff of what is happening on the campus. The program is broken down into four phases.

Phase one involves putting together the team. A core group of at least five parents willing to volunteer their time needs to be identified in a school. A lead person or team leader can be elected or appointed to organize the program.

Phase two involves training for the team. A member of the Violence-Prevention Team conducts the training. The training consists of gang identification, what volunteers can and cannot do, review of the *Rights and Responsibilities Handbook,* liability issues, and a session with the administration and staff of their particular school.

Phase three involves the dissemination of equipment. Each volunteer receives a matching T-shirt and windbreaker. Each piece of clothing has the word *parent* printed across the back and on the front left pocket.

Phase four is implementation. The team leader schedules hours that members can work. The peak hours needed are before school, after school and during lunch. The school administration must be made aware of the number of persons working and their hours.

One of the most important ingredients in the safety program is a group of five staff members comprising the Violence-Prevention Team. The Violence-Prevention Team offers not only an intervention capability but also a number of educational and service programs to schools. Several of these programs involve building self-esteem and training in positive methods of conflict resolution. Students need specific competencies to resolve conflicts with peers and authority figures. Conflict resolution is basic training in a needed life survival skill. The team provides a program called "Circle Group," which focuses entirely on esteem building and conflict resolution. This program is available for a variety of age levels.

The Violence-Prevention Team also supports "Project S.O.A.R." (Student Opportunity for Academic Renewal). This project involves a partnership with the College of Education at the University of Arizona, Office of Multicultural Recruitment and Retention, and the Violence-Prevention Team to develop and provide a mentoring program for at-risk students. The basic premise of this project is that every child needs one adult who is irrationally crazy about him or her. Many of our children suffer from affection starvation. Mentoring programs can have a powerful impact on children's sense of self.

Another program sponsored by the Violence-Preventon Team is "Who Cares?" This program is directed toward students and is designed to reward good citizenship. Students are recognized for making a difference in the safety and security of their school.

"Who Owns Me?" is a program designed to teach students how to make safe-choice decisions. This program serves intermediate-aged students.

The Violence-Prevention Team is always available for mediation and intervention in crisis situations. They serve as front line staff in preventing the escalation of explosive situations.

It is clear that the Violence-Prevention Team has an enormous responsibility for school safety. Their responsibilities cross prevention, intervention and safety needs. They develop, track and implement new programs related to violence prevention and school security. They are pivotal in prevention.

The Violence-Prevention Team has also developed a series of video training tapes. The tapes cover a number of gang-related topics including gang awareness which reviews reading graffiti, dress, trends and activities. Another tape covers legal issues including searches, liability, self-defense and the defense on others. It also addresses investigative training: covering evidence, preservation of the scene and questioning witnesses. Along this line, a tape of crowd control and weapon identification is also available.

Another avenue of tape training includes sensitivity training that covers topics of interest in prevention. These topics include dealing with diversity, learning to appreciate others and working together. Another tape deals with intervention skills which include mediation, crisis intervention, diffusing volatile situations and warning signs for potential suicide.

Individual School Sites

Another area that TUSD supports is effort by the individual school sites. Within TUSD, school sites have independently developed strategies and programs designed to first reduce and ultimately eliminate violence.

(1) Mediation specialist—A person who uses mediation techniques to reduce tension between individuals and to create feelings of acceptance and agreement about solutions developed. The parties involved agree to the conditions of mediation and schedule a convenient time and setting for a meeting.

(2) Support groups—Groups meet at a variety of times during the school day for different reasons:
- domestic violence, rape, molestation and incest
- children of alcoholics, addicts and rageaholics
- alcoholics, addicts, runaways, domestic violence, neglect and homelessness

These groups meet often enough to keep a "barometer check" on each other and their lives in and out of school.

(3) Transition—Students who are unsuccessful in the traditional classrooms can be placed from one to five periods in a newly developed transition classroom for reasons of attendance, failure, legal issues, parent and/or school requests.

(4) VIP program—This program selects sixty at-risk freshman students and places them in a human relations class for one period per day. Their progress is monitored on a daily, weekly and quarterly schedule. Tutorial assistance is also provided.

(5) Saturday Academy—This program is an intervention program for students and their parents who have attendance and/or academic problems. The sixteen-hour intervention includes study skills, career exploration and self-discovery components.

(6) Reenrollment program—At-risk youth with a range of attendance, academic and emotional problems are interviewed and reenrolled, referred to alternative education programs, or connected with community agencies as needed. At-risk students and their families are interviewed in an intake and referral format.

(7) Prevention education—Prevention education is a collaborative effort with the Girl Scouts Council. They teach life skills, leader-

ship skills and empowerment. This is integrated into freshmen PE classes.

(8) Development groups—A local counseling agency has a grant that supports counselor-led groups on campus. These groups focus on affective educational needs. The group goals include promotion of positive peer relations, communication skills and a sense of belonging.

(9) Parent resource center—Designed to promote parent participation in schools. The parent resource center holds bimonthly planning meetings, parent education meetings, facilitates parent volunteers and provides reference information for parents. Parents of at-risk students were initially targeted, but it is now open to all parents.

(10) Block—A four week alternative program for late reentry students. English, social studies and mathematics are taught in a four-week rotation for .5 credit. At the end of the semester, students enrolled in Block return to traditional programs. These students are monitored for attendance and provided assistance with school assignments.

(11) AIP—Alternative to suspension for students who have broken school rules related to attendance or disruptive behavior. Three follow-up contacts are made on each student upon their release from AIP to ensure student success.

(12) Student assistance programs—This student advocacy program was established under the direction of the dropout-prevention coordinator. Teachers volunteer to monitor students of their choice for attendance, credits and grades. Students entering the school system from the State Department of Corrections are referred to this program for monitoring also.

(13) At-risk program—This program serves students who meet the criteria as defined by the "at-risk" staff. The criteria includes failing of three or more classes, attending less than 60% of classes, referral from a teacher or administrator, and parent request or outside agency request. The program provides the opportunity for students to work in a smaller classroom setting with individualized instruction available to them.

(14) Student assistant service committee—The goal of this committee is to identify students with behaviors of concern by faculty, guardians and/or peers. This committee facilitates adult mentoring and assists with the out-of-school referrals process for students, when necessary.

(15) Reentry program—The reentry program provides for interviews of all students and their parents who reenter school after dropping out for reasons of nonattendance, juvenile adjudication or transfer from another school. A written monitoring program is provided for each student to assist them in becoming successful in school.

(16) Students of concern—All incoming freshman who demonstrate behaviors of concern are identified and provided with summer orientation and an acclimation program. Study skills are taught. The students are actively monitored until the identified behavior of concern is reduced. These students are identified by the middle schools with names forwarded to the receiving high school.

(17) Alternative instruction program—This program is designed to work with students in an attempt to have them make positive choices and decisions about their behavior and education. This includes Behavioral Education Skills Training (BEST), which assists students to catch up in their classes and make positive behavioral changes. The program also provides a contact person for them to talk to before school when they have problems.

(18) Academic support—Students experiencing difficulty in math or English can drop an elective class and enter academic support. Within the academic support classroom, individualized tutoring and instruction is provided.

(19) Star program—Two classes of ninth-grade English students tutor at an elementary school after training in the language experience approach, the use of math manipulatives and the facilitation of art projects. The objectives for this program are to decrease the freshman dropout rate, increase student self-esteem, increase basic skills levels and reduce violence in school.

(20) SOS program (Students Offering Service)—One class of ninth-grade English students performs volunteer work with the elderly at a retirement home. Students are paired with residents at the home. Students visit with and interview the residents regarding their lives. Students use their interview notes to write short biographies about their partners. The goals are improved communication skills, self-concept and heightened awareness of the worth of others.

(21) Student peer mediator program—A number of students are trained by a professional mediator to mediate student–student and teacher–student conflicts. Contracts between the parties are developed at the conclusion of the mediation process.

(22) Developmental group program—These groups are facilitated to provide students a safe place to discuss problems and investigate solutions. Problems deal with dysfunctional families, surviving abuse and substance abuse. The facilitator is an agency counselor from the community.

(23) Homeless student program—The school coordinates with community-based programs to serve homeless students enabling them to receive an education.

(24) Tucson teen congress program—A community-based training program is held for identified students from area schools. The purpose is to identify teen problems in the schools and community, and to work toward possible solutions. The goal of the program is to produce student-designed programs to improve school climate. Students attend monthly meetings.

(25) Transition program—The transition program was implemented to provide ninth- to twelfth-grade students with an individualized and alternative learning and guidance environment. Transition is based on the idea that students need a self-contained environment removed from traditional school in order to relearn educational procedures to become successful again. An integrated guidance program is a part of this program. Transition is a small personalized program that facilitates attendance and academic success.

(26) Homework clinic—This service is available three days each week in the library immediately after school for two hours. Tutors are available.

(27) Intramural program—This program offers students physical release through basketball, volleyball, weight room training and other activities before school and during lunch.

(28) Student tutoring services—This program involves students who have been trained as tutors and who are compensated for tutoring performed after school and on Saturdays.

(29) Power of Positive Students (POPS)—This is a bilingual, multicultural club designed to provide access to mainstream campus activities for monolingual Spanish-speaking students. POPS kids become involved in team sports, student government and other clubs due to the support and encouragement of the POPS sponsors and other members. Historically, these students hesitated to become involved in activities and often lacked essential information to continue their education in postsecondary institutions.

(30) Talent search—This program targets culturally diverse middle school students who have the potential to attend college. They are identified for participation in field trips and guest visits by professionals from a variety of professions. Students are followed through high school and encouraged to attend college. Tutors are available twice weekly for academic support. Students' attendance, grades and participation in extracurricular activities are monitored.

(31) PASS—This is an alternative program for seniors who need additional credits to graduate. Course packets are provided to students which must be completed to gain credit. Tutors are available. Students work at their own rate.

(32) Teatro Guerrero—This is a bilingual theater group that writes original plays and music for community performances. It is provided through the drama program. This group performs in the immediate community. The program provides for cultural exchanges with non-Hispanic student bodies and enhancement of bilingual abilities. It promotes pride in Latino culture and language.

(33) Pueblo Mariachi group—This is a musical performance group specializing in traditional Mexican folk music. Students have an opportunity to perform at community events.

(34) Tribal image classes—This program provides two classes for American Indian students covering history, language and culture of native peoples. Pride in culture and knowledge of traditions and values is obtained.

(35) American Indian tutor—This person supports American Indian students academically and emotionally to stay in school and graduate.

(36) Metropolitan gang task force—Administrators and campus monitors attend regularly scheduled monthly meetings. These meetings are designed to keep district personnel informed of any and all gang-like activities in the community as well as in the schools.

(37) Family resource and wellness centers—Using school sites as points of service-delivery for social, medical and psychological services, this program is the result of collaboration among metropolitan school districts.

It is easy to see that a great deal of energy and creativity has gone into meeting the diverse needs of students on individual campuses. Many of these programs offer students positive alternatives to gang membership.

Safety

At the point where the safety of staff and/or students is threatened, action must be taken to prevent the consequences of an occurrence of violence. Often, the action taken is in the form of procedural consequences found in the "Guidelines for Rights and Responsibilities" handbook. If the action of a student threatens the well-being of another, the student will often be suspended or perhaps even arrested.

Most incidents involving gang activity or violence on campuses are addressed through seven behavioral areas identified in the "Guidelines for Rights and Responsibilities" handbook:

(1) Reckless endangerment—Any willful act that is not intended to cause harm but in fact places others in jeopardy of injury, including possession of explosive devices.

(2) Illegal organizations—Clubs, fraternities, sororities, antisocial organizations, secret societies and other sets of individuals that are not sanctioned by the governing board and that are determined to be disruptive to teaching and learning. This includes wearing of symbolic apparel, making gestures, writing on and marking of property, or altering of personal appearance to symbolize membership in an organization with a history of, or determined to be, a disruption to teaching and learning.

(3) Assault—Unlawfully causing any physical injury to another; intentionally placing another in reasonable apprehension of imminent physical injury through verbal or physical means; knowingly touching another with intent to injure, insult or provoke such a person.

(4) Fighting—A hostile, physical encounter between two or more individuals.

(5) Aggravated assault without a weapon—Assault committed under either of the following circumstances: 1) causes serious physical injury to another person; or 2) is knowingly committed on a teacher, administrator, any other school employee or a peace officer.

(6) Aggravated assault with a weapon—Assault committed when a person uses a deadly weapon or dangerous instrument.

(7) Possession/or concealment of weapons—Self-explanatory.

In a summary of suspension and arrest statistics, TUSD reported that violent acts against persons increased by 29%, from 2137 in 1992 to 3009 in 1994. These acts of violence included: assault, aggravated assault with and without a weapon, fighting, reckless endangerment, possession and/or concealment of a weapon and illegal organization membership. These statistics indicate an increasing problem of violence on campuses. During the 1993-1994 school year, there were 274 arrests made on campuses for violence. The majority of these were for fighting (92), assault (80), or possession and/or concealment of a weapon (77). Arrest records on campuses were not available prior to this past school year. However, these records indicate a strong district stance against violence on campuses.

The Violence-Prevention Team maintains records on gang-related incidents. These figures reflect a directional shift from direct intervention to prevention activities. They reported intervening in 405 gang-related incidents during the past year. However, they also attended 259 speaking engagements and provided seventy-five consultations. Previously, the prevention activities had constituted less of a time commitment from the team than gang-related incidences.

TUSD has taken an assertive role against campus violence including the closed campus policy for high schools beginning the 1994-1995 school year. The Violence-Prevention Team plays a major role in these activities.

CONCLUSIONS

In summary, TUSD collaborates with community agencies to implement programs in K-12 that promote school safety. Many programs exist across the district that provide positive alternatives for student involvement. However, TUSD works collaboratively with the city police departments and juvenile authorities in holding a hard line with students who bring weapons to school, assault others and/or belong to illegal organizations in order to maintain safe schools.

REFERENCES

Newkumet, M. & Casserly, M. (1994). *Urban school safety: Strategies for the great city schools.* Washington, D.C.: Council of the Great City Schools.

Southern Arizona Committee & Tucson Police Department. (1991). *Pima County kids factbook.* Tucson: Children's Action Alliance.

CHAPTER 13

Technology to Create Safer Schools

ART TOWNLEY
KENNETH MARTINEZ

INTRODUCTION

SCHOOL should be a safe place! This six-word sentence seems so simple and such a universal truth. How could there be any disagreement about making it happen? It is such a basic right of children and parents that Congress, President Bush and President Clinton made it one of the nation's priorities. Congressional leaders recently approved a crime bill that authorizes millions of dollars in federal aid to be spent for policing the nation's schools.

Violence now rivals academics as the top concern of the nation's public schools, with shootings, stabbings and other serious assaults increasing in number and spreading from urban districts to suburbs and small towns. For the first time in twenty-six years, violence, fighting and gangs tied for first place as the biggest issue facing public schools, according to the annual Gallup Poll on education.

As violence increases on city streets and in communities, violence also increases in schools. This portrayal of crisis and danger in America's schools is frequently expressed in school safety articles and other professional publications (Nelson & Shores, 1994; Goldstein et al., 1994). According to a survey by the National League of Cities, America's schools are growing more violent: in small towns, in the suburbs and, most dramatically, in big cities. Forty-one percent of big-city schools reported deaths or serious injury to students in the past year (Shogren, 1994).

It has been estimated that 100,000 guns and 600,000 knives are brought to school each day. Each day, 8% of public school teachers report being physically threatened. Cincinnati public schools may be typical of the urban districts in the country in its efforts to cope with student violence. In 1993, out of a student body of 50,000, there were 1292 expulsions, 14,949 out-of-school suspensions and 16,464 in-school suspensions. In three years, the number of suspensions and expulsions in Cincinnati has nearly tripled. "Virtually everyone is frustrated by the current situation," wrote members of an advisory board charged with recommending ways to improve discipline. "Many are angry. Most who are daily engaged in the responsibilities of schooling and raising children are near their wits' end over what to do" (Bradly, 1994).

Cincinnati is not alone. Every year, three million thefts and violent crimes occur on or near school campuses. It is not uncommon for a school administrator to display a grab bag of weaponry representing a semester's collection: brass knuckles, a seven-inch "kung fu knife," several revolvers, toy guns and a penknife with a razor-sharp blade.

It has become more urgent now than at any time in the nation's history for educators and the citizens of this country to provide safe schools. One of the characteristics of effective schools is a safe and orderly school climate. Squires, Hitt and Segars (1983) linked school effectiveness to low amounts of violence and vandalism. The question is: How can the nation achieve this objective of making our schools a safer place? Greater use of technology can assist in this effort.

Technology

In many households, students start their day by turning on the computer to check the ball scores from the previous night, view the rating of the latest movie, and read the news from the Associated Press. They check to see if any messages have arrived by e-mail and, perhaps, search the ERIC file for articles they might use in writing a report for a science class. After turning off the computer, the student may make a call on the portable cellular phone to a friend to finalize plans for attending the school dance.

The world is poised on the brink of a telecommunications revolution. The President can be reached via modem on the national information highway, called the Internet, merely by having a desktop computer dial "President@WhiteHouse.gov." It is predicted that change will come with the same magnitude as with the invention of the automobile, the electric light and the printing press. Millions of Americans will carry pocket-sized personal communicators that will combine the capabilities of computers and telephones in one mobile gadget. The communicators will become fax machines, calendars, address books and sketch pads with the insertion of function modules the size of a credit card.

In nine years, projects a study by the Personal Communications Industry Association, more than fifty-two million Americans will have cellular phones, and thirty-one million will have phones using a new digital wireless technology called personal communications services, or PCS. Furthermore, sixty-five million people will have pagers or messaging services. This PCS technology will handle five to ten times more calls or channels than cellular and cost half as much. Considering future predictions and current state-of-the-art technology, how can technology be used to assist school personnel in providing a safe campus?

Safe Schools

Serious crime on school grounds is a relatively new phenomenon in the United States. Most schools in America were free of serious problems with drugs, gangs and weapons on campuses until the 1960s. It has only been in the past decade that many campuses experienced drive-by shootings and serious violent acts on school grounds.

Trying to cope with this new phenomenon, schools have employed security guards, and state legislatures have passed tougher laws that require the expulsion of students for a litany of violations. In urban areas, where school violence has increased dramatically, many districts have created a district police force in an attempt to maintain safe campuses. San Diego School District is an example: The School Police Department has an annual budget of $2.3 million that includes spending for both educational services and equipment. The district has an emergency operations center that rivals the best public police department. The center has a series of workstations with phone and radio connections to each school site. The district's administrators, head custodians, health director, counselors and security officers can mobilize their staffs within minutes in the event of a natural disaster or other crisis (Portner, 1994).

In addition to the use of technology to prevent violence on campus, districts have established a variety of curriculum reforms in an attempt to curb violence. Classes to create student self-esteem and anti-gang programs have gained in popularity. However, most districts have not utilized available technology as an important tool to assist in creating safer campuses. Moreover, technology that has been available for decades, such as the telephone, has been underutilized.

THE TECHNOLOGIES

The Telephone

When visiting some schools, the telephone appears to be a new invention. There is an antiquated switchboard with four to eight incoming lines and a dozen or so phones in the school. The National School Boards Association estimates that only 22% of the nation's classrooms have a phone (Brown, 1994). If educators expect students to participate in the education of the 1990s, then education must move into the nineties. Every classroom should have access to phone and television lines. Perhaps more importantly, every classroom should be connected to a computer information network.

The ability to call 911 in an emergency is a capability that a district must have for a secure and safe campus. Without access to a phone, the teacher must send a message with a student, and hope the student gets to the office and relays the message correctly. This loss of time can mean the difference between timely emergency help or the ability to deal with a potentially violent situation.

This mandate for school personnel to have access to a phone sounds simple enough, but it has not happened in many school districts. The rule should be, if students have access to an area, then a phone should be nearby. The most common places without phones are athletic areas: track and baseball fields, gym, swimming pools and tennis courts. The highest incidence of student injury is likely to occur during physical education classes. Therefore, a high priority should be placed on having a phone in these instructional areas.

Other campus areas that often do not have phones are the cafeteria and the auditorium, or the multipurpose area. Districts should complete an evaluation of phone service to classrooms and the areas where installment of phone equipment is needed and set aside funds for this purpose.

Two-Way Radios

Two-way radios, in conjunction with the telephone, can be a great asset to principals, teachers and staff in providing for a safe campus. The advantage of the hand-held radio is its portability, and if phones are busy, the radio serves as an additional communication device. School districts generally have two types of radios: The limited frequency for short distance campus use by staff, and the higher frequency for contact with the district office, law enforcement, fire department and medical personnel. Many school principals and assistant principals carry a radio when they are visiting classrooms or supervising the campus.

Generally the higher frequency radios, 800 megahertz systems, are used only in emergencies and require federal approval for their use. School districts are allowed only a limited number of radios that operate on these frequencies. In California and other states more prone to natural disasters, such as hurricanes, earthquakes, floods and fires, the acquisition of the higher range frequency radios is a *must* to assist students and staff in case of a major emergency.

Computers

Many American schools have at least one computer available for school management functions and one or more computers available for instruction. However, the majority of schools do not have computer capability for assisting with campus safety. A simple computer program can provide the assistant principal or principal with a student database that could include suspensions and expulsions. Furthermore, the computer should have a modem that would link the school to the district office and law-enforcement agencies.

Time, or the lack of it, is a problem in any school. The computer expedites efficiency. The first task should be to create a database of serious, habitual offenders. The database should include students who have been suspended, expelled, arrested, convicted of crimes, truant, affiliated with gangs, and students who have been assigned a probation officer. This data could be used when looking for suspects, confirming suspicious persons, or attempting to identify students. When nonstudents are detained on or around school grounds, a profile record could be stored on the computer for instant identification, thus avoiding potential problems.

Digitized Camera

Identification is a mandatory process for school administrators. It is important for the school administrator to have a way of identifying students and nonstudents. The traditional method is to look through the student yearbook. However, this is a slow procress with a high rate of error. The student may not have been enrolled when yearbook pictures were taken, may have chosen not to have his or her photograph taken, or the person's everyday appearance may look drastically different from a posed yearbook photo.

The digitized camera can be a great asset to the principal in quickly and efficiently identifying a student. The digitized camera does not use film; it uses a computer disk built for the camera. The disk is capable of holding a quantity of up to forty pictures. The images can be downloaded onto the computer. The picture can be matched with the database to determine the student's past record, noting any disciplinary problems. If the person is suspected of committing a crime on campus, the digitized picture can be transmitted by computer to the police department for further identification. Consequently, if the student has a weapon or is suspected of possession of stolen property, the picture can provide evidence for an expulsion hearing or further action by the police department.

Scanners

Another technological tool to assist school administrators in maintaining a safe campus is the computer scanner. A scanner is simply a copy machine for a computer. A photograph or written or typed document can be placed on the scanner and transferred to the computer. This information can be added to the student database.

School districts are spending thousands of dollars on graffiti cleanup and removal each year. Graffiti from textbooks or written on notepaper can be scanned and stored in the computer, helping to identify students who are members of gangs. Additionally, this information can help in the apprehension of students who vandalize school property.

Confiscated weapons can be scanned and the image stored in the database. This method of using the computer scanner can provide a computer search within seconds, an obvious advantage to the administrator.

Metal Detectors

Metal detectors can serve as a great asset to school administrators in maintaining a safe campus. Recognizing the political reality of campus violence, President Clinton in October of 1994 signed an order that would withhold federal funds from school districts that fail to expel students who bring guns to school. Shogren (1994) writes that nearly twenty percent of schools now use metal detectors to keep weapons out of schools.

Following two tragic deaths on Los Angeles high school campuses in spring 1993, the Los Angeles Unified School District accelerated its efforts to create safe schools. Each of the secondary schools was provided with two metal detectors, or wands, and directed to conduct daily random searches (Isaacs, 1994).

There are basically two types of detectors: The large ones that students have to pass through, similar to the familiar detectors at airports; the other kind is the hand-held metal detector. The logistics of several hundred students entering and leaving a campus make the large type impractical on most school campuses. Then too, students will employ many ways to circumvent a stationary metal detector.

The hand-held detectors are invaluable for conducting a search of a student who is suspected of possessing a weapon. They are nonintrusive and reliable. The hand-held detectors also can be used to randomly check student lockers or a classroom where a student may be concealing a weapon. Obviously, school personnel must be vigilant in the proper use of metal detectors and related technology to ensure that students' rights are not violated. In this regard, the California Attorney General has issued an opinion that the reasonable application of metal detectors in schools does not violate the Fourth Amendment or California constitutional and statuary standards. As a matter of policy, local school officials are the appropriate authorities to determine if, when, where and how metal detectors should be employed to deter the presence of weapons, given the unique circumstances of their school.

Video Cameras

School districts experience increased costs each year due to vandalism and theft. Classrooms are broken into, computers and other school equipment are stolen, and many students return to school on Monday morning to find gang graffiti all over the campus. Theft and vandalism of student property is also a common problem on many school campuses. Lockers are broken into and students' personal property is stolen or vandalized. An additional major security problem for schools is the student and staff parking lot where cars are stolen or vandalized. San Diego Unified School District has used electronic surveillance extensively to protect the schools in that district. Each school has a complete alarm system that includes infrared sensors that detect motion (Portner, 1994).

The strategic placement of video cameras in halls or parking lots that have been defaced could deter this type of criminal activity and assist in the apprehension of the culprit. The surveillance cameras could also be placed in hallways or other problem areas. Furthermore, the camera could aid in identifying people entering or leaving the campus. Any drug deals could be recorded on film. In addition, numerous school districts across the country are using cameras on school buses as another "set of eyes" to detect and record behavior which is detrimental to the welfare of students. Such cameras have proved exceptionally beneficial in the prevention and control of undesirable student behavior. Once again, as with metal detectors, a district must establish proper safeguards to ensure student and staff privacy and the protection of legal rights.

CONCLUSION

Providing safe campuses must be a high priority for the citizens of this nation. We must become more proactive with initiatives designed to reduce violence in the nation's schools. Los Angeles School Superintendent Thompson said, "There will be a price in time and money, a price we must pay" (Isaacs, 1994, p. 19). Unfortunately, a great share of the nation's educational resources must be devoted to these goals. The thoughtful and planned use of technology can greatly assist school administrators and teachers in providing a safe campus where students can learn without fear of violence to person or property.

REFERENCES

Bradly, A. (1994). The booming dilemma. *NASSP Bulletin*, 78(56).

Brown, D. (1994). Youth violence: Causes & solutions. *Thrust for Educational Leadership*, 24(2).

Goldstein, A. et al. (1994). *Student aggression: Prevention, management and replacement training*. New York: Guilford.

Isaacs, D. (1994). Safe island on the streets of Los Angeles. *Thrust for Educational Leadership*, 24(2).

Nelson, C. M. & Shores, R. E. (Eds.). (1994). Dealing with aggressive and violent students. *Preventing School Failure*, 38(3).

Portner, J. (1994). Cops on campus. *Education Week,* p. 33.

Shogren, E. (1994, November 2). Violence in schools on rise across U.S. *Los Angeles Times,* Los Angeles, CA.

Squires, D. A., Hitt, W. G. & Segars, J. K. (1983). *Effective schools and classrooms: A research based perspective.* Alexandria, VA: Association for Supervision and Curriculum Development.

Extracurricular Activities: Asset or Hindrance

JERI L. ENGELKING
MICHAEL R. HOADLEY

INTRODUCTION

EXTRACURRICULAR activities have been a part of the total educational program for many years. These activities over the past few decades have finally moved from being considered a frill or an add-on to the regular school program to receiving active support and being seen as having an educational value for students (Wood, Nicholson & Findley, 1979). Dependent upon how activities are organized and managed, the total activities program may be viewed as an asset by school administrators or they may be looked at as a hindrance to the overall goals of the school. A well-organized activity can be a great benefit to both the participant and the program, but if it is poorly organized and run, it can bring about more problems and headaches than it might be worth.

Student activities have been viewed as an important part of the school setting since highlighted in the National Education Association's Seven Cardinal Principles of Secondary Education in the early 1900s. Activities and their programs related to use of leisure time, citizenship, ethics and health have been determined particularly appropriate.

Student activities serve as a logical and practical extension of the school curriculum (Joekel, 1985). They should not be considered contrary to the goals of academia, but rather an avenue for students to express themselves and to gain relevant experiences.

Leisure, co-curricular and extra classroom activities fall within the purview of a school program. They provide opportunities that foster the value of school and community involvement, encourage a climate that develops leadership and skills for interacting with others in a social setting, and help meet the interests of special students (North Central Association, 1992). Extracurricular activities should be designed so they make a positive contribution to the educational development of students in the school system.

A well-balanced program provides students the opportunity to participate in a variety of activities. Every effort should be made to prevent the domination of activities by just a few students. All such activities need to have qualified supervisors who are employees of the school or nonemployees who have been approved by the administration. Programs should reflect the special needs of all students and should be designed to serve the needs of the community as a whole.

Extracurricular activities are available to those who choose to participate; therefore, participant and spectator safety need to be considered in all aspects of the program from the planning process through the completion of each activity. School personnel working for the safety of students in and around activities should also give special consideration to the total school environment in which activities take place.

PROGRAM NEEDS

Extracurricular activities denote activities in which students participate, but are not part of the main course of study at a school and are scheduled at times when attendance at school is not required (Gorton, Schneider & Fisher, 1988). Extracurricular activities provide another dimension to a school's program. These activities help students develop leadership skills, improve their self-concept, become motivated and apply the skills they have learned in class.

Students participate in extracurricular activities for a number of reasons, among which are the opportunity to socialize with peers, to achieve success and to gain recognition. Unfortunately some students are not able to participate because of after-school employment, lack of relevant activities and the number of competing activities available elsewhere. If activity is to be successful, then students must have some degree of control, involvement must be voluntary, the experiences must be real and valid, opportunities for socializing must exist, and experiences or rewards must be provided that would not be available otherwise.

The organization and leadership in an extracurricular activity must be provided by students. Administrators must also provide the necessary leadership to organize and stimulate activities, either directly or by appointing others and assigning that responsibility.

A concern for safety is inherent in both organized and unorganized activities that take place under the auspices of the school setting. The safety and success of any such activity depends to a large extent on the cooperation of the administration, the activity supervisor and the participants. This becomes the overall responsibility of the school administrator and the activity supervisor or coach. The activity supervisor or coach represents the front line of the safety program in extracurricular activities. They have the responsibility for preventing accidents and for educating participants about safety.

Risks are inherent in extracurricular activities, especially sports activities. Accidents and injuries cannot be avoided, no matter how safe the program, but school personnel must do everything they can to provide a reasonably safe program. One important action is to assemble a safety committee (Appenzeller, 1993). The purpose of the committee is to implement a safety review and policies for all activities. Periodic reviews by the safety committee include the identification of potential risks, assessment of reports to ascertain patterns associated with activities or their locations, review of inspections of equipment and facilities to better ensure all problems are eliminated or remedied, implementation of accident and injury reporting procedures and the development of safety policies. The safety committee should represent a number of interested groups including participants, teachers, administrators, parents and people from the community.

The entire extracurricular activity program, as well as individual activities, need written and well-defined objectives or purposes. Guidelines written by a committee of teachers, administrators, parents and students should be developed that outline the parameters to operate the program. Faculty sponsors should be recruited or appointed, especially those who are willing to properly supervise students. Training and other inservice programs should be offered, job descriptions should be developed to clarify the assignments, and evaluations should be conducted, especially for those sponsors who are compensated for their work.

Not only do supervisors or coaches explain and demonstrate to participants the safe performance of various activity skills and procedures, they must also work with the school administration, custodial and maintenance personnel to ensure that all equipment and facilities fall within the accepted regulations for each activity and are in good working order (Bever, 1988). Good rapport and a close working relationship with custodial and maintenance personnel will ultimately help control hazards and dangerous conditions before they can become a major problem.

When considering any type of activity program, the following questions should be asked by administrators, supervisors and/or the safety committee, and could ultimately act as a set of guidelines for the administration of an activity.

(1) What educational value does the activity hold for students?
(2) Are the students' needs and interests being met by the activity?
(3) What are the objectives of the activity?
(4) How are the activity's supervisors/coaches selected?
(5) What are the responsibilities of the administration to the activity?
(6) How are the rules/regulations for the activity formulated and by whom?
(7) What are the responsibilities of the supervisor/coach?
(8) Are there agencies other than the high school that govern this activity?
(9) What are the requirements/considerations for participation in the activity?
(10) How is the activity financed?
(11) Who is responsible for handling the finances for the activity?
(12) How and by whom is the activity scheduled? (contests, practices, etc.)
(13) What are the legal ramifications of students participating in the activity?
(14) What facilities are necessary to accommodate the activity?

OBJECTIVES OF THE PROGRAM

Not everyone will participate or take part in extracurricular activities, but the opportunity to participate should be available for anyone to try if they choose. According to the National Association of Secondary School Principals (1984), more than 80% of all students who attend high school participate in at least one activity during their four years of eligibility.

Extracurricular activities should be developed as a result of genuine interest by students and reflect a balance between various types of activities. For example, the amount of money spent and the personnel time involved in an athletic program should not be excessively out of line with the money and effort put forth for other student activities. There should also be a balance within activities providing activities for both boys and girls, and team activities balanced in relation to individual activities.

All event or activity plans should be in writing (Berlonghi, 1991). This not only provides documentation at the time of the event, but also can be used as a training tool to prepare others for similar events. It is also important that nothing be put in the plan unless it is going to be done because negligence is easily determined. Emergency response plans should also be outlined in detail.

If disabled students take part in an extracurricular activity, they must be protected from unreasonable risks. As best as possible, all physical barriers should be removed and provisions should be made to increase accessibility (Minor & Minor, 1991). More supervision may be needed and more extensive measures may need to be taken to provide appropriate instruction for students and their parents to help them understand any risks associated with the activity.

In the event an accident occurs, the courts will determine negligence by considering these questions (Minor & Minor, 1991, p. 2):

(1) Was a duty owed?
(2) Was the duty neglected?
(3) Was there actual harm?
(4) Was there a relationship between the harm and the behavior of the educator?

The probability of liability decreases for every "no" response to these questions.

SAFETY IN ACTIVITIES

An integral part of any extracurricular activity is an instruction phase followed by some type of practice or involvement phase in which safety education should be taught. Safety education in this context should be in the form of safety behaviors for each activity to ensure the greatest probability of accident-free activities

Obviously, it is impossible to eliminate all risks and hazards in activities. Skill development depends upon a participant's ability to reproduce patterns of motion in a consistent fashion. As long as the human element is involved, mistakes willl be made in activities and accidents will happen. Students participating in activities are going to run, jump, trip, fall down, run into one another and get hit by balls or other equipment. Every type of human motion in an activity creates some potential for an accident and resulting injury to occur. The more rapid and vigorous the motion, the greater the potential for an accident or serious injury, even when rules are closely followed and protective equipment is utilized correctly.

If transportation in a school vehicle is necessary for the extracurricular activity, proper planning must precede the trip (Minor & Minor, 1991). Parents must be notified of the activity, its agenda and the purpose of the trip. The vehicle being used must be inspected and should include concerns about safety belts, broken or worn seats and seating capacity. Students being transported must also be informed about all details of the trip and should be given clear, concise, and specific instructions on how to behave and what to do during the trip. If students are being transported in the personal vehicle of a teacher and an accident occurs, the teacher could be held liable for any injury that occurs. Informed permission slips should be signed by parents or guardians, but administrators must also understand that a waiver of liability is not a legal document. Liability cannot be waived for children under the age of eighteen and parents cannot waive liability when the possibility of injury to a child exists.

Special events at school may pose a special safety problem because they involve children. Techniques for making the special events as safe and secure as possible must be effectively integrated in all levels of the planning and operating of the events. As a result, reducing the risks at special events like extracurricular activities becomes the responsibility of everyone involved. Responsibility extends to individuals including teachers, organizers, volunteers, parents and everyone else present. If children are put in dangerous situations the school district's exposure to liability increases dramatically.

According to Berlonghi (1991), two primary concerns must be addressed prior to the occurrence of an extracurricular event:

(1) The competence and experience of the organizers in planning a safe and secure extracurricular activity.
(2) The knowledge of the organizers and supervisors in integrating risk management into the planning of an extracurricular activity.

Three circumstances which lead to chaotic situations for special events (and extracurricular activities) include the following:

(1) Number of participants increases as you get closer to the beginning of the event.
(2) Workload tends to increase, communication tends to decrease and details tend to get lost.
(3) Space becomes a premium and tends to disappear.

Some Ideas

- Contestants should be as equally matched as possible.
- Participants should have medical supervision throughout all seasons.
- Safe transportation should be provided to and from all activities.
- Limitations should be placed on number of events, practices, etc.
- Supervision and instruction are mandatory.

SCHOOL FACILITIES AND EQUIPMENT

A safe environment consists not only of the general physical plant (the buildings, grounds, parking lots, hallways, lunchrooms, commons areas, etc.), but also instructional areas and activity areas that can present specific hazards to students, such as locker rooms, training rooms, bleachers, theater stages, tracks, etc. Extracurricular programs require extensive facilities and equipment that need to be designed to limit the possibility of human error as students participate in physical activity.

Educators must be responsible for the proper maintenance of equipment used at the school. Equipment must be checked on a regular basis by supervisors and custodial staff. Users of equipment must be informed of any dangers or unsafe conditions that may exist (Minor & Minor, 1991). The areas must also be checked for potential hazards, which will vary depending on the time of the activity.

The general safety of the school grounds and playing fields (such things as lighting, mowing and general maintenance) is usually the responsibility of maintenance personnel, while the safety of inside activities areas and equipment are most often the responsibility of the teachers and activity supervisors (gymnastic equipment, PE equipment, locker rooms, gymnasiums, etc.).

Activity supervisors/coaches should be familiar with the care and operation of equipment used in their specific activity, especially if the equipment is to be used by participants. Students should not be allowed to use equipment until they have received instruction and training by the supervisor on how to use it safely. Instruction should include a demonstration of both equipment and any other necessary gear. Modeling of safety practices as an example enhances students' learning. Security procedures should also be designed and put into place to eliminate unauthorized use of equipment and facilities as a safety precaution.

Potential accident hazards or unsafe conditions should be noted by any staff members in an activity area and reported to activity supervisors, maintenance or custodial personnel, or administrators. Hazards such as projections, obstructions and unused equipment in and around activity areas should be eliminated before participant use.

Some Ideas

- Provide safe facilities for activities to take place such as level playing fields and floors with adequate playing and spectator space.
- Have facilities and equipment checked before each season as well as prior to each use.
- Identify and remove unsafe conditions, keep areas and surroundings free of obstructions.
- Avoid overlapping of areas during play or practice.
- Be sure that adequate illumination is provided for each area.

PARTICIPANT CONDITIONING

Most extracurricular activities require some type of instruction or coaching followed by a period of practice in order to develop skill and coordinate movement. The conditioning of participants before and during this period is crucual to accident and injury prevention and a safer activity environment. Proper stretching and appropriate warm-up activities before participation in an activity is important.

In addition, proper instruction must include specific procedures on how to perform the assigned activities and a determination that students clearly understand the procedures. The expectations of proper behavior must be understood by students and parents (Minor & Minor, 1991). Meetings should be held prior to the activities so everyone is properly informed and so they understand the consequences of any inappropriate or unsafe behavior.

CARE AND PROTECTION OF PARTICIPANTS

Whether they are termed co-curricular or extracurricular activities, the courts have determined that the right to participate in school activities is not equivalent to a student's right to attend school (Gluckman, 1985). Nevertheless, when it comes to the responsibility for the safety of students who participate in those activities, there is no distinction. The key element from the court's perspective is the school's sponsorship of the activity and the assignment of personnel to supervise it.

Questions of negligence typically center around the ability to foresee any injury and whether actions taken by the supervisor could have avoided it. In cases when a teacher or other supervisor has fulfilled his/her duty, the establishment of negligence is usually unfounded. The supervisor also should never assume the role of a qualified medical person in an accident situation. A good rule of thumb is to never treat beyond the limits of the first aid training you have received. Supervisors can be held personally liable for being negligent if they do not exercise prudence in caring for the injured person within their set limitations.

A risk analysis can be conducted to identify the specific and unique risks associated with an extracurricular activity or other special event. According to Berlonghi (1991), individual risk factors may not be a problem, but combining risks can greatly reduce the safety element. The risk analysis should also include information about what is being done to address or minimize the risks.

Athletic trainers, coaches, emergency personnel and team physicians play a key role in providing services for the range of activity programs found in today's schools. Continuous monitoring by supervisors/coaches during an activity is the best key to safety. In the event of an accident, all injuries should be reported to school officials as soon as possible. Should a student be injured during a school sponsored activity, every effort should be made to contact the parent or parents for instructions and/or information. Accident forms then need to be completed by the supervisor and turned in to administrative offices for purposes of insurance and tracking of injury incidents.

When students participate in an extracurricular activity they assume a certain amount of risk, but adequate supervision must also be provided and students should never be left alone. An adequate number of school staff must be present to exercise a reasonable standard of care to protect students from risks. Several factors must be taken into account for proper supervision, including the student's age and developmental level, as well as the novelty of the task and its inherent dangers. It is the responsibility of the sponsors to keep the students in small, manageable groups to keep them on task and to help prevent negative interactions (Minor & Minor, 1991).

Some Ideas

- Adequate supervision before, during and after each activity
- Available medical personnel during activities
- Proper conditioning before participation
- Participant information gathered regarding medical conditions, medicines, etc.

PRINCIPLES GOVERNING ACCIDENT/INJURY PREVENTION

Risk management has as its primary focus the safety of students, and its guiding principle is that all students have the right to be provided with an environment where quality educations occurs in a safe and orderly fashion (Minor & Minor, 1991). Managing risks is a moral responsibility of all educators in a school and the management of any risk is a legal responsibility that schools must accept. In the case of extracurricular activities, school districts can reduce their liabilities and other potential problems by controlling risks.

Participants—Some Ideas

- Be sure to have a physical examination and find out any limitations before entering into an activity that requires physical stress or strain.

- Warm-up muscles before each participation as a precaution against strains and sprains.
- Never continue participation when you are fatigued.
- Select activities to participate in that are within your range of ability.
- Attempt new skills that may be hazardous only under the direction of a qualified person, skills should progress from simple to the more advanced.
- Do not participate where equipment is improperly erected, if the floor surface is rough, slippery or has obstacles that can lead to injury.
- Wear proper personal equipment at all times for protection.
- Seek immediate and adequate attention for all injuries.
- Participants should think before they act in an activity.
- Knowledge of and adhering to the rules and regulations of an activity should guide a participant's actions.

Programs – Some Ideas

- Require a medical examination for each participant, with a physician's statement as to whether or not the student may participate.
- Develop and institute an accident reporting system among activities to provide uniform records of all injuries and accidents, to determine cause, and to institute preventive measures.
- Plan program activities appropriate to gender, age, ability, condition, etc., to equally match students as is possible.
- Insure that safety instruction is an integral part of all programs.
- Require or provide access to health or accident insurance for participants.
- Employ only certified and qualified personnel to direct programs.
- Participants who are injured may not return without the consent of a qualified physician.

Equipment – Some Ideas

- Frequent inspection and correction of any defects is required.

- Movable equipment should be put up in safe storage when not in use.
- Safety rules and regulations regarding use of equipment must be established and enforced in all programs.
- Only safe equipment should be used.

Personnel — Some Ideas

- Primary concern is given to the well-being of participants.
- Only qualified and certified personnel should supervise activities.
- Adequate personnel should be available for the number of participants in each activity.
- Effective officiating should be provided where necessary for contests.
- First aid as well as proper follow-up treatment must be provided for all injuries.
- Responsibility for their own and others safety should be taught to each participant.

REFERENCES

Appenzeller, H. (1993). *Managing sports and risk management stategies.* Durham, NC: Carolina Academic Press.

Berlonghi, A. (1991). Managing the risks of school district special events. *School Business Affairs,* pp. 12–16.

Bever, D. (1988). *Safety: A personal focus* (3rd ed.). St. Louis, MO: Mosby Year Book, Inc.

Gorton, R. A., Schneider, G. T. & Fisher, J. C. (Eds.). (1988). *The encyclopedia of school administration and supervision.* Phoenix: Oryx Press, pp. 112–113.

Gluckman, I. (1985). Legal aspects of student activities. *NAASP Bulletin,* 69(483):10–16.

Joekel, R. (1985). Student activities and academic eligibility requirements. *NASSP Bulletin,* 69(483):3–9.

Minor, J. & Minor, V. (1991). *Risk management in schools: A guide to minimizing liability.* Newbury Park, CA: Corwin Press.

National Association of Secondary School Principals. (1984). *The mood of American youth.* Reston, VA: NASSP.

North Central Association. (1992). *Policies and standards for schools.* Arizona State University, Tempe, AZ: Author.

Wood, C., Nicholson, E. & Findley, D. (1979). *The secondary principal: Manager and supervisor.* Boston: Allyn & Bacon.

PART IV

CONCLUSIONS AND RECOMMENDATIONS

CHAPTER 15

Educational Reform in Changing Contexts of Families and Communities: Leading School-Interagency Collaboration

LARS G. BJÖRK

INTRODUCTION

WIDESPREAD public concern that America's economic, political and military preeminence in world affairs was being eclipsed engendered an extensive and sustained educational reform movement during the past decade. The development of causal linkages between the perceived failure of schooling and the nation's economic decline provided reformers and critics with a platform and an explanation of the inadequacy of American schooling and the inability of business and industry to counter the rising tide of international competition. In this milieu, prominent businessmen, politicians and educators who served on education commissions viewed the task of reforming public schools as fundamental to safeguarding the nation's future. Consequently, national commissions and task forces investigating the condition of education raised serious concerns about declining student achievement scores, tenuous linkages between academic preparation and work, and indicted public schools for failing the nation's youth and the economy. While most reform reports offered remedies, ranging from enacting legislative mandates intended to fix the existing system to involving professionals to restructure schools, several reports emerging during the late 1980s and early 1990s recognized the magnitude and complexity of the social problems confronting children that hindered their success in school.

These reform reports and critiques offered by a number of eminent educators, researchers and policy analysts, questioned the veracity of claims made in earlier commission reports. The work of these revisionists (Björk, 1995) helped to bring attention to the strong associations between deteriorating social conditions and poor educational outcomes. These works acknowledged that schools would have to help ameliorate these problems before substantive improvement in academic outcomes could be expected. It was apparent to many analysts that attempts to solve these intractable social and educational problems would require financial and professional resources that exceeded the limits of most district level budgets. As many observers persuasively argued for schools to actively intervene on children's behalf, federal and state policy makers began shifting the burden of responsibility for solving these problems to local school districts. Consequently, school districts had a compelling interest in not only identifying the nature and scope of problems confronting school-aged children but accelerated redefining schools as integrated service systems to better serve these at-risk children.

THE EDUCATIONAL REFORM REPORTS

During the 1980s, public criticism of a broad range of public and private organizations was as frequent as it was intense. One of the most consequential challenges, however, was directed at the nation's public school system between 1983 and 1993. During this period, three successive "waves" (Firestone, Fuhrman & Kirst, 1990; Murphy, 1990) of reports released by national commissions and task forces examined the purpose, condition and performance of public schools. The landmark report *A Nation at Risk* (National Commission on Excellence in Education, 1983) launched the first wave of educational reform (1982–1986) which was followed in immediate succession by *Making the Grade* (Twentieth Century Task Force on Federal Educational Policy, 1983), *High School* (Boyer, 1983), *Action for Excellence* (Education Commission of the States, 1983) and *Educating Americans for the 21st Century* (National Science Board, 1983). These cardinal reports called for raising student test scores, increasing accountability, strengthening regulations and centralizing management control of schools.

While concurring with the need to pursue increased academic rigor, the reports released during the subsequent wave of educational reform (1986–1989), advocated the professionalization of teaching and expanding local discretion. These reports include *Investing in Our Children*, Committee for Economic Development, 1985; *A Nation Prepared: Teachers for the Twenty-First Century*, Carnegie Foundation, 1986; *Tomorrow's Teachers*, 1986; *Time for Results: The Governors' 1991 Report on Education*, National Governors' Assocation, 1986; and *Children in*

Need, Committee for Economic Development, 1987. These reports covered a wide array of remedies; however, three major policy recommendations emerged. First, the stultifying effects of school bureaucracies were identified as contributing to the failure of children in school. These reports recommended that states and school districts support the professionalization of teaching and increase participatory decision making at both the district and building levels. Second, these reports stressed the importance of employing instructional techniques that emphasize higher-order thinking skills, problem solving, computer competency and collaboration; and they advocated a dramatic shift in the teaching and learning process. Lastly, they made compelling arguments that connected national demographic trends with educational performance and advocated addressing the needs of all children, particularly those who historically had been poorly served by education: children of color and children at-risk who would comprise the majority of the nation's workforce during the twenty-first century (Murphy, 1990).

The third wave of educational reform reports, however, was highly critical of previous recommendations that focused primarily on structural and professional issues rather than on children. This new focus on children was evident in *Turning Points* (Carnegie Council for Adolescent Development, 1989); *Beyond Rhetoric: A New American Agenda for Children and Families* (National Commission on Children, 1991); *Visions of a Better Way: A Black Appraisal of Public Schooling* (Commission on Policy for Racial Justice, 1989); *Education That Works: An Action Plan for the Education of Minorities* (Quality Education for Minorities Project, 1990); and *National Excellence: A Case for Developing America's Talent* (1993). Two other reports were released during this time period; however, they were anomalous. The U.S. Department of Education (1991) released *America 2000: An Education Strategy,* which reflected the policies of the Bush administration, that converged on standards, achievement testing, accountability and creating "new American schools" within existing funding levels (Howe, 1991; Doyle, 1991). Subsequently, the Clinton adminstration released *Goals 2000: Educate America Act* (King, 1994), which was signed into law in April 1994. This legislation set in motion a series of initiatives designed to stimulate systemic reform at the local level using top-down strategies reminiscent of the first wave of educational reform. It required states to develop plans for new curricula, student performance standards and altering teacher preparation. Although *America 2000* and *Goals 2000,* released by the Bush and Clinton administrations, reflected themes that cut across the first two waves of reform, they were qualitatively different from the thrust of most third wave reports. The core of the third wave reports identified numerous contributing factors to student failure, broadening the reform debate, and grasped the irony of the world's richest nation failing both its poor and gifted children. Two simple, yet powerful, perspectives emerged from these reports: 1) substantive school reform must focus on children, and 2) restructuring schools should be based on how children learn. Backwardmapping (Elmore, 1979-1980; Odden, 1991) begins with an understanding of how children learn. This knowledge then defines optimum conditions for teaching and learning, schedules, structures and professional relationships. In other words, form follows function. This approach is contrary to common practice in which schools force-fit teaching and learning, schedules and relationships into an industrial bureaucratic framework. The notion that schools should serve children and that their needs should define structures influenced calls for radically different approaches for organanizing schools. One of the most striking characteristic shared by many of the third wave reports has been the need for schools to serve as "integrated interorganizational service" systems (Murphy, 1990, p. 29). This concept is reflected in Professional Development Schools, Cities in Schools, Sizer's Coalition of Essential Schools and Comer's School Development Programs (Fullan, 1993).

These perspectives challenged earlier solution-driven recommendations and argued that the policy initiatives launched during the previous "waves" of educational reform would not achieve substantive reform (Petersen, 1985; Clark & Astuto, 1994). It became increasingly apparent to policy analysts that any attempt to redesign school structures would require clarifying society's expectations for education, identifying optimal conditions for student learning, defining the nature and extent of support needed to enhance children's educational progress, and examine school budget constraints. The recent spate of educational reform reports recognize that adequately defining the condition and context of education was essential to restructuring schools and integrating their work with the work of other community-based service agencies to better serve at-risk students.

CHANGES IN PUBLIC EXPECTATIONS FOR SCHOOLING

The educational reform reports provided a forum in which politicians, economists, business leaders, educators and cultural entrepreneurs made confident pronouncements that current educational expectations had to be redefined to fit the emerging postindustrial work contexts and that schools had to serve a more diverse student population better. While the educational reform reports were highly critical of American public schools, they also confirmed our fundamental belief that education was linked to individual success and that a vigorous system of education was essential to the national well-being. Brogan (1962) noted that public faith in the benefits of education has been a conspicuous aspect of the American cultural experience and persisted despite criticisms leveled at schools (Cuban, 1990; Elam, Rose & Gallup, 1993). Consequently, it is not surprising that the same critics that indicted American public education for failing to educate American youth and jeopardizing the nation's economic future, asked schools to remedy the situation (Murphy, 1995).

One of the driving forces behind the educational reform movement of the 1980s was the projection indicating that a larger proportion of the nation's youth would have to be more highly educated to meet manpower demands during the next century. Demographic data clearly indicated that minority groups would provide the preponderance of workers in the twenty-first century. American business leaders, realizing that schools were strategically positioned to develop the nation's human capital during the coming decades (Björk, 1995; Wirth, 1992; Reich, 1983, 1991; Snyder, 1984), heightened their involvement in the school reform movement. In this context, the contentious dilemmas of access and excellence, which had troubled policy makers during earlier decades, were viewed as intrinsically related rather than mutually exclusive. As morality became pragmatic (Henderson, 1977, p. 235), liberal and conservative adversaries became natural allies in promoting the education of all children as a means of supporting the nation's quest for economic self-preservation.

Redefining educational expectations, however, inevitably led to questioning the deep structures of educational practice. Spring (1986) noted that in the past schools served as "sorting machines." Children who succeeded in the bureaucratic school contexts were viewed as having the greatest potential for fitting into regimented industrial settings. They were prepared to meet these work demands by being taught the importance of obeying superiors, following rules, complying with regulations, and rote learning in static classroom environments. Continuing these practices in a postindustrial economy, however, would be tantamount to preparing the next generation of American workers for planned obsolescence. In the future, work will demand an entirely different set of behaviors. Given the nature of the postindustrial economy, schools would have to alter practices and structures of schooling that served nineteenth century purposes and instead, educate all children well by optimizing learning; cultivating the ability to question the status quo; developing critical thinking skills; using technology to access, manipulate and analyze information; and working independently as well as collaboratively in solving real problems. Schools in the postindustrial era will have to employ learner-centered approaches to teaching and learning rather than continue to use traditional teacher-centered methods. In addition to redefining the very nature of teaching and learning, schools are being challenged to prepare a large segment of the nation's youth who not only have been poorly served by schools historically, but are also being affected by a wide array of social problems that inhibit academic success. Meeting these challenges will require a greater understanding of the changing social context and the nature of the problems facing American society and youth.

The Changing Social Context of American Education

Inquiries into the root causes of poor student performance, which the commission reports referred to as the "crisis" in American education, forced researchers to examine these issues in the larger social context. They found that many of the problems that negatively impact student success in schools could be traced to the deterioration of the nation's social fabric including nuclear family structures. Their findings coincided with those of the vast majority of Americans who understood that the rising number of illegitimate births, increasing divorce rates, climbing numbers of single-parent households headed by women, escalating drug use, violent crime and urban blight has created an imperiled generation of children (Goertz, 1990). It was clear that the social malaise affecting society was having a commensurate devastating impact on children and jeopardizing their potential for academic success. These observations were confirmed by Elam (1990) in the "22nd Annual 1990 Gallup Poll of the Public's Attitude toward Public Schools," with the finding that 73% of Americans believed that problems originating in society had a profoundly negative effect on the performance of many school children and that the blame for these problems should be placed with society and not with the schools. Schools, however, are confronted with both the consequences of these problems and the compelling need to find solutions.

Demographic Shifts

The growing segment of the nation's minority population will have a significant impact on public schools during the coming decades. The African-American cohort in the United States numbered 26.7 million in 1980 and increased by 16% to 31 million by 1990. Hodgkinson (1991) projected that this trend would continue and anticipated that by the year 2020 this segment of the population would increase by an additional 29% to 44 million (p. 5). Demographic projections for the Hispanic population followed a similar course. In 1980, they numbered 14.6 million and increased by 44% to 21 million by 1990. Their numbers are expected to swell by 53% to 47 million by the year 2020. While the nation's total population numbered 249.8 million in 1990, projections indicated that it will increase to 265 million by the year 2020 with more than 91 million Americans, more than one-third of the nation, being nonwhite (Hodgkinson, 1985).

These demographic trends have significant implications for schools. Minority students, who have the greatest level of need, are the fastest growing segment of the nation's school population. Between 1970 and 1980, the number of students attending elementary and secondary schools decreased 13.6% while the average number of minority students increased 6% (Sergiovanni, Burlingame, Coombs & Thurston, 1987, p. 48). Hodgkinson's (1991) demographic projections suggest that the proportion of minority school children will increase from 30% in 1990 to 38% of the total in 2020. Nearly 10% of these minority students do not speak English at home, "do not function at high levels in schools" (Sergiovanni, Burlingame, Coombs & Thurston, 1987, p. 50), lack parental support needed to succeed, are often alienated, perceive themselves as failures in school (Hodgkinson, 1985) and are at risk of dropping out.

In spite of these constraints, public schools have made considerable progress and should be given credit for increasing the graduation rate of students, particularly minority students. During the 1940s, the lack of school provisions for working with pregnant, handicapped, learning-disabled or troubled children prevented many students from benefiting from public education. In addition, segregation systematically "excluded three-fourths of all minority and low-income students"

(Males, 1992, p. 55). For example, in 1950 only 56% of the nation's white students and 25% of the nation's African-Americans graduated from high school. Thirty-eight years later, however, most schools had made provisions for working with these students and enabled 85% of the white students, 81% of the African-American students, 62% of the Hispanic students (National Center for Educational Statistics, 1988, p. 28) and 55% of Native Americans to graduate from high school (Commission on Minority Population in American Life, 1988, p. 8). As a result, "illiteracy today is one-fifth its 1940 level . . . [and] college enrollment has quadrupled" (Males, 1992, p. 55).

These statistics, however, only reflect students who graduate on time after twelve consecutive years in school. If students who leave school and return later to complete their studies or finish a General Educational Development (GED) certificate program are factored into the equation, the percentage increases rather dramatically. Bracey (1992) calculated that "more than 91% of the class of 1980 had completed high school or its equivalent by 1986" (p. 107). While schools have struggled to serve the nation's at-risk population, success came at a high cost to local school districts. The diversity, magnitude and severity of emerging problems coupled with remote prospects for increasing district expenditures may restrain, if not reverse these positive trends.

Changes in American Families

The long-range consequences of children living in poverty are so profound that many view it as a twentieth century American tragedy. In the larger sense, both Mitchell (1990) and Eisner (1992) believed that the nation's social, educational and economic policies were inextricably linked. Clark & Astuto (1990) argued that these problems must be addressed before society can expect children to obtain the education needed to both escape from poverty and contribute to the economic vitality of the nation.

During the last half century, changes in the configuration of families have had profound repercussions on children. Shortly after the end of World War II, more than 80% of the children grew up in "Ozzie and Harriet" families made up of two married biological parents and two children (Whitehead, 1993). By 1990, however, only 6% of American families included both biological parents, with the mother at home, a working father and two school-age children (Hodgkinson, 1991, p. 10).

There are indications that this percentage may decline even further during the coming decade. The deterioration of the nuclear family has been accelerated by a number of root causes.

First, the divorce rate increased more than 200% between 1960 and 1991 moving from 9.2% per thousand married women in 1960 to 20.9% in 1991 (Bennett, 1993, p. 13). This resulted in a substantial increase in the number of single-parent families. For example, by 1990, 50% of all children under age eighteen lived in single-parent families, with 87% of them being headed by women. The divorce rate has increased disproportionately among minority groups. Hodgkinson (1991) reported that more than 52% of African-American children, 24% of Hispanic children, 12% of white children and 10% of Asian children live in single-parent families (p. 11).

The dramatic rise in illegitimate births over the past three decades (1960-1990), increasing more than 400% (Bennett, 1993, p. 9), has also contributed to the increasing number of single-parent families in the United States. The illegitimate birth rate rose disproportionately among some population groups. For example, between 1960 and 1990 the rate increased from 2.3% to 21% for whites and from 23% to 65.2% for Arican-Americans (Bennett, 1993, p. 9). It is evident that single-parent households, rather than being the exception in American society, are now becoming the norm.

The relationship between growing up in single-parent families and being poor is troubling. Children living in poverty are not only a sober predictor of low performance on standardized tests, but poverty has profound consequences on success later in life (Kirst & McLaughlin, 1990). In 1984, the Congressional Budget Office released *Poverty among Children,* which described the harsh circumstances in which an increasing proportion of the nation's children lived. Reed and Sautter (1991) reported that by 1989, 20% or 12.6 million children below the age of eighteen years of age accounted for nearly 39% of all the poor in the nation. Sergiovanni, Burlingame, Coombs and Thurston (1987) provided additional insight into the plight of young children noting that 44% of African-American children lived in poverty in 1986. That percentage increased to 56% if they lived in a home headed by a single mother (Reed & Sautter, 1991, pp. K3-K4). Hispanic children living in poverty accounted for 37.5% of the total in 1989 and escalated to 59% if they lived in a home headed by a single mother (Reed & Sautter, 1991, pp. K3-4).

Crime and Violence

There is little doubt that the nation's unenviable record of violent crime, four times that of other Western European nations (Elam, Rose & Gallup, 1994), has influenced perceptions that the United States is the most violent country of the industrialized world (Sautter, 1995). There is little disagreement that crime is a significant problem in American society and recent students have painted a bleak picture of its impact on children. The violence and crime in communities throughout the nation are permeating school boundaries and are raising concerns about the capacity of the schools to counteract this violence.

For more than a quarter century, the annual Gallup poll has chronicled public concern for the lack of discipline in schools. In 1994, however, public response to the category "fighting violence and gangs" catapulted the issue of crime and violence in schools into first place. Eighteen percent of respondents indicated that it was the most significant problem facing schools today (Elam, Rose & Gallup, 1994), paralleling concern for the lack of discipline. If the responses for the two categories, "fighting violence and gangs" (18%) and the "lack of discipline" (18%) are combined (p. 44), the data indicate a significant level of concern. Although Elam, Rose and Gallup (1994) have reported that Bureau of Justice statistics indicate that the crime rate has been declining since 1981, they also have noted that the rate among African-Americans has escalated by 65%. Serious crimes including rape, assault, robbery and murder are disproportionately impacting the African-American segment of the nation's population. Rather than reporting the distressing level of crime afflicting the African-American communities on a daily basis, the news media sensationalized violence in schools, which in comparison, is at a minimal level. The public, however, understood that the origins of problems facing public schools were rooted in society. "At least 70% of respondents rate the increased use of alcohol and drugs, the growth of youth gangs, the easy availability of weapons, and a general breakdown in the American family as very important causes of violence in the nation's schools" (Elam, Rose & Gallup, 1994, p. 43). Sautter (1995) reported similar findings indicating "that the grinding poverty, inequitable educational opportunity, latchkey homes, child abuse, domestic violence, and family breakups, as well as general abandonment of children to a constant barrage of televised mayhem, would result in escalating real world violence" (p. K6).

Crime in the United States is at a twenty-year low, dropping from 35.7 million in 1973 to 33.6 million in 1992. Statistics show that youth crime is also down. In 1975, 26% of all arrests were accounted for by individuals under the age of eighteen. By 1992, that figure had dropped by 16%. The most troubling statistic, however, is the fact the number of violent crimes committed by very young children is increasing at a significant pace. The number of individuals under the age of eighteen arrested for murder in 1960 was 513. During 1992, that figure stood at 2829. Nested within these 1992 figures, is the troubling fact that African-American males between the ages of twenty and twenty-four years of age are four times more likely to be shot than their white counterparts (Sautter, 1995, p. K4).

During the early 1990s, schools accounted for 11% of all crimes committed in the nation, a rate three times that recorded for the American workplace (Sautter, 1995, p. K5). Many of these "crimes," however, were related to simple battery, petty theft and infringements of school discipline policy. They, nonetheless, were entered into national crime databases. Although the statistics on crimes committed in schools appears high, homicide data indicate that 99% of all deaths of those under the age of eighteen occur outside of school. Statistics on death rates in our nation's communities indicate that homicide is the leading cause of death for children between the ages of five and fourteen years, the second leading cause of death among those ten to twenty-four, and the leading cause of death among African-Americans between the ages of fifteen and thirty-four. Even more troubling is the fact that as the proportion of fifteen to twenty-nine-year-olds in the population is declining, the percentage of crimes being committed by individuals who fall into the group is increasing. For example, between 1963 and 1990, the juvenile arrests for murder increased 332% (Sautter, 1995, pp. K4-K7).

The trend is "likely to continue, driven by deepening child poverty, destabilization of families and more guns, drugs, and nihilism among people" (Marriott, 1994, p. 122). According to the American Psychological Association's (1993) recent report, *Violence and Youth: Psychology's Response,* much of the social violence in society is learned behavior occurring early in a child's development. The causes of children as perpetrators of violent acts on others frequently is based on their being victims of abuse and neglect. While many of the more serious crimes are not being committed in schools, they are being committed by school-aged children in their communities or affect young victims in sobering ways. James Fox, Dean of the College of Criminal Justice at Northeasten University, at a recent meeting of the American Association for the Advancement of Science, observed that as some 40 million young children mature into their teens, the murder rate will surge. He noted that current government intervention programs have had little impact on correcting the problem. He believes that an investment in children as young as six or seven years old may be part of the solution strategy (Recer, 1995).

It is clear to professional school staffs and policy makers that the effect of crime is having a significant impact on the ability of a substantial number of children in schools, and the measures currently employed to counteract its force are having little effect. The problem of violence in society and its impact on children in schools cannot be addressed by teachers or administrators working alone. It will require the integration of a very large array of community-based services that may help identify antisocial behavior among very young children in schools and provide intervention services designed to prevent future violence. As the context of schooling changes, we must be cognizant that if academic performance is falling, we may be failing children by not focusing on their more fundamental human needs.

The Problem of Drug Abuse

Public concern about drug abuse as an important social problem comes in cycles. Although psychoactive drugs have been used for centuries, it wasn't until recent decades that the issue of drug abuse emerged as a central social issue facing the nation. During the 1980s, the level of concern over drug abuse was heightened by most politicians seeking public office, some interested in profits and others attempting to divert public attention away from other economic issues. Politicians and the news media understood that "fearmongering sells programs and newspapers" (Goldstein, 1993, p. 9) and both estates portrayed drug abuse as the nation's number one problem (Goode, 1993) to advance their careers or increase profits. Whether the public or educators are well-served or pawns in the public's hysteria may be a moot point; however, having dependable data on the dimensions of drug abuse in American society and understanding its intrusion into schools may lead to better policy decisions and more viable intervention strategies.

Aside from sensationalized coverage of drug busts and scandals in the media, the abuse of legal or controlled substances impairs the functioning of users, threatens the well-being of very young children and diminishes their success in school. Although drugs are classified according to their effects on the central nervous system, some are legal while others are illicit. All, however, are psychoactive and may alter the healthy, normal functioning of users varying with the amount used. The abuse of legal drugs in the United States, particularly alcohol and tobacco, however, has a more devastating social impact that those classified as illicit drugs. For example, more than 70% of adults in the United States use alcohol. Out of the estimated 110 million drinkers, 10 million are considered problem drinkers (Hawley, 1991). In addition, alcohol abuse has nearly doubled the social cost of all illegal drug abuse in society and has been related to 80,000 to 100,000 deaths annually. Out of this total, 23,990 teenagers have died in alcohol-related auto accidents (Stevens, 1987). Alcohol abuse has been identified as a major factor in nearly half of the nation's accidental deaths (other than auto accidents), suicides and murders (Kinney, 1991). In addition to its association with vehicular deaths, alcohol is directly linked to more than 150,000 premature infant deaths per year. Alcohol abuse alone has an estimated social cost of over $200 billion a year in medical treatment and loss of productivity (Goode, 1993).

Another legal drug, tobacco, has similar detrimental effects. Its consumption not only creates a significant level of nicotine dependence, but cigarette smoking carries with it significant social costs. Not long ago, the outspoken U.S. Surgeon General, C. Everette Koop, asserted that nicotine was as addicting to users as heroin and cocaine (Tolchin, 1988). Nicotine has been associated with increased risks of high blood pressure, heart disease and cancer, and poses a significant health risk for pregnant women. The Center for Disease Control has linked cigarette smoking to more than 320,000 deaths each year. In 1990, The American Lung Association reported that 419,000 deaths were caused by smoking and the U.S. Occupational Health and Safety Administration attributed an additional 47,000 deaths each year to second-hand smoke. Sachs (1986) estimated that 18% of the nation's total health care costs, a staggering $365 billion a year, could be directly attributed to smoking. While many have come to the defense of smokers in the growing national debate on the effects of smoking, the American Medical Association has taken issue with the tobacco industry noting that during "Joe Camel's" first four years in the spotlight, sales of Camel cigarettes to adolescents increased from $6 to $476 million (Downs, 1994). In comparison, Goldstein (1993) estimated the number of deaths attributed to smoking crack cocaine at 300 per year suggesting a misplaced emphasis of concern on the use of illicit drugs, while socially accepted abuse of both alcohol and tobacco are having a more devastating impact on society.

Substance abuse affects school children regardless of economic background or geographic region. School administrators are particularly concerned with the use of illicit drugs because of their link to declines in academic performance, school dropouts, discipline problems, crime, and the fact that they are frequently distributed on school property (Gaustad, 1993). Although it is encouraging that several national surveys indicate that the level of drug use among school-age children in general is declining, the significant level of illicit drug use, however, is unsettling. Drug use has been cited by the general public as a major problem facing schools for the past fifteen years. In 1980, for example, 14% of the general public indicated that the use of drugs was a problem, increasing to 22% in 1994 (NCES, 1993, p. 30). There is some basis for this concern particularly as it relates to school children experimenting with drugs at very early ages. More than 59% of the students surveyed indicated that they first tried alcohol in the fifth grade. More than 37% of the eighth graders and 60% of the tenth graders reported using alcohol six or more times. The survey indicated that 38% smoked their first cigarette between the fifth and eighth grade. Nearly 12% indicated that they had tried marijuana in the fifth to eighth grades; however, only 6% of the eighth graders indicated that they had used it more than six times. Nearly 17% of the tenth graders admitted to using marijuana that frequently. Only 3.6% of the eighth graders responding to the survey indicated that they had used cocaine more than once with nearly 8% of the tenth graders admitting to this level of use (NCES, 1993, p. 139). Examining the trends in drug use of high school seniors between 1975 and 1992 is also useful in defining the scope of the problem. More than 84.8% of those responding to the 1975 NCES survey indicated that over the previous twelve-month period they had used alcohol. In 1992, 76.8% indicated that they had used alcohol during this extended period. In 1974, 15.3% indicated that they had smoked marijuana; however, this percentage dropped to 8.1% in 1992. The use of cocaine by high school seniors declined from 1.9% in 1975 to 1.3% in 1992 (NCES, 1993, p. 141).

Discussion

The deterioration of family structures has compromised the future of our nation's children and has been identified as the central cause of many of the nation's most exasperating problems: poverty, crime, drug abuse and declining school performance. An overwhelming portion of the incidence of children living in poverty during the 1980s may be attributed to changes in the nuclear family structures. The direction and magnitude of these trends does not bode well for either the ability of schools to increase their effectiveness with low-income and minority children, or for the future contribution of these cohorts to the productivity of the nation. Without a long-term intervention strategy, the short-term costs of sustaining the welfare system will increase the financial burden as well as exacerbate the loss of the nation's human capital.

The dramatic rise in school discipline problems in both urban and suburban schools, including students attacking other students and teachers, antisocial behavior, and emotional outbursts in class, have eclipsed levels experienced during previous decades. The increase in both dysfunctional behavior among students in schools and urban crime over the past several decades has been attributed to the deterioration in the family structure. The findings of social science research, controlling for income level and race, indicate that more than 70% of male juveniles incarcerated in state correctional facilities come from homes in which the father is absent (Whitehead, 1993), and they are more likely to end up in penitentiaries when adults. The relationship between poverty, single-parent families and juvenile crime has been chronicled as being both significant and persistent.

Children of dysfunctional families often find it difficult to sustain their interest in mundane education and need increasing amounts of academic and therapeutic remediation (Whitehead, 1993). The burden of mitigating the effects of family disruption has fallen on schools. In order to stave off the effects of drugs in society, many schools have expanded counseling and psychological services, established parental advisory groups, developed drug education programs, offered courses of conflict resolution, installed metal detectors and hired security guards. There is little evidence, however, that these well-intended efforts have helped raise standardized test scores for a growing segment of children. During the past twelve years, society has demanded that schools prepare all students well to ensure their contribution to the nation's quest for economic survival. Although numerous proposals including strengthening academic rigor, linking scholarship with work, allowing parental choice, and engaging in school-based management have been advanced, none can ameliorate the effects of disrupted families. Fixing the problems associated with social dislocation will require the resolve of both the federal government and states, as well as time. Schools impacted by the immediate consequences of deteriorating family structures are faced with the burden of resolving these intractable issues with limited budgets and professional resources.

Implications of the Changing Social Context for School Leaders

During the decade of reform (1980-1990), the number of alternative perspectives bent on fixing and reinventing American schools increased. Concepts including decentralized governance, site-based management, teacher empowerment, transformational leadership, and principles emerging from effective school efforts were provocative. The most pronounced call for changing the role of teachers and principals emerged from the third wave reform reports which advocated "child-centered," integrated service delivery systems. This new structural configuration came with corresponding demands that principals manage schools, facilitate broader participation in decision making, and broker services available through a wide array of private-philanthropical, county, state and federal agencies. These changes had profound implications for both the structure of schooling and the administrator's role particularly with regard to the emerging emphasis on soliciting participation of those who inhabit schools and those who share responsibility for addressing social problems affecting student performance.

Integrated Services

The reports released during the third wave of educational reform responded more directly to public demands for systemic changes designed to better serve all children. These reports revealed that schools failed to address the needs of the academically gifted as well as those at-risk. They made a significant contribution to raising the consciousness of the public, policy makers and educators to the discernible linkage between low academic performance and the deterioration of the social fabric of the nation. Their recommendations for establishing integrated service systems to better serve a growing segment of the student population considered at-risk suggested schools be linked with a very large array of human service organizations in their respective communities.

Three different but related dimensions of this policy initiative contributed to generating broad-based interest. First, the emphasis placed on the need for schools to better serve all children reflected an important social theme of the decade-long educational reform movement. The corporate sector embraced this concept; however, the impetus for their escalating participation in the educational reform movement arose from trepidation that the next generation of workers may not be adequately prepared to perform in a highly competitive, information-based economy. Fulfilling expectations for increasing levels of participation and performance would require systemically reforming the current education system. The magnitude and complexity of the social problems that inhibit educational progress for at-risk children contributed to expanding the scope of school responsibility. Traditional educational perspectives hold that the principal task of schools is to attend to academic and pedagogical matters. The emerging perspective, however, posits that the education of children be more holistically addressed by requiring that problems impinging on their lives be ameliorated before they can succeed academically. Thus, academic success was no longer defined solely as a school-based issue but one dependent upon the successful intervention of a broad spectrum of community-based human service agencies.

Second, because "schools provide the organizational context for the most sustained and ongoing contact with children outside the family setting" (Smrekar, 1994, p. 422), reformers argued that they should serve as the hub in which problems could be identified and treated through expanded child-centered services. At this juncture, a number of initiatives at the national, state, county, city and site-levels illustrate the potential for intervention.

The Philadelphia Children's Network recognized that the fragmentation of child support systems was part of the problem and argued that altering existing interrelationships among these agencies was part of the solution. This capacity-building effort fostered community coordinated child services to ensure young children's readiness to learn and the reengagement of young fathers with their children (Smith, 1992).

The School Development Program, which began as a collaborative effort between the Yale Child Study Center and the New Haven Public Schools, focused on early detection, prevention, strengthening of interpersonal relationships among school personnel, families and the community to address both the causes and the symptoms of low student performance in schools (Comer, 1980).

The city of San Diego, California, recognized that its crisis-oriented service delivery system was fragmented, wasteful and inconsistent with the notion of helping children. The New Beginnings program developed a collaborative approach that systemically altered the manner in which services to children and families were organized and delivered. With schools serving as the hub, agencies shifted from inflexible, narrowly focused traditional social service providers to becoming family advocates. These advocates worked toward increasing accessibility of school staff and families to human service agencies (Payzant, 1992).

The League of Schools Reaching Out housed at Boston University linked academic success of at-risk children and developed an ecological approach to school restructuring that integrated family services, education and economic development, and utilized classroom teachers to increase involvement of families and community agencies (Davies, 1991). The initiative launched by the City of New Orleans blended community resource streams to connect parish schools with families and community services through collaborative action (Garvin & Young, 1993). The Cities in Schools program (Smrekar, 1994) established 217 alternative projects coordinating social service, health and educational services to at-risk children.

The Annie E. Casey Foundation's "New Futures" grants to the cities of Savannah, Dayton, Little Rock and Pittsburgh established case-management systems that integrated a wide array of human services to school children and their families. New Jersey's Department of Human Services has integrated "employment counseling, drug and alcohol abuse counseling, health services, and recreation services" (Smrekar, 1994, p. 422) at twenty-nine school sites. California recognized that the existing structures for delivering services to children and families were inadequate in meeting the needs of many families and were incompatible with the state's vision of future service systems. The Healthy Start program was established by Senate Bill 620 and designated the responsibility for developing comprehensive, integrated school-linked service models. These systems coordinated education, social services, health services, mental health and drug and alcohol programs (White, 1993). The notion that schools have a fundamental interest in establishing integrated service systems extended several major themes proposed in the second wave of reform reports including increasing local control, school-based management and community participation. The concept of forging these new interagency partnerships was legitimated by the reform reports and conformed to site-based management initiatives in an increasing number of districts. The concept of site-based management was based on management theories that pointed to the benefits that may be derived from increasing participation of individuals who inhabit organizations. While these initiatives first emerged in the corporate sector (Peters & Waterman, 1982; Kantor, 1983), research findings on large-scale change initiatives released by the Rand Corporation (McLaughlin, 1991) confirmed their applicability in educational settings.

Third, while the concept of integrated service systems extended child-centered agendas and reflected corporate human resource management initiatives, they also were greeted with approbation among conservative proponents of the "new federalism." The conservative Republican philosophy articulated by Presidents Nixon, Reagan and Bush asserted that the devolution of decision-making authority to the lowest levels of government was a fundamental doctrine of the American democratic system of government. Proponents of the "new federalism" in education held that states have the responsibility for schooling rather than the federal government. Those who promote this view maintained that both local districts and schools are better positioned to understand the nature of their problems than central authorities and should have the authority to solve them (Dye, 1990). An integral part of the conservative agenda is to reduce the size of government and levels of public spending. Over the past decade, the demand for educational reform, social disintegration, and the effort to reduce the size of government and its spending have forced the reexamination of how schools are organized and led.

Under normal circumstances, organizations compete for public tax dollars; however, in circumstances of heightened competition in which the survival of the organization is in jeopardy, organizations may collaborate in areas that are mutually beneficial (Bjork, 1983). In these emerging contexts, school districts have found themselves in the uncomfortable position of having to compete directly with other public agencies for scarce tax dollars. School district personnel are acutely aware of the increasing demand for compehensive school-based services to at-risk children and the shortfall in public funding to support the expansion of services to at-risk children. Policy analysts suggest that there is increasing awareness among many human service agencies that adequately serving an increasingly at-risk population will strain separate school, agency and private resource budgets (Doyle, 1987; Arthur & Bauman, 1994). These circumstances have forced school and agencies to examine the efficacy of traditional service delivery approaches and explore alternative avenues through which at-risk children may be better served. Many view this crisis as an opportunity to redefine the nature and structures of schooling as well as the relationships among professional educators. An expanded view of schools suggests they are keys to forging interagency and intergovernmental partnerships that serve as central coordinators of services for children and families. These partnerships may be a way to reduce the duplication and fragmentation of services, more efficiently utilize limited public resources and increase assistance to children.

The increasing number of interagency partnerships that have been forged between schools, private and public agencies during the last decade (1985-1995) may indicate a willingness to reframe problems and solutions associated with at-risk children as common endeavors. Although American schools have implemented various models of coordinating human services in schools, strong leadership appeared to be an important characteristic observed by the U.S. General Accounting Office (1993). While these programs may increase the likelihood of better serving at-risk student populations, few impact studies and cost-effectiveness evaluations have been conducted to assess their contributions.

IMPLICATIONS FOR CHANGING ADMINISTRATOR ROLES

The creation of integrated service systems not only blends provider disciplines and agencies in a unified structure (Morrill, 1992), but requires adoption of an ecological perspective on how children are educated. This paradigm shift will move the focus of schooling and human services away from narrow, problem-based assistance with accountability based on procedural compliance, toward an emphasis on both comprehensive neighborhood-based support and measuring success in terms of positive outcomes for children (Mitchell & Scott, 1993; Pounder, 1994). In turn, collaborative structures will redefine and expand the roles of teachers and principals as well as the relationship among schools, parents and community-based human service agencies. The characteristics of restructured schools identified by the Education Commission of the States (1983) include: 1) deregulation, 2) shared decision making, 3) parent involvement, 4) accountability based on outcomes, and 5) redesigning work. These general characteristics have significant implications for altering the roles of teachers and principals who share responsibility for leading schools.

The notion of deregulating schools is based on the assumption that the best decisions are made at the lowest level of the organization resulting in shifting decision making from state and district authorities to school sites. It implies the suspension of external regulatory controls and budgetary constraints, the transfer of decision-making authority, the utilization of the professional expertise of teachers and the accountability for outcomes. The shift towards site-based management broadens and intensifies collaboration among principals, teachers and parents. The areas of collaboration may include making decisions on curriculum and instructional methods, fashioning school policies and governing through council structures, establishing collaborative relationships with other human services organizations, allocating school resources and hiring personnel.

Over time, the role of the principal has changed. For decades, administrators have used management techniques that emphasized the use of formal authority and hierarchical arrangements characteristic of Weberian bureaucratic organizations. The shift away from reliance on formal, hierarchical authority toward increased participatory decision making will dramatically alter authority relationships in the school. As the demand for school reform has heightened, the emphasis on management shifted to more collegial models of interaction appropriate for decentralized, professional systems (Wise, 1989). The shift toward more effective human relations strategies intended to strengthen school performance encouraged the use of instructional leadership and, more recently, transformational leadership techniques (Hallinger, 1992). Transformational leadership is characterized by building on the capacity of expert teachers to participate in managing the school, building leadership teams and facilitating their work in achieving school-defined goals. Techniques associated with transformational leadership may enhance the success of school linkages with other governmental agencies. Thus, restructuring schools as integrated service systems will redefine the personal and professional roles of teachers and administrators, realign parent involvement and renegotiate roles vis-à-vis shared service boundaries with other professionals in the public and private sectors.

The reform literature that framed issues associated with teacher empowerment, professionalism and their participatory management indicated that those in the classroom largely have been left out of school-based decision processes. Their sense of alienation (Bacharach, Bamburger, Conley & Bauer, 1990) has limited the ability of districts and schools to change classroom practices and accelerate substantive, child-centered reforms. As a result, many view teacher participation in developing curriculum as a means through which decisions affecting classroom instruction may be improved (Pierpoint, 1989) and child-centered policies implemented (McLaughlin, 1991). The recent shift toward integrated service sytems has enhanced teacher empowerment initiatives and expanded their participation as members on site-based councils.

Although these councils may have varying degrees of authority over school affairs, they provide an important vehicle through which teachers and parents may influence the course of neighborhood schools. For example, in the past, teachers and school administrators were only expected to be concerned about what children did in the classroom. When schools serve as the hub of integrated service systems, however, teachers will be asked to understand what happens to children when they are at home (Smrekar, 1994), help identify their needs and connect them to available community resources. While teachers may help to identify problems among children in their classrooms, working with parents and agencies to find solutions will require a different level of activity. Linking schools with community-based service systems may be facilitated, in part, through broadly representative building level councils.

CONCLUSION

The move towards increased participation and integrated service systems is being driven by public demand that schools be more accountable for educational outcomes of all children. In this context, schools are being compelled to view the educational process from an ecological perspective (Mawhinny, 1993) that implies that children at-risk are unlikely to learn and progress unless the fundamental causes of their problems are addressed. Meeting these new public expectations will call for changing the structures of schooling, transforming teaching and learning and altering leadership roles of both teachers and principals.

Transforming the roles of teachers and principals to fit restructured school contexts will not be easy. Redesigning work not only will violate broadly accepted norms of privacy, cordiality and equality (Lortie, 1975), it will require renegotiating structures, professional norms and career expectations. Teachers and principals, identified as key stakeholders in integrated service systems, will be compelled to alter distinctive patterns of employee relations and authority in schools. In most instances, "differences in capacity and expertise are recognized in differentiated power, workloads, tasks, and rewards" (Pounder, 1994, p. 154). Altering school structures will also alter the concept of leadership, expanding it to include teachers serving in a variety of new capabilities including formal leadership roles such as lead teachers, mentor teachers and master teachers (Pounder, 1994); members of instructional teams in redefined classrooms (Sizer, 1984); and human resource coordinators. While redesigning work contexts has been the focus of an increasing number of reform initiatives over the past decade, the implications of these changes for building principals needs to be more extensively examined.

It is inevitable that efforts at restructuring education will have a concurrent impact on the roles of principals and their place in the social system of the school. The changes envisioned for American schooling will require delineating the emerging behaviors expected of them and reframing their role expectations. According to Pounder (1994), emerging school contexts are characterized by the displacement of stability with fluidity, hierarchical decision-making authority with dispersed expert authority, and managing the status quo with facilitating change. These new circumstances will place greater emphasis on 1) building the capacity of teachers and schools as an antecedent condition to change, 2) focusing on accountability for individual performance and school outcomes, 3) validating authority through teacher empowerment in redefined work settings, 4) redesigning and coordinating work and 5) serving as transformational leaders. Developing skills in these key areas will accelerate school reform and enhance educational progress for all children which Fullan (1993) portrayed as the moral purpose of schooling.

REFERENCES

American Psychological Association. (1993). *Violence & youth: Psychology's response to, Volume 1*. Washington, D.C.: Author.

Arthur, G. & Bauman, P. (1994). School-based community services: A study of public agency partnerships. *Journal of School Leadership*, 4(6):649–671.

Bacharach, S., Bamburger, P., Conley, S. & Bauer, S. (1990). The dimensionality of decision participation in educational organizations: The value of a multi-domain evaluation approach. *Educational Administration Quarterly,* 26(2):126–167.

Bennett, W. (1993). *The index of leading cultural indicators.* Washington, D.C.: The Heritage Foundation.

Björk, L. (1983). *Organizational environment and the development of a research university.* Unpublished doctoral dissertation. Albuquerque, NM: University of New Mexico.

Björk, L. (1995). Substance and symbolism in the education commission reports. In R. Ginsberg and D. Plank (Eds.), *Commission reports and reforms: Fashioning educational policy in the 1980's and beyond.* New York: Praeger (In Press).

Boyer, E. (1983). *High school.* New York: Carnegie Foundation for the Advancement of Teaching.

Bracey, G. (1992). The second Bracey report on the condition of public education. *Phi Delta Kappan,* 74(2):104–117.

Brogan, D. (1962). *The American character.* New York: Vintage Books.

Carnegie Council for Adolescent Development. (1989). *Turning points.* Washington, D.C.: Author.

Carnegie Foundation for the Advancement of Teaching. (1986). *A nation prepared: Teachers for the twenty-first century.* New York: Author.

Clark, D. & Astuto, T. (1990). The disjunction of federal educational policy and national educational needs in the 1990's. In D. Mitchell & M. Goertz (Eds.), *Educational politics for the new century.* London: The Falmer Press.

Clark, D. & Astuto, T. (1994, March). Redirecting reform: Challenges to popular assumptions about teachers and students. *Phi Delta Kappan,* 75(7):512–520.

Comer, J. (1980). *School power: Implications of an intervention project.* New York: Free Press.

Committee for Economic Development. (1985). *Investing in our children.* New York: Author.

Committee for Economic Development. (1987). *Children in need.* New York: Author.

Commission on Minority Population in American Life. (1988). *One third of a nation.* Washington, D.C.: American Council on Education/Education Commission of the States.

Commission on Policy for Racial Justice of the Joint Center for Political Studies. (1989). *Visions for a better way: A black appraisal of public schooling.* Washington, D.C.: Joint Policy Center for Political Studies.

Congressional Budget Office. (1984). *Poverty among children.* Washington, D.C.: Author.

Cuban, L. (1990). Four stories about national goals for American education. *Phi Delta Kappan,* 72(4):264–271.

Davies, D. (1991). Testing a strategy for reform: The League of Schools reaching out. Paper presented at the annual meeting of the American Educational Research Association, Chicago (ERIC Document Reproduction Service No. ED 331 178).

Downs, G. (1994, August 14). Smoking guns. *Savannah-News Press,* pp. E-1, E-3.

Doyle, D. P. (1991). America 2000. *Phi Delta Kappan,* 73(3):184–191.

Dye, T. R. (1990). *American federalism: Competition among governments.* Lexington, MA: Lexington Books.

Education Commission of the States, Task Force on Education for Economic Growth. (1983). *Action for excellence: A comprehensive plan to improve our nation's schools.* Washington, D.C.: Author.

Eisner, E. (1992). The federal reform of schools: Looking for the silver bullet. *Phi Delta Kappan,* 73(8):722–733.

Elam, S. (1990). The 22nd annual Gallup poll of the public's attitudes toward the public schools. *Phi Delta Kappan*, 72(2):41-55.

Elam, S., Rose, L. & Gallup, A. (1993). The 25th annual Gallup/Phi Delta Kappa poll of the public's attitude towards the public schools. *Phi Delta Kappan*, 75(2):137-157.

Elam, S., Rose, L. & Gallup, A. (1994). The 25th annual Gallup/Phi Delta Kappa poll of the public's attitude towards the public schools. *Phi Delta Kappan*, 76(1):41-64.

Elmore, R. (1979-1980). Backwardmapping: Implementation research and policy decisions. *Political Science Quarterly*, 94(4):601-616.

Firestone, W. A., Fuhrman, S. & Kirst, M. W. (1990). An overview of educational reform since 1983. In J. Murphy (Ed.), *The reform of American public education during the 1980's: Perspectives and cases*. Berkeley: McCutchan.

Fullan, M. (1993). *Change forces: Probing the depths of educational reform*. New York: The Falmer Press.

Garvin, J. & Young, A. (1993). Resource issues: A case study from New Orleans. In L. Adler & S. Gardner (Eds.), *The politics of linking schools and social services*. Washington, D.C.: The Falmer Press.

Gaustad, J. (1993). Substance abuse policy. *ERIC Digest*. Eugene, OR: ERIC Clearinghouse on Educational Management, University of Oregon.

Goertz, M. (1990). Education politics for the new century: Introduction and overview. In D. Mitchell & M. Goertz (Eds.), *Education politics for the new century* (pp. 1-9). London: Falmer Press.

Goldstein, R. (1993). Getting real about getting high: An interview with Andrew Weil, M.D. In E. Goode (Ed.), *Drugs, society, and behavior* (pp. 9-11). Guilford, CT: The Dushkin Publishing Group.

Goode, E. (1993). *Drugs, society, and behavior*. Guilford, CT: The Duskin Publishing Group.

Hallinger, P. (1992). The evolving role of American principals: From managerial to instructional to transformational leaders. *Journal of Educational Administration*, 30(3):35-48.

Hawley, R. (1991). Legalizing the intolerable is a bad idea. *Phi Delta Kappan*, 73(1):62-64.

Henderson, H. (1977). A new economics. In D. Vermilye (Ed.), *Work and education*. San Francisco: Jossey-Bass.

Hodgkinson, H. (1985). *All one system: Demographics of education, kindergarten through graduate school*. Washington, D.C.: Institute for Educational Leadership.

Hodgkinson, H. (1991). Reform versus reality. *Phi Delta Kappan*, 73(1):8-16.

Howe, H. (1991). American 2000: A bumpy ride on four trains. *Phi Delta Kappan*, 73(3):192-203.

Kantor, R. (1983). *The change masters: Innovation for productivity in the American Corporation*. New York: Simon & Schuster.

King, E. F. (1994). Goals 2000: Educate America Act. *School Law Bulletin*, 25(4):15-27.

Kinney J. (1991). *Loosening the grip: A handbook of alcohol information*. St. Louis: Mosby-Yearbook.

Kirst, M. & McLaughlin, M. (1990). *Rethinking children's policy: Implications for educational administration*. Bloomington, IN: Indiana University, Consortium on Educational Policy Studies.

Lindbloom, C. (1980). *The policy making process*, (2nd ed.). Englewood Cliffs, NJ: Prentice-Hall.

Lortie, D. (1975). *Schoolteacher: A sociological study*. Chicago: University of Chicago Press.

Males, M. (1992). Top school problems are myths. *Phi Delta Kappan*, 72(7):566-568.

Marriott, M. (1994, December 26). Young, angry and lethal. *Newsweek*, 74(26):122.

Mawhinny, H. (1993). Discovering shared values: Ecological models to support interagency collaboration. In L. Adler & S. Gardner (Eds.), *The politics of linking schools and social services: The 1993 yearbook of the Politics of Education Association* (pp. 33–50). Washington, D.C.: The Falmer Press.

McLaughlin, M. (1991). The Rand change agent study: Ten years later. In A. Odden (Ed.), *Education policy implementation* (pp. 143–156). Albany: State University of New York Press.

Mitchell, B. (1990). Children, youth, and educational leadership. In B. Mitchell and L. Cunningham (Eds.), *Educational leadership in changing contexts of families, communities, and schools*. Chicago: The University Press of Chicago.

Mitchell, B. & Scott, L. (1993). Professional and institutional perspectives on interagency collaboration. In L. Adler & S. Gardner (Eds.), *The politics of linking schools and social services: The 1993 yearbook of the Politics of Education Association* (pp. 75–93). Washington, D.C.: The Falmer Press.

Morrill, W. (1992). Overview of service delivery to children. *The Future of Children*, 2:32–43.

Murphy, J. (1990). Educational reform of the 1980's: A comprehensive analysis. In J. Murphy (Ed.), *Educational reform of the 1980's: Perspectives and cases* (pp. 3–56). Berkeley, CA: McCutchan Publishing Corporation.

Murphy, J. (1995). Changing role of the teacher. In M. O'Hair & S. Odell (Eds.), *Educating teachers for leadership and change* (pp. 311–323). Thousand Oaks, CA: Corwin Press.

National Center for Educational Statistics. (1988). *The condition of education 1988, vol. 2*. United States Department of Education, Washington, D.C.: Government Printing Office.

National Center for Educational Statistics. (1993). *Digest of educational statistics 1993*. Washington, D.C.: United States Department of Education, Government Printing Office.

National Commission on Children. (1991). *Beyond rhetoric: A new American agenda for children and families*. Washington, D.C.: Author.

National Commission on Excellence in Education. (1983). *A nation at risk*. Washington, D.C.: U.S. Department of Education.

National excellence: A case for developing America's talent. (1993). Washington, D.C.: United States Department of Education.

National Governors' Association. (1986). *Time for results: The governors' 1991 report on education*. Washington, D.C.: Author.

National Science Board. (1983). *Educating Americans for the 21st century*. Washington, D.C.: National Science Foundation.

Odden, A. (1991). *Education policy implementation*. Albany: SUNY Press.

Payzant, T. (1992). New Beginnings in San Diego: Developing a strategy for interagency collaboration. *Phi Delta Kappan*, 74(2):139–146.

Peters, T. & Waterman, R. (1982). *In search of excellence: Lessons from America's best run companies*. New York: Harper & Row Publishers.

Peterson, P. (1985). Did the education commissions say anything? *Education and urban society*, 17(2):126–144.

Pierpont, B. (1989, January 22). The price of excellence. *CBS Sunday Morning*.

Pounder, D. (1994). Educational and demographic trends: Implications for womens' representation in school leadership. In Prestine & P. Thurston (Eds.), *Advances in educational administration: New directions in educational administration: Policy, preparation, and practice* (pp. 135–150). Greenwich, CT: JAI Press Inc.

Quality Education for Minorities Project. (1990). *Education that works: An action plan for the education of minorities.* Cambridge, MA: Massachussetts Institute of Technology.

Recer, P. (1995, February 19). Research warns a sharp increase in murder rate within decade. *Savannah News Press,* 29(53):4-A.

Reed, S. & Sautter, R. (1991). Children of poverty: The status of twelve million Americans. *Phi Delta Kappan,* 71(10):K1-K12.

Reich, R. (1983). *The next American frontier.* New York: Times Books.

Sachs (1986). Cost benefit analysis of tobacco dependency treatment. In J. Ockene (Ed.), *Pharmacologic treatment of tobacco dependence: Proceedings of the World Congress,* November 4-5, 1985 (pp. 270-280). Cambridge, MA: Harvard University School of Government.

Sautter, R. C. (1995). Standing up to violence. *Phi Delta Kappan,* 76(5):K1-K12.

Sergiovanni, T., Burlingame, M., Coombs, F. & Thurston, P. (1987). *Educational governance and administration.* Englewood Cliffs, NJ: Prentice-Hall, Inc.

Sizer, T. R. (1984). *Horace's compromise: The dilemma of the American high school.* Boston: Houghton Mifflin.

Smith, R. (1992). Help the children. Fix the system. *University of Pennsylvania Law Journal,* 27:20-23.

Smrekar, C. (1994). The missing link in school-linked social service programs. *Educational Evaluation and Policy Analysis,* 16(4):422-433.

Snyder, D. (1984). *The strategic context of education in America 1985-1995.* Washington, D.C.: National Education Association.

Spring, J. (1986). *The American school 1642-1985.* New York: Longman.

Stevens, W. (1987, October 29). Deaths from drunken driving increase. *The New York Times,* p. 12.

Tolchin, M. (1988, May 17). Surgeon general asserts that smoking is an addiction, *The New York Times,* pp. 1, 26.

Twentieth Century Task Force on Federal Educational Policy (1983). *Making the grade.* New York: Twentieth Century Fund.

U.S. Department of Education. (1991). *America 2000: An education strategy.* Washington, D.C.: U.S. Government Printing Office.

U.S. General Accounting Office. (1993, December 30). *School-linked human services: A comprehensive strategy for aiding students at risk of school failure.* Washington, D.C.: U.S. Government Printing Office GAO/HRD-94-21.

U.S. News and World Report. (1987, November). Coming to grips with alcoholism, pp. 56-63.

White, W. (1993). California's state partnership for school services. In L. Adler & S. Gardner (Eds.), *The politics of linking schools and social services* (pp. 171-178). Washington, D.C.: The Falmer Press.

Whitehead, B. D. (1993). Dan Quale was right. *The Atlantic Monthly,* 27(4):47-84.

Wirth, A. (1992). *Education and work in the year 2000.* San Francisco: Jossey-Bass Publishers.

Wise, A. (Ed.). (1987). *Public sector payrolls.* Chicago: University of Chicago Press.

Wise, A. (1989). Professional teaching: A new paradigm for the management of education. In T. J. Sergiovanni & J. Moore (Eds.), *Schooling for tomorrow* (pp. 270-280). Boston: Allyn & Bacon.

CHAPTER 16

Violence in Our Schools

M. SUE TOLLEY

INTRODUCTION

THIS study was undertaken to analyze the problem of violence in our schools and possible remedies suggested by various sources. "Because states mandate compulsory attendance by youth, the right to learn in a safe environment should be provided. Without a safe environment, educators assert that students cannot focus their attention on acquiring the knowledge to be a citizen in a democracy" (Hiatt, 1987, p. 1). "Our nation's schools, once thought to be safe havens, have fallen victim to an increase in gun violence, and educators and children are caught in the crossfire" (Center to Prevent Handgun Violence, 1990, p. 2).

Violence has become news in the nation's public schools, touching rural and suburban schools as well as those in the inner city. Many school administrators are going through a period of denial, refusing to admit the presence of violence in their schools. However, the problem must be assessed and the "blinders" removed as we face a changing world with changing problems.

There must also be communication within the community. "The more informed the school community is about school problems and the steps the school district is taking to eliminate them, the higher the probability of success of the district's efforts" (New Jersey State Department of Education, 1992, p. 18).

This chapter will focus on the extent of violence in our schools. Factors that influence violence and suggested corrections will be examined.

REVIEW OF THE LITERATURE

Los Angeles County Commission on Human Relations. (1989). *Intergroup conflict in Los Angeles County schools. Report on a survey of hate crime.* Los Angeles, CA: Author (ERIC Document Reproduction Service No. ED 312 362).

"As could be expected, schools which were homogeneous in their student population were less likely to suffer incidents than their heterogeneous counterparts. It appears that a greater incidence of hate crime begins to appear when any one minority ethnic group (be it White or non-White) begins to exceed 10 percent of the student population" (p. 2).

"In 1980, the Los Angeles County Commission on Human Relations began compiling statistics on criminal acts motivated by racial and religious bigotry. The Commission approached the Los Angeles County Office of Education in November 1987 about the feasibility of a joint project. . . . The survey was drafted and distributed to all 1,570 schools in the county" (p. 5).

"In all, 956 schools, or 61 percent of the total, responded to the survey. Of these, 354 reported that they had incidents of hate crime over the past year, and 602 responded negatively. Overall, 37 percent of those responding had incidents of hate crime" (p. 5).

"Across the board, more schools reported anti-Black incidents than any other type" (p. 7).

"In comparing the responses of differing school levels, there seems to be a slightly higher probability of incidents occurring in the junior high school population when compared to the elementary and high school levels" (p. 7).

"The second most common manifestation of conflict was physical violence, which occurred almost 25 percent of the time" (p. 7).

"It must be noted here that there is a substantial difference between White supremacist or "skinhead" gangs and gangs in the traditional sense of the word. While gangs such as Crips or Bloods draw upon their own ethnic group for their affiliations, their primary reason for existence is to provide social support and (illegal) economic rewards. In addition, most of these gangs usually victimize others of their own population. In the case of White supremacist groups, however, their primary activity is to threaten, intimidate, or physically assault non-Whites under the rubric of "racial superiority" and "White pride" (p. 11).

It was interesting that this study found in the majority of instances where students were victims of hate crime, perpetrators were counseled and returned to class. In the majority of instances where a school employee was the victim, perpetrators were suspended. Does that mean that educators are more valuable than children? Do they deserve more protection?

Another interesting finding was that there was no relationship between the socioeconomic status of students and the incidence of hate crime in the county's schools. Obviously, education and a higher socioeconomic status does not always "broaden minds" and allow people to accept others as equals.

Newman, I. M. (1991). *Violence, victims and suicide: Nebraska adolescents' attitudes and behaviors* (Tech. Rep. No. 23). Lincoln: University of Nebraska, Prevention Center for Alcohol and Drug Abuse (ERIC Document Reproduction Service No. ED 340 995).

"As part of the Nebraska Adolescent Student Health Survey of 1988, a sample of Nebraska students in grades 8 and 10 in 37 school were asked about their involvement in physical fights; about their access to weapons; about being victims of robbery, physical assault, threats and attempts at forced sex; about their attitudes to violence and coercion; and about attitudes toward and attempts at suicide" (p. 8).

"A fight was defined as a physical fight . . . when two people hit each other or attack each other with weapons, not when they yell or shout" (p. 10).

"Thirty percent of the females reported fighting at least once during the past year. Fifty-eight percent of the males reported having been in a physical fight during the past year" (p. 10).

"About one-fifth of all students felt that threatening to use a weapon was an effective way to avoid fighting. Almost one-quarter of all the male students felt that carrying a weapon was an effective way to avoid fighting" (p. 11).

"About one-fifth of the male students also felt that joining a gang for protection was an effective way to avoid fighting" (p. 11).

"A substantial majority (69%) of the tenth grade males reported they could get a gun if they wanted" (p. 13).

"These findings suggest that fighting, approval of coercive methods and the availability of guns are part of a general climate of violence for some Nebraska students" (p. 15).

"Almost half the students reported having been threatened with physical assault both at school and outside of school" (p. 19).

In this study the author suggests that Nebraska needs to become aware of the growing problem of violence in school and outside of school. He reminds the reader that the rate of adolescents fifteen to nineteen years of age dying from violence increased 23% from 1984 to 1988. In 1988 Nebraska ranked thirty-second in the nation's fifty states in violent teenage deaths.

Mr. Newman thinks violence can be prevented if educators will focus on four points. They are: the tendency to violence is learned, violence is frequently enabled by the use of alcohol and other drugs, incidences of violence can be reduced through appropriate education programs, and programs must involve and generate support from all levels of the community. He goes on to say that parents must recognize that young people learn from their parents' behaviors. Therefore, parents must also develop skills to handle stress and tension that do not include violence.

Mr. Newman believes media portrayals of violence need to be counteracted with realistic information. Instances of violence reported in the press and shown on television do not constitute the norm for society. Also, I think the media and schools should consistently inform children that joining a gang is not the best means of avoiding a conflict that might result in fighting.

In his conclusion, Mr. Newman states that only when all segments of the community become aware of the violence-related problems and direct prevention services appropriately can we expect to note significant reductions in the types of violence described in his study.

Several sensible program components were provided by Mr. Newman that should be implemented in our schools today to prevent violence. Suggestions included: encourage the development of a strong sense of personal worth and self-esteem in children; involve parents in all aspects of a child's education; teach people the signs of high-risk individuals; develop peer support groups at school and in the community; and, establish meaningful relationships between schools, law enforcement and the judicial system.

Hunsaker, A. C. (1982). The impact of location alteration on school attendance of Chicano gang members (ERIC Document Reproduction Service No. ED 223 388).

> "The high school completion rate for Chicanos is only half that of non-Hispanics. For Chicano gang members, the completion rate is lower than that of the Chicano population as a whole" (p. 1).

"One study of six gang cliques in East Los Angeles found that high school completion rates were less than 11% for five of the six cliques" (p. 1).

"Of the various reasons cited for dropping out of school, at least one may be specific to the Chicano gang member: problems emanating from on-campus interaction with members of rival gangs. If the school is located within a territory claimed by one barrio, the campus may become a battleground for members of other barrios who wish to attend" (p. 1).

"The setting for this study was a community-based delinquency and gang violence prevention project. Preliminary studies indicated that gang members who dropped out of school frequently mentioned inter-barrio fighting as the most important reason for failing to continue school" (p. 2).

"The Alternative Studies Program (ASP) provided a flexible approach to education in which students contracted with tutors to meet educational goals within specified time periods" (p. 2).

"The ASP was moved to a neutral site in order to encourage gang members to attend" (p. 2).

"Thirteen males between the ages of thirteen and eighteen admitted to the gang violence prevention project during a one-year period served as subjects for this study" (p. 2).

The results of this study may be limited, possibly invalid, since such a small population was studied. The author stated that of the thirteen subjects selected to participate in the study, only five (38%) elected to return to school when offered the alternative site within their home barrio. However, he emphasized that the baseline rate of return-to-school for Chicano gang members is not greater than 10%. Therefore, the alteration of school site increased the rate of return-to-school by 28% at least.

In his conclusion, Dr. Hunsaker said the study demonstrated that the alteration of school sites can have a significant impact on the school attendance behavior of Chicano gang members.

As numerous communities are faced with acknowledging the presence of undesirable gangs in middle and high schools, it is our responsibility as educators, administrators, parents and community members to find "creative" strategies (such as the alternative school site in this study) to address their presence and overcome the negative impact they have on a school environment. They are children who deserve an education as all children do in our society. Too many times we expel children who belong to gangs because of their behavior on the school campus with no thought to what they will do once they are out of the school environment. Once expelled from the school setting, statistics indicate that these children become more involved in community crime, specifically in drugs. Isn't there something we can do to prevent this from happening?

Toby, J. (1983). *Violence in schools. Research in brief.* Washington, D.C.: National Institute of Justice (ERIC Document Reproduction Service No. ED 319 837).

"According to two national studies of school crime, most school crime, like most crime outside of school, is nonviolent" (p. 2).

"One study, conducted by the National Institute of Education (NIE) in 1976 was a victimization survey of 31,373 students and 23,895 teachers in more than 600 public secondary schools in the United States" (p. 2).

"The survey results showed that teachers were in much greater danger of losing their property through stealth than of being assaulted or robbed. . . . Both teachers and students tend to be victimized more violently in the larger cities" (p. 2).

"The second study was derived from a National Crime Survey data collected in 1974 and 1975 by the Bureau of the Census in 26 big cities" (p. 3).

"Based on these data, nonviolent offenses also predominate in the central cities" (p. 3).

"Although school violence is less common than nonviolent theft, even in the schools of the biggest cities, violent school crimes arouse destructive fears among students, parents, and teachers. . . . Four percent of all secondary school students in smaller public schools said that they stayed home from school out of fear at least once in the month before the survey" (p. 3).

"In large cities 7 percent of the senior high school students and 8 percent of the junior high school students said they had stayed home from school out of fear at least once in the month before the survey" (p. 3).

The NIE study concluded that students were the main perpetrators of school violence because most victims of assaults and robberies identified the perpetrators as students. The author states that the majority of perpetrators of school violence are strangers to the victims. The bulk of the perpetrators in the twenty-six-city study were adolescent or young-adult males. Although blacks constituted only 29% of the general population in the twenty-six cities, three-quarters of the perpetrators of violent offenses were black. Finally more than a quarter of the robberies and the aggravated assaults were carried out by groups of three or more perpetrators.

The author states that the rate of assaults and robberies of students are greater at the junior high level than at the senior high level, possibly because junior high schools contain a higher proportion of involuntary students. These facts suggest that student initiated violence in public schools could be reduced provided that attending students wanted to be in the school for educational purposes rather than to comply with the law.

The author speculates that one way to achieve greater voluntary participation in school enrollment is to try harder to persuade adolescents that education is worth taking seriously. Also, he would like to see the compulsory attendance age lowered to fifteen to eliminate those students who view school as a prison or as a "compulsory recreation center." Thus, the environment would be safer for those who want to attend.

Mr. Toby believes continued vigilance is necessary to prevent intruders, including dropouts, from making disruptive forays into school buildings. He believes that we should not accept violent schools with fatalistic resignation.

Hiatt, D. B. (1987, November). Avenue to safe schools: Research, policy and practice. Paper presented at the annual meeting of the California Educational Research Association, Malibu, CA (ERIC Document Reproduction Service No. ED 299 686).

"Because states mandate compulsory attendance by youth, the right to learn in a safe environment should be provided. Without a safe environment, educators assert that students cannot focus their attention on acquiring the knowledge to be a citizen in a democracy" (p. 1).

"Believing in the right to safe schools, the Ninety-third Congress of the United States in 1974 passed the Safe School Study Act. As a response to this legislation, the National Institute of Education (NIE) designed a three-part study to acquire information on the current status of safety in public schools in America" (p. 1).

"Phase I of the NIE study was a survey of 4000 elementary and secondary school principals. For a monthly period, they were asked to make daily reports on the incidence of illegal or disruptive activities" (p. 2).

"During Phase II of the study, 642 public junior and senior high school principals were surveyed by on-site field representatives" (p. 2).

"Phase III of the study was a series of case studies of schools which had changed from a large incidence of crime and violence in the school to a safer school environment or those which continued to have serious problems with crime and violence" (p. 2).

Even though this study was conducted several years ago, many of the findings are relevant in the schools today. It was noted that schools which reside within a high crime community report more violence and vandalism. Looking at the age of children, the study found that students in junior high schools are more likely to report victimization than older students. Apparently younger students are victimized by older students.

Many other results were noted in this study. Larger schools report a greater percentage of violence and vandalism. Intense stress among students for leadership increases vandalism. Schools with clear rules of conduct enforced by the principal report less violence and vandalism. Schools with students that report fair discipline practices report less violence and vandalism. Small class size results in less violence and vandalism. Schools in which students indicate the relevance of school to their lives report less violence and vandalism. A principal who appears to be ineffective or invisible to students reports more violence and vandalism in that school. Schools with principals that provide opportunities for the teachers and students to be participatory members of decision making report less violence and vandalism. Cohesiveness among the teaching staff and the principal result in less violence and vandalism.

The findings of the interviews indicated that 38% of students had been a victim of robbery, assault or larceny. Younger students tended to be more frequently or more seriously victimized. Whites were most likely to be the victims, but Asian minorities reported that all other ethnic groups victimized them. Being fearful "on occasion" within the school was mentioned by 28% of students and 36% indicated they avoided places at school due to fear for their personal safety.

Lavatories seemed to be the most dangerous location as reported by students. Weapons appeared to be common in school as 28% reported that they had carried a weapon one or more times to school and more than 50% indicated that weapons were regularly carried by some of the students.

Center to Prevent Handgun Violence (1990). *Caught in the crossfire: A report on gun violence in our nation's schools.* Washington, D.C.: Author (ERIC Document Reproduction Service No. ED 325 950).

"Our nation's schools, once thought to be safe havens, have fallen victim to an increase in gun violence, and educators and children are caught in the crossfire" (p. 1).

"Gang or drug disputes were the leading cause of school gun violence (18%)" (p. 2).

"The Center to Prevent Handgun Violence examined gun violence in both public and private schools during the past four academic years. The information in this report was abstracted from more than 2,500 news stories in our nation's newspapers" (p. 2).

"For purposes of this study, we examined all incidents which we were able to uncover where shootings occurred at school during school functions or where individuals held others hostage at gunpoint on school property during school functions" (p. 2).

"The Center examined 227 such incidents in this report" (p. 2).

The Center's results were alarming to say the least. During 1986 to 1990, seventy-one people have been killed with guns at school. At least another 201 were severely wounded. In addition, at least 242 individuals were held hostage by someone with a gun.

These statistics are not localized to one area of the country. School shootings occurred in thirty-five states and the District of Columbia. There were no clear geographic patterns. High schools were more than twice as likely to host these events of terror than middle or elementary schools. Intentional shootings were reported four times more frequently than accidental shootings or suicide. Males were far more likely to be the offenders in school shootings and hostage takings. They were also more likely to be the victims or targets.

The study revealed that youngsters aged thirteen to seventeen were most likely to be the offenders and victims of gun violence. When students, twelve and under, were the victims of gun violence in schools, 94% of the students were victimized by adults. When students, thirteen and older, were victims, 82% of the offenders were other students or other teenagers who came onto school campuses.

Researching media coverage showed that there was not one overriding cause for gun violence in school. Rather, there were five causes that sparked most of the incidents: gang-drug related activity, continuations of long-standing disagreements, playing with or cleaning guns in schools, fights over material possessions and romantic disagreements. Handguns were the weapon of choice for students and adults who committed gun-related violence in schools.

Most of the shootings and hostage taking occurred inside schools with hallways and classrooms as the most common locations. A sizable number occurred on the grounds of the school.

In the Center's conclusion the potential for additional gun violence was examined. With an estimated 400,000 boys carrying handguns to school yearly, there is a fear that we may experience even greater rates of death, injury and violence.

The Center offered many reasons why gun violence is increasing in our schools. One reason is the sheer availability of guns in America. For every household in America there are two guns in the hands of private citizens.

The Center believes that it is going to take the efforts of parents, educators, lawmakers and law-enforcement officials working together to change this situation. Students must be educated about the great danger involved in carrying guns and the real facts about gun violence. We need to provide information to the parents on how to reduce the potential for violence. It has to be the lawmakers and law-enforcement officials responsibility to work together to make sure that those who carry guns and those who commit gun violence on school property are severely punished. It is important to pull together now and fight back against the epidemic of violence in our schools.

Peach, L. (1991, February). A study of violence and misconduct perpetrated agasinst teachers by students in selected rural Tennessee schools. Paper presented at the annual meeting of the Eastern Educational Research Association, Boston, MA (ERIC Document Reproduction Service No. ED 338 462).

"The purpose of the study was to determine certain incidence of violent acts and other types of malicious conduct by students against teachers in selected rural Tennessee public schools" (p. 3).

"Because of the diverse make up of the student population in most schools, disruptions within the school environment and carry-over disturbances from external sources pervade public school campuses" (p. 3).

"The problem is of such a magnitude in some localities that the normal operation of school is curtailed" (p. 3).

"The National Association of School Security Directors estimate that violent acts in schools cost the American taxpayer nearly a billion dollars annually" (p. 4).

"A questionnaire was sent to 35 high school principals in certain rural regions of the State of Tennessee" (p. 4).

"The study was limited to situations where the students involved were placed on suspended status or expelled from school. Also, the violence or misconduct occurred on school premises or during school sponsored activities" (p. 4).

"A total of 27 school principals (77%) returned completed questionnaires" (p. 4).

Dr. Peach's findings in this 1991 study show that in three years there were some 229 violent acts committed by students toward teachers in the twenty-seven high schools responding to the questionnaire. These incidents included one murder, two armed robberies, one reported rape, 129 acts of vandalism, eighty-six threats against teachers, one case of arson and nine acts of physical abuse.

One interesting result that came to light in the study was that most students involved in disruptive acts were from single-parent home situations. This gives us a fact to use in parenting classes to help single mothers see the need for a father figure or a mentor in their children's lives.

The author said schools must take the responsibility to address violence. Dr. Peach said an action plan should include the development of meaningful school programs, improved guidance services and better communication between the home and school.

He lists eight specific guidelines which he thinks should help to decrease violence and make schools safer places to teach and learn. They are

(1) Controlled access to school buildings and other facilities
(2) Proper identification of students and visitors
(3) Adequate supervision and observation techniques
(4) Programs designed to meet diverse student needs
(5) Student and parental input into school rules and regulations
(6) Regular reporting of misconduct
(7) Cooperation with law enforcement agencies and positive security planning
(8) Meaningful school board policies and participation in the management of critical situations that occur at school or at school-related events
(9) The availability of counselors and other qualified personnel to respond to student needs

Violence in schools needs to be treated as a societal problem. Combating this problem requires improved cooperation between the school, the parents, the community, the law enforcers and the lawmakers. It is going to take a joint effort to make a difference.

Regnery, A. S. (1985, April). Current problems encountered by American youth: Delinquency, crime, school violence, school discipline, and related matters. Paper presented at the Conference on the Development of Civic Competence and Civic Responsibility, Irsee, West Germany (ERIC Document Reproduction Service No. ED 299 178).

"It would thus be worthwhile, and would give a good indication of our crime problem to start by making comparisons between American and German crime rates" (p. 1).

"During 1982 in the United States, there were 22,500 murders: there were 3,012 in Germany" (p. 1).

"While there were 30,500 arrests for robbery in Germany, there were 574,000 in the United States" (p. 1).

"Taking just the violent crimes, we find that there were more than 12 times as many arrests for crimes in the United States than in Germany; compensating for the difference in populations, we found nearly 4 times as many arrests per hundred thousand people as did the Germans" (p. 2).

"In the United States about 33% of all violent crimes are committed by juveniles. In Germany about 14% of the violent crimes are committed by juveniles" (p. 2).

"As much as 80% of juvenile crime is committed by a small number of offenders, not more than 5 or 10% of the juvenile population" (p. 3).

"Our most serious juvenile crime problem is with the chronic offender" (p. 3).

"There is little doubt that the family breakdown has contributed considerably to our juvenile crime problem" (p. 4).

"For both violent crimes and property crimes, those 12 to 19 years of age are nearly four times as likely to be victimized as those over 35 years of age" (p. 4).

"Murder remains the most likely cause of death for black males under twenty-five in the United States" (p. 4).

"The good news is that most American children do not get into trouble" (p. 5).

When looking at the comparison of crime between the United States and Germany in 1982, it makes one wonder about the direction in which we are headed in education. Why do countries such as Germany and Japan have a significantly lower crime rate? Is this a reflection on the quality of our public schools? Would improving discipline in the schools decrease violence as well as helping us increase educational excellence? One has to remember that although the statistics are shocking, most incidents of crime and violence in the schools are committed by a relatively small percentage of the students. However, educators realize that it does not take more than a few students who choose to victimize their school and their fellow students to cause major disruption to a school system.

Mr. Regnery states a relevant fact about our juvenile justice system. He says that it is undergoing a dramatic revolution. Frustrated by its inability to control juvenile crime, many state legislatures have made important changes to the system. He thinks that with time the juvenile justice system will become simply another criminal justice system. Increased juvenile violence and crime will lead to more stringent laws and penalties for breaking the laws.

Bull, K. S. (1991, March). Minority dropouts: Do rural, urban, and suburban administrators perceive causes affecting minorities as priority items? In *Reaching our potential: Rural education in the 90's*. Symposium conducted at the Rural Education Conference, Nashville (ERIC Document Reproduction Service No. ED 342 553).

294   CONCLUSIONS AND RECOMMENDATIONS

"About 25% of American students fail to complete twelve years of education" (p. 3).

"Urban students drop out more frequently than rural students. Rural educators claim that a rural education is different, better than in the more crowded and congested urban areas, with fewer problems leading students to drop out" (p. 3).

"Minority students are more likely to drop out than are their white, middle class peers. As many as 56% of a school minority population drop out of school before graduation" (p. 3).

"The purpose of this study was to examine the perspectives of administrators concerning the priority of causal variables contributing to minority students dropping out of school" (p. 4).

"The instrument for this study was created by Bull, Salyer and Montgomery" (p. 8).

"The subjects were randomly selected principals (650) and superintendents (650) drawn from *Patterson's American Education*" (p. 8).

"The sample contained 752 identifiable males and 119 females. Subjects averaged 10.7 years in administration and 12.3 in teaching" (p. 9).

This article examined how peer violence was ranked by administrators as a cause for minority students dropping out of school. The author gives the following rankings: parental problems (88%); no hope of graduating (87%); no parental support (80%); pregnancy (65%); no peer support (65%); poverty (54%); migrant family (50%); failure to pass; or anticipation of failure on, minimum competency tests (50%); no community support for education (46%); lack of teacher role models (34%); personal, cultural and linguistic dehumanization (30%); peer violence (22%) and discrimination (17%). Surprisingly, peer violence ranked low for minority dropouts in the school systems. Many researchers speculate that peer violence would have kept many minority students away from school, eventually causing them to drop out if they were severely threatened.

Mansfield, W. & Farris, E, (1992). *Public school principal survey on safe, disciplined, and drug-free schools* (Report No. ISBN-0-16-036133-8; NCES-92-007). Rockville, MD: Westat, Inc. (ERIC Document Reproduction Service No. ED 342 131).

"The tabular summaries in this report are based on data collected from the *Public School Principal Survey on Safe, Disciplined, and Drug-Free Schools* for the National Center for Education Statistics. The survey was conducted by Westat, Inc., a research firm in Rockville, Maryland, through the Fast Response Survey System" (p. 11).

"A stratified sample of 890 schools was drawn from the 1988-1989 list of public schools compiled by the National Center for Education Statistics. The schools were stratified by type of locale and level of instruction" (p. 19).

"A response rate of 94% was received" (p. 19).

The survey results indicated that 69% of public school principals across the nation said police provided assistance or educational support to a great or moderate extent in promoting safe, disciplined and drug-free schools. About half of the school principals indicated that social service agencies and parent groups provided the same level of support.

Thirty-three percent of secondary school principals agree that alcohol is a serious or moderate problem in their school. Sixteen percent of secondary school principals thought student drug use was a serious or moderate problem in the school setting. For every 100 students, public school principals reported an average of about six in-school suspensions due to disruptive behavior or student alcohol and drug use, possession or sales during the fall 1990 semester.

Over 90% of public schools, elementary and secondary, offer referrals to social services outside the school system for disruptive students. About 70% of public schools offer such outside referrals for students using alcohol, drugs or tobacco.

The national survey indicated that 35% of public school principals said their ability to maintain order and discipline in their school was limited to a great or moderate extent by a lack of or inadequate alternative placements/programs for disruptive students.

Schools are seeing the need to be proactive with discipline and drug programs. School alcohol prevention programs and policies were considered highly/moderately effective by 27% of public school principals. General discipline programs and policies were considered highly/moderately effective by 78% of public school principals. The average number of hours drug use education was taught in each public school grade during the 1990-1991 school year ranged from about ten hours in kindergarten to about twenty-six hours in grade 7 and to about fifteen hours in grade 12.

The above data focuses on the significance of disruptive behavior and drugs in our schools today. Using proactive measures and the expertise of outside agencies possibly will help reduce our need to devote so much time to nonacademic matters.

New Jersey State Department of Education, (1992). *Violence, vandalism, and substance abuse in New Jersey schools* (General Report No. 140). Trenton, NJ: Author (ERIC Document Reproduction Service No. 350 539).

"This report presents an analysis of data from New Jersey school districts on incidents of violence and vandalism in the public schools of the state during the 1990-1991 school year" (p. 1).

"An incident is defined as an act of malicious intent to injure another individual; willfully destroy property; or possess, sell, or distribute controlled dangerous substances" (p. 1).

The Commissioner's Report contained six major findings for the state of New Jersey. They are

(1) The total of all incidents of violence, vandalism and substance abuse increased by 10% from 17,414 in 1989-1990 to 19,193 in 1990-1991.
(2) The increase in incidents of violence can be accounted for principally by an increase in the number of fights recorded.
(3) The increase in incidents of violence was most pronounced in counties in the northern and southern regions of the state.
(4) Seven-year trends show a decline in the number of incidents of vandalism and substance abuse and a return to the level of prior years of incidents of violence.
(5) Along with the general decline in the number of incidents of vandalism, the cost of vandalism declined significantly.
(6) Actions taken by districts increased significantly in two of the three major action categories: discipline and suspension.

In the first finding, the incidence of violence increased in percentage, but the number of incidents of vandalism and substance abuse remained relatively constant. Incidents of violence increased by 49% with an increase from 4,932 in 1989-1990 to 7,300 in 1990-1991. The incidents of gang fights increased more than fights or vandalism.

Assault with a weapon increased by 48% and possession of a weapon by 7%. The number of incidents of robbery increased by 98%. It was interesting to note that the level of substance abuse has declined steadily since 1986.

New Jersey seldom uses expulsion. Only forty students were expelled during 1989 and twenty-five during 1990-1991. Instead, in June of 1985, the New Jersey State Department established a grant program to reduce student disruptions in school. The program focused on those students whose disruptions were serious enough to warrant removal from the school for varying lengths of time.

This New Jersey study noted several important considerations for reducing violence in school: 1) schools are not totally responsible for the problems of violence and vandalism; 2) other elements of the community share responsibility on both ends of the continuum, from identifying causes of problem behavior to providing prevention and treatment; 3) school districts should create a climate of full participation and cooperation with all elements of the community; and 4) teachers and parents should be engaged as partners in learning and school improvement.

The department also recommends that local school officials work cooperatively with law-enforcement agencies and family court authorities to develop specific plans to reduce violence and vandalism. Finally, the report said that there must be communication across the community. The more informed the school community is about school problems and the steps the school district is taking to eliminate them, the higher the probability of success of the district's efforts.

Van Meter, V. L. (1991). Sensitive materials in U.S. public schools. *School Library Media Quarterly,* 19(4):223-227.

"The holdings of elementary and secondary media centers of the topics of AIDS, child abuse, family violence, homosexuality, and incest were examined" (p. 223).

"The importance of the school library media center and the library media specialist in providing materials to support the curriculum and to meet the individual needs of students is well established" (p. 223).

"The purpose of this study is to provide information concerning the holdings on the topics of AIDS, child abuse, family violence, homosexuality, and incest in public elementary and secondary schools in communities of all sizes across the nation. The data is descriptive, and there is no known basis for comparison" (p. 223).

"During the 1988-1989 school term, a nationwide survey was conducted to determine the following: the quantities of materials relating to these sensitive social issues available in the surveyed schools: whether access is restricted: whether the topics are included in the curriculum of the school: and, if so, whether the library media specialists have looked for materials" (p. 224).

"Of 157 questionnaires sent to elementary schools, seventy-one were returned. It is granted that the rate of return is not as high as would be desired, but the sensitive nature of the topic determined that complete anonymity must be guaranteed and that no follow-up of respondents was possible" (p. 224).

Children can learn to accept violence as an acceptable part of life if they are constantly exposed to it in the home. One way to judge how we, as schools, are addressing this problem is to look at the availability and amount of nonviolence instructional materials in the media center. To our credit, the study shows that child abuse and family violence are the most highly represented in the fiction collections of both elementary and secondary schools. Over 49% of the media centers in elementary schools report holding one or more vertical file items on AIDS, child abuse and family violence.

A surprising finding to me was that AIDS, child abuse, and family violence are covered in the curricula of over 62% of the elementary schools responding. However, of those respondents who indicate that these topics are in the curriculum, a range from 15.2-25% say that they have not looked for appropriate materials to teach it.

Due to the small number of schools participating in this study it would not be wise to generalize these findings for media centers across the nation. A follow-up study is needed to verify the results.

Krysinski, P. R. (1993, October). Emerging issues of violence: Impact on leading and learning in schools. Paper presented at the annual meeting of the University Council for Educational Administration, Houston, TX (ERIC Document Reproduction Service No. ED 364 957).

"In order to better understand the lives of students, I undertook a qualitative research study of teenagers who live and attend high schools in an urban school district in northeastern United States in Washington, D.C. In the early stages of study in the summer of 1992, my initial interest was in school and student culture, student expectations, school curriculum, achievement, attendance, and drop-out rates. The over-riding question was to see if minority youth are well served by the public schools" (p. 2).

"As the study progressed, it became clear to me that the dominant theme pervading the lives of students was survival—in the streets, in the homes, to and from schools, and in the schools. From the perspective of students, the major issue facing them was surviving, first in communities and now in the schools where violence or the threats of violence were commonplace" (p. 2).

"As an initial step, I visited high schools within a single urban school district of 45,000 students in the northeastern section of the United States. For one month I observed, interviewed, and collected field notes. Following the visits, I collected primary data such as observations and in-depth semi-structured interviews with students, administrators, teachers, security officers, health care professionals, and police officers" (p. 5).

"Secondary data collection included contemporary records, confidential student journals, public reports, student poetry and songs, student newspapers, school district public reports, crime reports, and census data" (p. 6).

"I depended on the personnel of each school to ensure an appropriate representation of teenagers" (p. 6).

The validity of this study is questionable. The entire data collected seems to be from interviewing students dealing with violence and their reactions to the violence. What's the possibilities for these children? The author's account of the lives of these children forces the question, "how can we expect teenagers to get out of these conditions, enter school without fear, to go to college, and to lead productive lives?" There doesn't seem to be an easy answer.

Greenlee, A. R. & Ogletree, E. J. (1993). *Teachers' attitudes toward student discipline problems and classroom management strategies.* Chicago, IL: Chicago Public Schools (ERIC Document Reproduction Service No. ED 364 330).

"One new program which prompted this research study on student discipline problems stemmed from involvement in the newly implemented program in the Chicago public school system which is the Teachers for Chicago Program" (p. 2).

"Questions of the Study: What are teachers' perception of the characteristics of students viewed as discipline problems? What are teachers' attitudes toward classroom management strategies? What are teachers' attitudes toward the most frequently occurring discipline problems? What are teachers' attitudes toward the major causes of discipline problems? What are teachers' attitudes toward strategies to improve student discipline?" (p. 13).

"The population in this 1993 study will include 50 Chicago school teachers" (p. 13).

"Questionnaires were distributed and collected as contact was made with teachers while attending a university course, professional interviewing workshops, and in the school where the researcher is employed. Professional colleagues also distributed questionnaires in their schools and those were distributed and collected via personal contact" (p. 13).

The data shows that teachers were in strong agreement on three of the questions on the questionnaire. They were

(1) Good teachers must be competent in curbing disruptive behavior in the classroom (forty-nine out of fifty agreed).
(2) Stress related to classroom management is the most influential factor in failure among novice teachers (thirty-nine out of fifty agreed).
(3) Teachers need more skill and training in how to deal with disruptive classroom behavior (forty-one out of fifty agreed).

The teachers indicated the top four most frequently occurring discipline problems are disrespect for fellow students, disinterest in school, lack of attention and excessive talking. The three major causes of disciplinary problems indicated by the teachers were violence in the media, broken families and drugs/alcohol.

The top four ways to improve discipline in the schools according to the teachers are counseling/guidance, administrative procedures, stricter/consistent discipline and school/community communication improvement.

Specific criteria associated with effective classroom management strategies must be developed and utilized in order to solve many of the discipline problems that can lead to violence in our schools today. Also, as the survey indicated, teachers' attitudes play an important part in effective school discipline. They must feel competent in their ability to discipline and be consistent with their practices. Behavior management training needs to be provided to all teachers experiencing difficulties with discipline problems. Peer groups, counseling sessions and mentors may be helpful in reducing the harmful effects of this type of behavior. One of our worst enemies in combating disruption and violence in the classroom is that of violence in the media. As the survey indicated, many teachers agree.

Trump, K. S. (1993). *Youth gangs and schools: The need for intervention and prevention strategies.* Cleveland, OH: Cleveland State University, Urban Child Research Center (ERIC Document Reproduction Service No. ED 361 457).

"Increased attention to youth violence, especially organized gang activity, has led to heightened interest in containing, controlling and preventing gang activity" (p. 4).

"With drug trafficking comes better armed and more violent gangs, as indicated by increases in drug-related homicides, "drive-by" shootings and other forms of open violence. Drug trafficking and the tendency of youth to settle disputes with the use of firearms, graphically illustrated by a 117 percent increase in the arrests of persons under 18 for murder since 1984, justify the concern over increased youth gang violence" (p. 4).

"Schools are clearly not immune from the impact of gang activity in the broader community. A 1989 Department of Justice survey of 10,000 youth, ages 12 to 19, found 14 percent of the white students, 20 percent of African-American students, and 32 percent of Hispanic students reporting the presence of gangs in their schools, with drug availability reported more often by those reporting gangs at their school (78%) than those where gangs were not present (66%). Students with gangs at school were twice as likely as those without gangs to fear attacks at, to, and from school (U.S. Bureau of Justice Statistics, 1992)" (p. 5).

Mr. Trump captures the reader's attention as he clearly defines what part gangs play in destroying the image of a safe school in the minds of our parents and children. He thinks there are twelve reasons that kids join gangs today. They are breakdown of the family; the need "to belong"; low self-esteem; youth socialized in a nonwork and/or criminal environment; poverty; substandard living conditions; failure of public educational institutions; failure of the criminal justice systems; teen unemployment; increased availability of alcohol, drugs and weapons for youth; economic incentives of crime and an inability of social institutions to handle increased demands resulting from the above conditions. However, many of the items existed in our society when gangs were not prevalent. Gangs did not emerge due to the presence of poverty, teen unemployment, substandard living conditions and the need to belong.

Mr. Trump has an interesting description of how gangs actually form and mature. He says many gangs start as small groups of youth with common interests. The social factors most often attributed to gang formation—power, status, security, family, friendship, love—attract youth at impressionable ages, most noticeably around twelve or thirteen years. As these groups grow in size, leadership develops informally and the group adopts an offensive posture toward nonmembers through protection of turf and school rivalries. The groups change over a period of time from the original social group to defensive groups to fighting gangs. Members of the gang often become involved in criminal offenses beginning with charges stemming from fighting and later extending to criminal offenses initiated from economic motivation (theft and drug trafficking).

Mr. Trump's study looked at a school program to prevent gangs in Cleveland, Ohio. The Youth Gang Unity serves as a specialized resource team for maintaining regular interaction and coordination of services with a network of school officials and designated community organizations. The unit represents a balanced approach within the school district to direct efforts of containment, control and prevention of youth gangs.

Results show that during its first year of operation, the unit handled over 380 incidents and identified over 950 gang members while training over 7400 staff, parents and students. The effectiveness of the program is illustrated by a 26% reduction in gang-related incidents during the first eight weeks of the 1992 school year as compared to the same time period in 1991.

Smith, F. (1992). *Family violence: Educational implications and recommendations* (ERIC Document Reproduction Service No. ED 353 674).

"In August 1990 the Office for the Education of Homeless Children and the Texas Education Agency conducted a study to better understand the educational needs of one sub-population of homeless children, children who are homeless as a result of domestic violence. Statistical information was gathered on the numbers of children and youth and the difficulties they encountered in accessing appropriate educational programs and services" (p. 2).

"It is hoped that the information from this study will assist educators and legislators in recommending state and district policies or procedures as they endeavor to ensure academic success for all our children, regardless of population, color, creed, gender, or economic status" (p. 2).

"Frequently the emotional and physical safety needs of children from violent families interfere with their attendance and academic success in school" (p. 2).

"Information on the educational needs of children and youth in Texas who were homeless as a result of domestic violence was gathered from three primary sources: The Texas Council on Family Violence, four domestic violence shelters representing three of the major population centers and one of the rural areas of the state, and a survey was sent to all domestic violence shelters in Texas. This survey solicited information concerning those children and youth who had resided in domestic violence shelters in Texas during 1989" (p. 2).

"The Council staff representatives emphasized the importance of school for children who are homeless as a result of domestic violence by providing a sense of stability and continuity for children at a time when everything feels chaotic and disconnected" (p. 3).

"Appropriate discipline strategies at school would focus on developing a child's self-esteem and emphasize that people are not for hitting rather than rewarding or punishing certain behaviors" (p. 3).

The survey of all the domestic violence shelters in Texas yielded a view of the magnitude of the problem children are facing in violent homes. As the study stated, children from these homes come to school thinking it is proper to settle their problems by hitting other children.

The number of replies to the survey questions (37.8%) was not as high as the author anticipated. The average monthly population in the shelters was twenty-five children. The greatest number of children reported in any one month by a single domestic violence shelter was 120.

The average length of stay for these children was twenty-two days. Many children (65.4%) did not attend school because it was not considered safe for them.

To serve these children in our school system and turn their thoughts away from violence, we must have a greater sensitivity and awareness on the part of our staff, develop appropriate counseling and academic programs and link them to services to ensure that the needs of the children are being met.

Unfortunately, this study confirms that the schools in Texas did not always welcome children from domestic violence centers. These children, especially, need to feel "wanted" in a public school setting.

Mrs. Smith lists the following important recommendations for administrators and staff:

(1) Schools must implement practices and procedures that facilitate the enrollment of children who are homeless as a result of domestic violence.
(2) Schools must maintain confidentiality regarding the child's enrollment status, including the transfer of records to new schools.
(3) School staff who work with children and youth who are homeless as a result of domestic violence must have comprehensive in-service training.
(4) Children and youth who are homeless as a result of domestic violence must be given immediate approval for such services as the federal meal program.
(5) Children who are homeless as a result of domestic violence must be exempt from discipline policies involving corporal punishment.
(6) Schools must create open, effective, responsive and responsible lines of communication with shelter personnel.
(7) Every attempt must be made to mainstream children, temporarily residing in a domestic violence shelter, throughout the regular educational program.

Task Force on School Violence. (1993). *Task force on school violence. Executive summary.* Raleigh, NC: Author (ERIC Document Reproduction Service No. ED 357 462).

"Violence in North Carolina, as well as in the rest of the country, has increased substantially in the past few years. In fact, the reported violent crime rate in this state has increased by more than 35 percent in just the last five years" (p. 6).

"Studies have shown that the conditions of schools are strongly influenced by the conditions of their neighborhoods" (p. 6).

"Since 1987 the number of reported arrests of young people, 15 years of age or less, for violent offenses increased by 100 percent" (p. 6).

"As part of the work of the Governor's Task Force on School Violence, the Department of Public Instruction administered a survey to more clearly identify the extent of school violence and to hear suggestions from the 129 school systems for solutions to the problem" (p. 7).

"Of the 129 systems in the state, 129 responded for a rate of 100 percent" (p. 7).

To correct a problem, one needs to gather as much information about the problem as possible. North Carolina's 1991–1992 survey provides a clear picture of violence in their schools. Pertinent survey results are

(1) Fifty-nine percent of the responding school systems reported an increase in violent behavior over the past five years. More guns and knives were found in the schools than five years ago.
(2) During the 1991–1992 school year, 27,135 students were placed in in-school suspension for assault or battery of students by students. A total of 693 students were arrested for assault and battery.
(3) A total of thirteen students were suspended for using a firearm in a violent act while sixty-three were placed on long-term suspension for that offense.
(4) A total of 161 students were sent to in-school suspension or suspended for using knives in a violent manner.

The Task Force composed a list of recommendations that are tough and directly to the point. Highlighting those we find:

(1) Establish weapon-free school zones.
(2) Limit access by minors to handguns.
(3) Consistently expel students who are violent in the school.
(4) Transfer students who threaten violence to alternative schools or programs.
(5) Provide high quality alternative programs.
(6) Require schools to report violent offenders to law officials.
(7) Require court counselors to confer with school officials.
(8) Expand immediate school actions to make school safer.
(9) Take privileges away from students.

(10) Teach violence prevention.
(11) Set up local task forces.
(12) Improve the juvenile code.
(13) Create the North Carolina Center for the Prevention of School Violence.

Wyne, M. D. (1979, April). The national safe school study: Overview and implications. Paper presented at the annual meeting of the American Educational Research Association, San Francisco, CA (ERIC Document Reproduction Service No. ED 175 112).

"In 1974, the 93rd Congress mandated the Secretary of Health, Education and Welfare to conduct a national study of the incidence and seriousness of school crime; the number and location of schools affected; the costs; the means of prevention in use, and the effectiveness of these means" (p. 3).

"Phase 1 involved a mail survey of principals in a representative sample of more than 4000 elementary and secondary schools" (p. 3).

"In Phase 2, a nationally representative sample of 42 public junior and senior high schools was surveyed using on-site field representatives" (p. 3).

"In Phase 3, ten schools were selected for intensive, qualitative analysis using a case study approach" (p. 3).

"How serious is the problem? In a word, the problem is as serious as it has ever been, but no more so. It appears to have peaked in late 1960s and early 1970s and, if anything, is on the decline. However, the risks of violence for young adolescents in cities are greater than anywhere else" (p. 5).

According to the study, there are many factors that affect violence in the schools: the crime rate and the presence or absence of fighting gangs in the school's attendance area; the proportion of students who are male; the grade level in secondary school and the age of the students; the size of the school; the principal's firmness, fairness and predictability in enforcing rules; the size of classes; the students' feelings of control over their lives; coordination between faculty and administration; teacher attitudes toward pupils, toward school and toward teachers; and the importance of leadership status. These factors discovered in the seventies are basically what we believe to be true today.

This study stressed that a strong, clear, consistent school governance, particularly by the principal, can help in reducing school crime and misbehavior. Investigators found a recurring tendency to minimize the extent of the problem—a "This is to be expected," and "We've learned to live with it and survive" attitude. Today the problem has escalated to the point that we are no longer willing "to live with it." Action groups in the schools, community and the board office are looking at ways to combat the growing problem of violence in schools.

Ottinger, C. & Root, M. (1994). *Critical education trends: A poll of America's urban schools.* Washington, D.C.: Council of the Great City Schools (ERIC Document Reproduction Service No. ED 369 875).

"The purpose of this report is to describe and forecast the main problems facing city school districts from the perspective of urban school leaders, school boards, superintendents and school administrators" (p. 4).

"The results are based on an August 1993 survey of the leadership of the Council of the Great City Schools (GCS) on enrollment trends, suply and demand of teachers, financial conditions and school reform. In addition, urban leaders were asked to identify the 10 most pressing current and 10 most likely future issues facing urban education" (p. 4).

"The first section of the survey addresses several overarching questions: What is happening with urban enrollments? What changes are occurring with the urban teaching force? Are urban school districts engaged in reform and the restructuring of schools? What is the state of the economic resources in urban schools?" (p. 5).

The report contained many interesting findings about urban schools and their concerns. Almost three out of five GCS leaders indicated that the accountability of administrators, restructuring the management of schools and school reform is a current concern. In comparison, 20% of national school leaders noted that they are facing these issues. GCS leaders were two times more likely than national leaders to indicate that site-based management was an issue of concern. GCS are large and complex entities: they employ 297,654 teachers; the student population totals 5.4 million; there are 7,392 schools, and total revenues of $31.8 billion.

Since this paper focuses on violence and gangs in the schools, the top ten current issues identified in the survey by Great City School Leaders, 1993, are presented. Also provided is a comparison of the nation's concerns on the same issues.

	GCS (%)	Nation (%)
1. Violence and gang-related activity	82.7	18
2. Parent involvement	71.2	44.4
3. Bilingual education and non-English students	64.4	13.0
4. School reform and restructuring	59.3	20.0
5. Site-based management	44.0	22.0
6. Early intervention education	38.9	12.0
7. Adequate finance/funding of schools	35.6	34.0
8. Increasing achievement of all students	30.5	NO
9. HIV/AIDS education	30.5	17.0
10. Equity issues	28.8	14.0

As one can see, violence and gang-related activity is the top concern of urban school leaders (82.7%). Isn't it amazing that only 18% of national leaders cited this as a current issue? The study further indicates that violence and gang-related activity is expected to be a future concern to 40.7% of the GSC leaders in comparison to 27% of the national leaders. It will be interesting to see if these predictions are correct.

Urban schools need be restructured to meet the needs of the student population. Violence, gangs, drugs, overcrowding, poor maintenance of facilities, poverty and lack of parental support will push our leaders into acting on behalf of children in urban schools.

Schoolland, K. (1986). Ijime: The bullying of Japanese youth. *International Education*, 15(2):5–28.

"Ijime, which means the intimidation of the weakest people in a social group, has become prevalent in the Japanese educational system" (p. 1).

"Between April and October of 1985, 155,066 cases of bullying were reported in Japan's schools" (p. 1).

"The educational council cites the rigorous discipline measures undertaken by teachers as the cause of rising violence by students" (p. 1).

"The education council has said that the most important reform is to eliminate the uniformity and inflexibility which are thought to be at the root of these educational problems" (p. 1).

"The council members hope to accomplish this by respecting the dignity of individuals" (p. 1).

"This view would recognize that young people have the right to be protected from the use of aggression and coercion" (p. 1).

"In pursuit of normalcy, the Japanese have been struggling with education reforms that could eventually result in the most significant changes since World War II. This upheaval has been inspired by widespread recognition that Japan's education system has deeply rooted problems that are certainly not to be admired and not to be imitated" (p. 5).

"The young people of Japan are subjected to a system of strict regimentation in which they have little or no voice" (p. 6).

"If a child is not doing his homework, talking in class, or even associating with a student who has a bad reputation, then it is possible that the student will receive a very hard blow across the head or face. The hitting of students is so widespread that it is beginning to cause a nationwide furor" (p. 8).

Several anonymous statistics were gathered in a poll by the Japan Youth Research Institute. The poll surprisingly showed that 55.7% of Japanese parents approve of physical punishment, versus 29.9% in the United States. In Japan 81% of the populace believe that corporal punishment may be inevitable, depending on the situation. Out of 393 cases of corporal punishment in 1984, involving 2433 students, it was revealed that about 70% of the students received injuries and one student died. The author of this article believes that young people learn by imitating their elders, and if the young learn nothing else from brutal teachers, they learn how to bully others. The incidence is rapidly on the rise.

One Japanese parent explained the problem of violence this way: "It's the atmosphere of coercion and violence in this school that gave rise to my son's being beaten up," declared the parent. "And can you blame the kids for thinking like that? They figure if it's all right for the teachers to hit people it's all right for them to do the same."

Americans need to look at the last example. We may not have violent teachers in the classroom but we certainly expose our children to outrageous violence on video games, movies and the television. Exposure to violence of this nature does foster violence on the school campus. As in Japan, children in America learn by imitating. Media officials need to rethink what it is we should encourage our children to imitate.

Fontenot, R. (1993). *The culture of school violence* (ERIC Document Reproduction Service No. ED 369 730).
"Eight middle schools with a total of 3,212 black and 6,460 white students were surveyed to identify the most frequent incidents of rule violations and school violence by ethnicity" (p. 2).
"The middle schools, which included the fifth through eighth grade levels, were randomly selected as the population for this study" (p. 2).
"Fighting, disturbance, disrespect for authority, violation of school rules, and cutting class were considered the most frequent incidents of school violence" (p. 3).

The findings in this study indicate that a larger percentage of black students are engaged in fighting at school, causing disturbance in class, disrespect for authority, violation of school rules and cutting classes than are white students in the middle school grades surveyed.

The author argues that the cultural differences between black and white Americans, such as life styles and the appreciation of school learning must be truthfully faced and acknowledged. He says that for too long there has been a taboo against discussing the differences that exist between and among various ethnic and socioeconomic groups in our country. "Until the truth about the ethnic, cultural, and value differences are confronted and discussed, we will not be able to design a better and more productive school environment that is conducive to school learning."

He continues to elaborate as he says, "The causes of school violence are many and complex. Most of the school's violence arise from cultural, ethnic, and special education classifications that make the schooling process nearly impossible to implement. The cultural, ethnic, special education classifications, and diversity appear in the manner of work ethics, rule and regulations adherence, and the desire for school learning. The characteristics and behavioral patterns of these children form a counter school culture which prevents the 'average' non-violent, obedient school directed learner to their right to an equal educational oportunity. It is the average obedient school directed student in our schools that is the most discriminated against and the most neglected in terms of educational opportunities."

Mr. Fontenot lists seven suggested remedies for alleviating the violence in our public schools:

(1) Clearly define the school's mission and purpose.
(2) Honestly acknowledge the cultural and ethnic differences in the lifestyles, values and beliefs that exist.
(3) Give teachers time and freedom to teach, and children time and freedom to learn—freedom from fear, intimidation, bodily harm, murder and rape.
(4) Establish orientation programs to teach the school's culture; require attendance for all students.
(5) Establish peer mediation teams and conflict resolution teams in each school.
(6) Establish a transition school for students who are disruptive elements in the regular school environment.
(7) Teachers and school personnel must be helped by the central office staff and personnel to be firmly in control of the schooling enterprise. They must be free to teach and discipline students within the school's cultural and learning environment.

White, L. E. (1994). *Violence in schools: An overview. CRS report for Congress.* (Report No. CRS-94-141-EPW). Washington, D.C.: Library of Congress, Congressional Research Service (ERIC Document Reproduction Service No. ED 369 159).

"The sixth National Education Goal is to make every school in America free of drugs and violence and offer a disciplined environment for learning" (p. 1).

"This report discusses the nature and extent of violence in the Nation's schools and reviews prior and current congressional efforts to address this problem" (p. 6).

"In 1990, when President Bush presented the sixth National Education Goal, the discussion predominately centered around drug use, awareness, and education. Over the past few years, however, increased attention has been given to achieving safe and violence-free schools" (p. 6).

"Goal six has also been a catalyst for highlighting the relationship of violence and discipline problems to teaching and learning" (p. 7).

The last major comprehensive study of violence was the Safe School Study commissioned by Congress and issued in 1978. The findings of the report indicated that crime was a serious problem that had peaked during the 1960s and 1970s. According to Ms. White, recent reports and studies suggest a resurgence of the problem. She presented selected findings froma number of publications depicting trends and current conditions in schools. Highlights of her findings are

(1) During the past twelve years, threats and injuries to high school seniors and theft of their property have risen.
(2) Eighty-two percent of 729 school districts responding to a National School Boards Association survey said that violence in their schools has increased over the past five years.
(3) Reported crime and violent incidents in the New York City public schools rose 16% between the 1991-1992 school year and the 1992-1993 school year.
(4) In 1992, 2% of eighth graders, 4% of tenth graders and 3% of twelfth graders nationwide reported that they regularly carried a weapon to school.
(5) In 1992, 14-19% of eighth, tenth and twelfth graders nationwide reported being threatened with a weapon and 25-29% reported being threatened without a weapon in school.
(6) In 1992, 5-9% of eighth, tenth and twelfth graders, nationwide reported being injured with a weapon in school.
(7) In 1991, more than 30% of all high school teachers felt that student misbehavior interfered with their teaching.
(8) In 1991, 19% of public school teachers reported that they had been verbally abused in the last four weeks, 8% reported being threatened with injury in the last twelve months, and 2% reported being physically attacked in the last twelve months.

Ms. White stresses that violence has spread from central city schools to the suburbs and rural areas. She states that responsibility for school safety rests with State and local officials and communities. However, inadequate financial resources and limited research on the scope of the problem and effective remedies hamper efforts to provide a disciplined, violence-free environment in many schools. For these reasons, she indicates that some have advocated Federal intervention to provide funding for school safety programs, research on the causes of school violence and effective remedies, and national leadership on this issue which affects schools across the country.

Currently there are three federal programs to address violence in the schools. They are the Gun-Free School Zone Act which makes it a Federal crime to possess or to discharge a loaded firearm on school property or within 1000 feet of an elementary or secondary school; "Safe Havens," which is a part of the Weed and Seed program that provides educational, recreational and cultural activities for high-risk youth in a safe setting after school; and, "Project Smart" which helps schools collect and analyze data relating to school crime, drug use and disciplinary infractions.

Since violence in schools is a nationwide problem, I think it is appropriate for Congress to respond with funding, research and training programs for teachers, students and the communities. Also, the problem needs to be addressed at the state and local levels. The real challenge for all levels will be in determining what will actually stop the violence and prevent it from reoccurring.

Capaldi, D. M. & Patterson, G. R. (1993, March). The violent adolescent male: Specialist or generalist? Paper presented at the biennial meeting of the Society for Research in Child Development, New Orleans, LA (ERIC Document Reproduction Service No. ED 357 844).

"Can we predict who will become violent and what are the developmental histories, characteristics, and family background of those who become violent?" (p. 3).

"There is a growing body of evidence that specialization in violent crimes is rare and that it is hard to identify distinguishing characteristics of violent offenders. We take the position that violence is a manifestation of high rates of antisocial behavior in general and that the violent adolescent offenders is a member of the broader category of multiple offender" (p. 3).

"We tested the hypothesis that violent adolescent offenders would be indistinguishable from frequent offenders for an at-risk sample of 200 boys in the Oregon Youth Study" (p. 3).

"The four hypotheses to be addressed in this article are as follows:

- Violent offenders are more likely to be multiple offenders.
- High rate or chronic offenders are at risk for committing violent crimes by ages 16 to 17.
- There would be no difference between violent and nonviolent offenders on contextual, family management, or earlier

measures of boy's behavior once frequency of arrests was controlled.
- Violent offenders would not self-report more violent acts than nonviolent offenders matched for frequency of arrests" (p. 4)

Ms. Capaldi's 1993 study concluded that violent offenders are indistinguishable from more frequent offenders, and all but one of the youth studied had arrests for nonviolent offenses. Children do not suddenly become violent adolescents. If one checked the discipline records of violent teenagers through elementary school, a pattern of disciplinary referrals would be evident including some notations concerning violence.

Ms. Capaldi found few differences in family backgrounds and developmental histories of violent and nonviolent juvenile offenders. There was a trend to lower per capita income and higher father arrest rates for the violent group. It may be that lower income families with a criminal father are better known to the police and justice system, and that adolescents in those families are more vulnerable to arrest.

The results indicated a trend for families with violent adolescents to have lower per capita incomes and higher antisocial behavior among the fathers. Also, the mother's antisocial behavior was well above the sample mean for both groups.

In the fourth hypothesis there was no tendency for the violent multiple offenders to report more violence in the past year than the nonviolent multiple offenders.

Ms. Capaldi concludes by stating that programs to prevent violence in adolescence should be synonymous with programs to prevent high-rate chronic offenders. She adds that the best predictor of chronic offending in adolescence is childhood antisocial behavior. We see children in the elementary setting who never interact with other children in the classroom or on the playground unless we force the interaction. There must be a way to target these children in Pre-K with counseling services, programs and other interventions to help the children overcome their antisocial behavior.

Educational Fund to End Handgun Violence. (1993). *Kids and guns: A national disgrace.* Third Edition. Washington, D.C.: Author (ERIC Document Reproduction Service No. ED 365 897).

"This 1993 report presents the statistical documentation of the toll gun violence takes on young people" (p. 1).

"Currently guns are used to murder at least one American child every three hours and at least 25 children, the equivalent of a classroomful, every three days" (p. 4).

"Juvenile gun homicides have more than doubled since 1983" (p. 4).

"For young black men, the rate nearly tripled just from 1985 to 1990" (p. 4).

"If action is not taken soon to rescue the children trapped in this ever increasing cycle of violence, then the United States is at risk of losing an entire generation. The victims will not only be those who were killed, but also the survivors, scarred by growing up in virtual war zones" (p. 7).

"Historically, the rate of homicide has always been higher for males than females and much higher for black males than white males. So much higher, that every year since 1969 the leading cause of death for black males 15 through 19 years of age has been firearm homicide" (p. 9).

"The availability of firearms has made firearm injuries the second leading cause of death behind motor vehicle accidents for youth ages 10–19" (p. 9).

"James Fox, one of the authors of the Northeastern University report, points out the difference between a 45-year-old with a gun and a 14-year-old with a gun. A 45-year-old with a gun in his hand, although he may be a better shot, is not as likely to use that gun as a 14-year-old. Fourteen-year-olds tend to be trigger happy. They'll pull the trigger without thinking about the consequences" (p. 11).

"One should consider that if the rest of the population was being murdered by firearms at a rate equal to that of young black males, over 260,000 Americans would be shot to death each year" (p. 11).

The last part of this article is devoted specifically to gun violence in schools. In a 1990 survey conducted by the Centers for Disease Control, the author says the survey found that on an average day approximately 100,000 students across the country bring guns to school. The Joyce Foundation study discovered that only 29% of parents believe that most children are safe from violence while in school.

The author says gun violence in schools is not a problem confined to large cities. Paul Kingery, a Texas A&M researcher, reports that rural students are twice as likely to carry a gun to school than the national average. The willingness of youth to carry guns to school combined with the easy accessibility of firearms has placed a deadly obstacle in the already difficult path of obtaining a quality education in schools throughout the country.

Looking specifically at learning, the author indicates that it is difficult to determine the effect gun violence has upon the learning of each student. The Joyce Foundation poll examined students' attitudes toward gun violence and found that only 21% of the students feel they are safe from violence in the schools and only 30% feel they are safe traveling to and from school.

There are differing estimates about where children get their guns. School security experts and law-enforcement officials estimate that 80% of the firearms students bring to school come from home. The Joyce Foundation discovered that only 43% of parents with children under eighteen years old who own a gun keep that gun safely locked. Until this nation and its leaders decide that gun violence is a serious problem which must be dealt with appropriately, our children will continue to suffer.

Cesarone, B. (1994). *Video games and children. ERIC digest.* (Report No. EDO-PS-94-3). Urbana, IL: ERIC Clearinghouse on Elementary and Early Childhood Education (ERIC Document Reproduction Service No. ED 365 477).

"This digest examines data on video game use by children, explains ratings of video game violence, and reviews research on the effects of video games on children and adolescents" (p. 1).

"This study of seventh and eighth graders found that 65% of males and 57% of females played 1 to 6 hours of video games at home per week and 38% of males and 16% of females played 1 to 2 hours of games per week at arcades" (p. 2).

"Among five categories of video games, games that involved fantasy violence were most preferred by the students surveyed" (p. 2).

"A 1989 survey of video games conducted by NCTV found that 71% of the games received one of three violent ratings" (p. 2).

"Contrary to early research, recent studies on the effects of video games on children have found connections between children's playing violent games and later aggressive behavior" (p. 3).

"A research review done by NCTV in 1990 found that 9 out of 12 studies on the impact of violent games on children reported harmful effects" (p. 3).

"Some professionals speculate that performing violent acts in video games may be more conducive to children's aggression than passively watching violent acts on television" (p. 3).

"Another problem cited by critics of video games is that these games stress autonomous rather than cooperative action. Furthermore, children's attitudes toward gender roles may be influenced by video games, in which women are usually cast as persons who are acted upon, rather than as initiators of action" (p. 3).

Many children go home to an empty house while they wait for their parents to return from work. When asked what they do when they get home, most children will say they get a snack and play a video game or watch television. Teachers know children will retain more if allowed to manipulate materials, such as math manipulatives. It is reasonable to assume that the same concept applies to video games. Manipulating characters in acts of aggression on the video screen has to have a residual effect on the behavior of children.

Bergman, L. (1992). Dating violence among high school students. *Social Work*, 37(1):21-27.

"Students from three midwestern high schools were surveyed regarding their experience with sexual, physical, and verbal dating violence. There were 631 respondents from suburban, rural, and inner-city schools" (p. 21).

"This study's purpose was twofold. First, it was designed to estimate the proportion of high school students who have experienced sexual dating violence, physical dating violence, and severe violence, the recurrence of violence in these relationships, and the incidence of violence on the first date. Second, the study was designed to determine if gender, age, grade point average, dating frequency, age at which dating began, number of dating partners, and community, which varied in regard to racial mixture, income averages, and employment trends, were significantly correlated with high school dating violence" (p. 21).

"This study's population consisted of all students attending three midwestern high schools: a suburban, a rural, and an inner-city school. The three communities in which these schools were located differed significantly in racial composition, average family income, and occupational trend" (p. 22).

"A total of 738 questionnaires were distributed; 631 were returned completed, or a response rate of 86 percent" (p. 23).

The average of number students in the sample reporting sexual dating violence was 10.5%. For physical violence, the average was 12%. The highest average was 17.7% for a combination of physical and sexual violence. From the survey it was discovered that the majority of the respondents told no one about the violence. The majority of respondents who reported physical violence also continued to date the perpetrators. Repeat violence appears to be a fairly consistent variable, whether the violence was physical or sexual and whether the victim was male or female.

The results of the survey indicated that the number of dating partners a respondent reported was the most significant positive correlate of dating violence. The second best predictor was the self-reported grade point average with dating frequency coming in third.

The highest incidence of dating violence was consistently found in the suburban school, the second highest in the inner-city school and the third highest in the rural school.

The author pointed her finger at the media as a contributing factor in teenage violence. She said media messages aimed at teenagers continue to support stereotyped sex roles and immediate gratification that reinforces violent behavior. Also, violent dating behavior patterns probably can be correlated to violence in schools. This would be an interesting point to investigate.

ANALYSIS, CONCLUSION, AND IMPLICATIONS

My analysis of the recent material concerning the presence of violence in the schools indicates that the number of violent incidents on school campuses rose significantly over the last several years. The rising number of violent acts have grown in tandem with a rising concern for children's welfare expressed by school administrators, parents and the community. According to Ms. Krysinski (1993, p. 29) many children now must face the new responsibility of survival in the schools where violence or the threats of violence are commonplace. In New Jersey schools (New Jersey State Department of Education, 1992,

p. 25) during 1990-1991, for example, assaults with a weapon increased 48%.

Mrs. White (1994, p. 49), who presented findings from the National School Board Association, highlighted the growing concern over violence as she reported that 82% of 729 school districts across the nation experienced an increase in violence over the past five years. No areas—rural, suburban, or inner city—were immune to the devastating effects of violence.

Guns and weapons are a growing concern to educators because of the fatal implications they can create for our society. Many explanations have been advanced for the increased use of violence using weapons including: gang-related activity, fights over material possessions and romantic disagreements. Unfortunately, The Educational Fund to End Handgun Violence (1993, p. 54) informs us that the availability of firearms has made firearm injuries the second leading cause of death behind motor vehicle accidents for youth ages ten to nineteen.

Other factors cited throughout the studies as contributors to children perpetrating violent acts included living in single-parent homes, imitating parents' violent behavior, watching violent acts on the television, participating in violent video games and protecting oneself in gang encounters.

The implications for the future are stark and clear. If we do not stop violence in our schools, educators will completely lose the "safe haven" we want to provide for our children when they step onto the school campus. Mr. Newman (1991, p. 5) aptly expresses the need for involvement. "Only when all segments of the community become aware of the violence related problems and orient prevention services appropriately can we expect to note significant reductions in violence." The Center to Prevent Handgun Violence (1990, p. 15) clarifies our need to be united by stating: "It is going to take the efforts of parents, educators, lawmakers, and law enforcement officials working together to change this situation."

Numerous strategies and suggestions were offered for combating violence in our schools. A compilation of the most frequently suggested strategies is listed below:

- Abandon corporal punishment on the school site.
- Establish weapon-free school zones.
- Consistently expel students who are violent in the school.
- Limit access by minors to handguns.

- Transfer students to alternative schools or programs if they threaten violence.
- Require schools to report violent offenders to law officials.
- Teach violence prevention.
- Require court counselors to confer with school officials.
- Set up local task forces.
- Improve the juvenile code.
- Maintain open communication throughout the system and community.
- Encourage the development of a strong sense of personal worth.
- Involve parents in all aspects of the child's education.
- Teach people the signs of high-risk individuals.
- Develop peer support groups.
- Develop clear rules of student conduct at school enforced by the principal.
- Reduce school and class sizes.
- Provide opportunities for the students to be participatory decision makers.
- Provide police assistance on the campus.
- Provide federal intervention to provide funding for school safety programs.

The safety of our children today and in the future depends on our ability to successfully address a new and pressing problem created by a changing society. As never before, we will need to work together across the community to stop a "killer" in our schools.

Epilogue

> A mind is its own place, and in itself, can make a heaven of hell or a hell of heaven.
> —John Milton, *Paradise Lost*

THE concept of creating a safe school should not be a topic for discussion. This book should never have been necessary. As a society we should treasure our most valuable resources, the children, more than any other commodity. However, as the American society evolves, forces are continually at work that force all stakeholders to examine their established institutions, particularly the schools (Horowitz & Boardman, 1994). Violence is with us every day, most graphically evidenced by the bombing of the federal building in Oklahoma City. The most violent acts of mankind are played and replayed on television monitors for all students to see. Is it any wonder that the violence seen on television and at the movie theaters is acted out on the streets and in the schools on a daily basis (Ordovensky, 1993)?

One of the more ironic debates in the recent Congress concerned maintaining funding for the study of safe schools. At one of the most challenging times for schools in the history of this country, Congress decided that the safe schools project did not deserve continued funding. Surely such thinking is short-sighted at best, and ridiculous at worst. The comparison between the basic cost of educating a child for one year and the cost for maintaining an inmate in prison has been reported many times (Hill & Hill, 1994). Apparently our elected officials do not remember the old commercial which stated that "you can pay me now, or you can pay me later." Is it not time to examine the end product of our schools and provide the remediation on the front-end, rather than back-loading and sustaining criminals in prisons? According to most economists the largest single increase in governmental spending in the next decade will be for prisons (Bushweller, 1993).

The most obvious statement in this volume, "schools have changed," is also the most difficult to explain and even more challenging to change. Sure schools have changed in the past three decades, from the quest for expression of the 1960s, through the turbulent 1970s, to the retrenchment of the 1980s, and the quest for quality in the 1990s. But though schools have changed, a corresponding change has taken place in society which is not totally reflected in school cultures (Foster, 1994). Most school reform of the 1980s and 1990s focused on the structure of the school organization, not on the internal variables which create the school culture. Technology has changed, but often teaching techniques remain the same as they were fifty years ago, or even longer.

It is the incongruence between school goals and societal goals that challenges all stakeholders toward a realistic discussion of safe schools: how to create one and how to recognize one. Although we have not provided the "one best answer" in this volume, we have attempted to provide a framework to channel discussion and establish a new collaboration to achieve the goal. The real challenge awaits educators, politicians, citizens and students as we move rapidly toward the twenty-first century (Linquanti & Berliner, 1994).

REFERENCES

Bushweller, K. (1993). Guards with guns. *American School Board Journal*, 180(1):34–37.

Foster, L. G. (1994). Discouraging gangs in schools: A prescription for prevention. *NASSP Practitioner*, 19(4).

Hill, M. S. & Hill, F. W. (1994). *Creating safe schools: What principals can do.* Thousand Oaks, CA: Corwin Press.

Horowitz, S. V. & Boardman, S. K. (1994). Managing conflict: Policy and research implications. *Journal of Social Issues*, 50(1):197–211.

Linquanti, R. & Berliner, B. (1994). Rebuilding schools as safe havens: A topology for selecting and integrating violence prevention strategies (ERIC Document Reproduction Service No. ED 376 600).

Ordovensky, P. (1993). Facing up to violence. *Executive Educator*, 15(1):22–24.